LADY INTO WOMAN

By the same Author:

Biography

Testament of Youth
Testament of Friendship
In the Steps of John Bunyan (U.S.A.: Valiant Pilgrim)
Testament of Experience (in preparation)

Fiction

The Dark Tide
Not Without Honour
Honourable Estate
Account Rendered
Born 1925

History

Women's Work in Modern England
The Story of St Martin's
Lady Into Woman

Travel

Thrice A Stranger
Search After Sunrise

Verse

Verses of a V.A.D.
Poems of the War and After

Miscellaneous

Halcyon or the Future of Monogamy
England's Hour
Humiliation With Honour
Seed of Chaos
Above All Nations (Anthology with George Catlin and Sheila Hodges)
On Becoming A Writer

Lady into Woman

A HISTORY OF WOMEN FROM
VICTORIA TO ELIZABETH II

by

Vera Brittain

LONDON
ANDREW DAKERS LIMITED

First Published 1953

PRINTED IN GREAT BRITAIN BY
THE DITCHLING PRESS LIMITED, DITCHLING, SUSSEX.

'There is no more striking difference between our age and all its predecessors than that human beings are no longer born into a class and chained down to it.'

Professor Preserved Smith. *A History of Modern Culture.* (1930)

'Among all the achievements of the past century, those discoveries and developments that have transformed the life of man and altered the very meaning of time and space, it may be doubted whether any is so profoundly significant and in the long run so beneficial as the emancipation of women.'

Canon Charles E. Raven. *Fellowship Magazine*, U.S.A. (1951)

ACKNOWLEDGEMENTS

MY MOST grateful acknowledgements and thanks are due to the Women's Service Library, 50 Tufton Street, Westminster, for the use of their invaluable collection of books, pamphlets and press-cuttings. I am especially indebted to their able and devoted librarian, Miss Vera Douie, for her constant help and advice, and for reading and checking the manuscript. She is, of course, in no way responsible for the opinions expressed or the use that I have made of facts supplied by her.

I am also grateful to Madeleine Henrey (Mrs Robert Henrey) for kindly allowing me to quote from her letters in Chapter 14; to Sir Eardley Holland for the generous gift of his published William Meredith Shaw Memorial Lecture on the death of Princess Charlotte; to the *Evening Standard* for permitting the quotation of a copyright article by Frederick Cook; to the *News Chronicle*, Mr A. J. Cummings, and the Gallup Poll for the use of copyright material, and to the Editor of this newspaper for the many valuable and relevant contributions to my subject which have appeared in his pages.

The following have been good enough to supply information which I gratefully acknowledge: Mrs Corbett Ashby, especially on the international side of women's history, and the International Alliance of Women; Mr George Ivan Smith and the London Centre of the United Nations; Miss M. Hermes and the International Federation of University Women; the General Register Office, Somerset House; Mrs Julia Samson, Assistant Press Officer, Ministry of Health; the Chief Press Officer, Information Division, Ministry of National Insurance; Dr G. Rosen, Counsellor to the Diplomatic Mission of the Federal Republic of Germany; Mr Arthur Bax and the Press and Publicity Department of the Labour Party; Mrs Dorothy Warner, Women's International League for Peace and Freedom; Miss Violet

McEwen, Honorary Secretary to the Women's Publicity Planning Association; Miss A. M. Pierotti and the National Union of Women Teachers; Miss Monica Whately and the Six Point Group; the International Federation of Business and Professional Women; the Chelsea Babies' Club; the Rev. Constance Coltman; Miss Olive Stone, barrister; Dr Horace King, M.P.; Miss Sybil Morrison; Mrs Grace Lankester; Miss Agatha Harrison; Mr Harry Silcock; Professor N. Gangulee; and Mr A. C. Barrington of New Zealand.

I am also indebted to the authors, editors and publishers of the many books, pamphlets and newspapers which I have used, and especially to those responsible for the books recommended in the Reading List at the end.

AUTHOR'S NOTE

Owing to the large canvas covered by this book and the space limitations imposed by modern publishing upon both publisher and author, I have been obliged to draw many of my facts and illustrations from the country which as a British woman I know the best.

But from the abundant examples that I have been able to use of progress elsewhere, I think it will be clear that—allowing for national differences of background, education, legal system, and social custom—the pattern of women's history during the twentieth century has shown, throughout the world, a remarkable consistency.

CONTENTS

ILLUSTRATIONS

COPYRIGHT OF ILLUSTRATIONS

By Picture Post Library:

Facing page	48	
,, ,,	208	*bottom right*

By Mirrorpic:

Facing page	49	*top left and top right*
,, ,,	64	*bottom right*

By Fox Photos:

Facing page	49	*bottom left*
,, ,,	192	*left*

By Exclusive News Agency:

Facing page	192	*right*
,, ,,	208	*top left*
,, ,,	209	*top left*

By Planet News Ltd:

Facing page	193	*right*
,, ,,	209	*top right*

By P. A. Reuter Photos Ltd:

Facing page	65	*top left*

By the Indian High Commission:

Facing page	65	*bottom right*

By the Nissho Company Ltd, Osaka:

Facing page	193	*left*

By Scandia Press:

Facing page	209	*bottom left*

By the Hogarth Press:

Facing page	209	*bottom right*

DEDICATION TO MY DAUGHTER

who suggested the title

My dear Daughter,

I owe you much gratitude for the title which you were resourceful enough to suggest.

You were right to propose a form of words which implies that the democratic movement described in this book has not been concerned exclusively with sex equality.

Not only has the sheltered 'lady' of the Victorian epoch become the self-sufficient 'woman' of today; the political and social changes of the past half-century have brought her close in experience and understanding to the millions of women in all past ages who were never sheltered and always had to work.

You will find that I have not attempted to be soberly impartial about the emancipation of women, past, present, or future; with Canon Raven I believe it to be more significant, and more beneficial, than any great constructive change of the past fifty years. But I do not expect every reader of this book to agree, for the backwoodsmen are still with us.

Up to date they have hardly troubled you, but unlike many of your contemporaries you do not regard the women's movement as a bygone issue. Even from your brief experience you know that it is continuing, and still has far to go.

When you were growing up you sometimes suggested, as you had every right to do, that certain aspects of your upbringing might have been better. But you have had three advantages which you do, I believe, acknowledge as likely to be of special service to you in your life and work.

First, you owe to the Infant Welfare movement in general, and the Chelsea Babies' Club in particular, the vital energy and powers of endurance which have enabled you to show that the physical inferiority of women was a myth based upon faulty training and a traditional expectation of feminine weakness.

Secondly, you have been free from the implanted sense of inferiority that handicaps so many women by undermining the self-confidence which is the basis of all achievement, both masculine and feminine. You were deeply desired as a *daughter*, and it was always taken for granted by both your parents that your education and opportunities would be equal to your brother's. The women of your family had sought these benefits before you. Your paternal grandmother was a pioneer suffragist; your mother grew up with that eager generation of young feminists who were the first to inherit the freedom won for women by women. You have repaid us both by making a full and early use of your heritage.

Thirdly, you belong to a household in which a woman's work has been constantly in progress, and professional standards obeyed with the same sense of obligation by a wife and mother as by a husband and father. You have never been made to feel that the profession adopted by a woman is somehow less important than the one chosen by a man, or that her failure to do as well as she is able should be condoned and excused because of her sex.

My work, it is true, has been more interrupted than yours, I hope, will be, for I belong to a generation in which most families still took, and take, for granted that a woman's vocation should be laid aside for parental illness, the troubles of relatives, and domestic trivialities of every description.

I could have written much better if I had been interrupted much less, and should have proved altogether a more effective person had I not been obliged—and not only in my youth—to spend time and energy in learning to believe in myself and my purposes despite the enervating influence of an Edwardian childhood.

That you, who have been spared that particular battle, will live to see women ascend to heights of achievement hitherto undreamed of and make your own contribution to this future stage of a great revolution, is the constant and joyful hope of

Your Mother.

I

A REVOLUTION IN PERSPECTIVE

When I agreed to write this book, I protested to its publisher that the history of women in the 20th century has been, in effect, the history of the human race. A book on women as such tends to perpetuate the still too common practice of treating them as though they constituted a special and somewhat peculiar category.

The revolutionary changes brought by this century to the position of women have deeply affected both men and children. Additional volumes on these great human divisions are needed to complete the story. So far as space allows, I have tried to indicate their part in the social transformation which it describes.

With my contemporaries I have witnessed the most dramatic stages of that movement towards freedom and equality which began with Mary Wollstonecraft's *Vindication of the Rights of Woman* a century and a half ago.

My mother, the conventional and protected young married woman of 1901, had survived before her death in 1948 to see a society in which women Secret Service agents were dropped on the Continent by parachute, and women air-raid wardens in Britain dealt with incidents caused by bombs.

My daughter, born in the nineteen-thirties, had travelled alone by air to a Youth Conference in post-war Germany before she was eighteen. To her, my mother's early years appeared as horrible and incredible as the adventures of the youngest generation seemed wild and foolhardy to my mother. Being a member of the generation which grew up with the women's revolt, it has been my privilege to bridge that enormous gulf.

Retrogressive as our epoch has been in the realm of international morality, here at least it can register some progress. A theoretical acceptance of women as equal citizens has been virtually established, though its logical consequence in a fifty-fifty share of public responsibilities has yet to be achieved. The inculcation of women's values in social and political thinking—an accomplishment far more difficult than equal franchise and changes in legal status—still lies in a future which has also to decide the related problem of human survival.

When women first entered public life, their induced sense of inferiority operated against their own recognition of their special interests; they confused human achievement with masculine achievement and sought to imitate men. Today most thoughtful women and many far-sighted men (such as Mahatma Gandhi in India and Canon C. E. Raven in Britain) have perceived that civilisation itself may reach a premature end unless the significance of feminine qualities is recognised in time. Such qualities include compassion, forbearance, and a concern for individual life, which especially during this century have been disregarded in the callous and aggressive policies periodically dominant in national programmes and international relations.

The chief error of the older feminists was to use men as yardsticks. What matters to the modern woman is not how men have tackled problems in the past, but how she herself is going to tackle them in the future.

The history of 20th-century women has been determined partly by great revolutionary forces which have changed life for all mankind, and partly by the conscious and deliberate effort of intelligent minorities created by those forces and working within their scope. To the complex interaction of personal and impersonal influences, the women's movement owed the richness of its initiative, the sacrificial vitality of its resistance to political opposition, and the bright colours of its individual adventures.

The minority which made that movement knew what they wanted, and at times, as in the British and American militant suffrage campaigns, their courage rose to epic heights of heroism. So substantial were their achievements that the story of women in this century has largely to be related in terms of the revolution which they led. But they did not always understand the primitive origins and defensive strength of the opposition that met them, for few paused to study the historic process of which their crusade was part.

That crusade sprang from the revolutionary epoch to which it belonged, and still belongs. In Britain almost a hundred years separated the Catholic Emancipation Bill of 1829—the first 19th-century measure to enfranchise a politically helpless minority—from the Represention of the People Act of 1928, which gave citizenship to women under thirty and completed the democratic struggle. The American, French, Russian and Indian Revolutions, and others less familiar in such widely-separated countries as Ireland, Turkey, Ceylon, China, and Indonesia, have simultaneously represented both the death-throes of the age which began in Europe with the Renaissance and the Reformation, and the birth-pangs of another whose shape as yet can barely be perceived.

The American and French Revolutions owed much of their inspiration to the English Revolution of 1688, which crowned with triumph the struggle for freedom of speech and worship in the period associated with Milton and Bunyan. But the British revolution of the nineteenth and twentieth centuries followed a different pattern from that of its own predecessor, and of the national revolutions in Europe and Asia with which it appropriately coincided. It took the form, not of a united movement designed to overthrow the government, but of persistent attempts by organised pressure-groups to change the policies of governments from within the constitutional framework.

The anti-slavery, Chartist, Trade Union, Fabian and feminist movements all shared this revolutionary spirit. In the 20th century it has found further expression in the movements to eliminate colour-bars, and to substitute peace for war. The changes in women's position in Britain and elsewhere are thus part of a world picture which must be viewed as a whole before each section can be seen in its true perspective.

This convulsive age of transition has produced gigantic wars, which are sometimes said to have been responsible for women's emancipation. Like the political and social revolutions of the period, these wars were symptoms of its apocalyptic quality. Just as the seeds of change, growth, disease, and decay interact upon one another in the human body, so there has been a process of interaction between the various conflicts of our time.

Wars have speeded revolutions by violently destroying antiquated structures which in quieter periods collapse more slowly and less painfully. Hence comes the paradox by which war—so hostile to women's social and biological values, and so essentially the expression of masculine aims and methods—has appeared in this century to advance women's interests. But war and revolution, the one destructive and the other creative, spring from the same underlying causes, and can fully accomplish their historic purpose only if their origins and potential outcome are alike understood.

A revolution can nevertheless be carried forward by men and women of restricted vision who perceive only immediate objectives. For this reason the position of women has altered with relative speed where it has depended on definite and limited reforms, such as equal franchise and the attainment of legal justice. In the field of employment and particularly of industry, in marriage, in the home, and in the vast inchoate sphere of manners and morals, change has come more slowly, for it has been at the mercy of long-established customs, traditions and prejudices rooted in still older superstitions and primitive taboos.

Even today these superstitions and taboos, rather than existing facts reinforced by proof, determine much of the popular attitude towards women. They explain the readiness with which a majority of both men and women regard a woman's ability as inferior before it has been tested, and her purity as a vulnerable asset which must be jealously guarded by others because she is incapable of defending it herself.

Occasionally the brutal assault does happen, just as we still read of tavern brawls in a country rapidly growing temperate owing less to the activities of temperance societies than to changing standards of social conduct. But these chance throw-backs to an older order no more mean that all women live in perpetual danger of criminal assault than that we are all victims of a drunken civilisation. The very featuring of isolated assaults and brawls by the Press shows how totally different are the expectations of behaviour upon which society as a whole depends.

Yet the conception of women as fragile creatures whose virtue must be guarded by the dominant male has contributed, at least as much as the practical duties involved by the rearing of children, to the conventional assumption—today largely driven underground, but still far from dead—that woman's 'sphere' is the home. Until recently those women who sought any other outlet were felt to be somehow unnatural, even if they were no longer described as 'unsexed' or 'strong-minded'.

The customs and prejudices which lie behind these suppositions are far more difficult to alter than the law, for their range is illimitable and sometimes appears inexplicable (though the explanation once existed, ceased to be relevant, and was then forgotten). Their field of operations is that of minds and habits, so much less definite and accessible than Statute Books. By the large majority of human beings, that which is established and familiar tends to be regarded as right and proper just because their particular country or generation has known nothing else.

From a world standpoint, this obstinate domination of custom accounts for the unevenness of feminine progress. While some Eastern women are becoming Ministers and Ambassadors or exercising the personal influence of a Madame Chiang Kai-Shek, China's 'First Lady' from 1927 to 1948, others remain in physical or mental purdah until they are shocked out of it by the initiative of such rare pioneers as Begum Liaquat Ali Khan of Pakistan.

While a white South African woman, Margaret Ballinger, was climbing to the top of the political tree, which she reached as the first woman to represent a native constituency in her country's Parliament, native South African girls—as the Duchess of Atholl informed a shocked House of Commons in 1929—were still being submitted to the grim and superstitious rite of female circumcision.* While such exceptional Middle Eastern women as Halidé Edib of Turkey were fighting for the education of their sisters in their own backward communities, Eleanor Rathbone was battling, with her characteristic bull-in-a-china-shop indignation which always accomplished so much more of greatness than anyone thought possible, to raise the age of marriage and the value set on women amongst the Arabs in Palestine.

* And still are. See chapter 5, p. 62.

Even in the relatively progressive West, we have all grown up with clichés which have survived as the expression of once widely-accepted beliefs. 'God made them high and lowly and ordered their estate' was taken less critically for granted by our grandfathers than today by ourselves, but what would-be modern peacemaker has not been challenged by the moss-encrusted argument: 'There have always been wars and there always will be; you can't change human nature'?

Translated into terms of problems which have already been solved by the subordination of primitive human qualities, these defeatist dogmatisms reveal their absurdity. 'There have always been slaves and there always will be.' 'Women have always had to suffer or die in childbirth; it's the law of God and the curse of Eve.' In Parliamentary debates on the use of anæsthetics by midwives we still hear echoes of this unscientific and irreligious sentiment, for which Martin Luther's dictum provided an august precedent: 'If a woman becomes weary and at last dead from bearing, that matters not; let her die only from bearing, she is there to do it'.

But the statesmen, civil servants, scientists, doctors and nurses who between them have reduced the annual number of maternal deaths from 4,000 in 1900 to under 700 in 1950, know that this 16th-century attitude has no relation to the proved facts of modern life. The economist studying industrial regulations becomes similarly aware that much so-called 'men's work' is no more than a cherished Trade Union phantom, since the muscular strength once required to perform it was replaced by mechanical power half a century ago.

Entrenched prejudice, like self-interest rooted in custom, may resist the forces of a new age long after the society to which it was relevant has passed from human memory. But the impetus of men and women in the van of thought and experiment has yet been, within the past fifty years, incredibly swift.

Through the dust arising from the violent collapse of outworn institutions, we can already see the outlines of the age which should replace our own.

It will actually arrive only if its vulnerable architects are not sacrificed to those incidental products of contemporary science by which man's diabolical ingenuity has rendered incalculable and uncontrollable the consequences of war. We live, work, and alter at a speed which would have appeared intolerable to the Europeans and Americans who established, a century ago, the earliest schools and colleges for women, and started the process by which their pupils' successors have gradually been transformed from third-class parasites into first-class citizens.

With the speeding-up of our mental and physical lives has come a new development of the human spirit; a growth of insight already manifesting itself in religion, literature and art, and in political and social change. Something has been lost; the creative contemplation of the slower ages has gone, and can now be recovered only by the deliberate allocation and organisation of time. But time itself, for the individual, has changed its character. Normal life has not only secured a larger quota of years, but fills those years with a fresh richness of experience attainable through the modern rapidity of travel and production, the shrinkage of the world, and the consequent impact of all its races, classes, and types, and both its sexes, upon one another.

In such a period, the history of women must be presented mainly as the story of a conscious revolution. Its shape and colour are unaffected by the fact that some of the most striking changes in women's habits and behaviour—for example in sport—appear to have no political significance. Every development in the position of women, every new field which they have entered or further explored, has been due to a change of perspective directly related to the women's movement.

Apart from the right to education secured for women in the 19th century, the first effective part of this movement was political because, as Chapter 3 shows, it had to be. Legal and social reforms depended upon a change of status which could be accomplished only by political means. From the stimulus of that political campaign, new life flowed into every effort made by women everywhere.

They still owe much of their inspiration to those suffragist forbears, though the middle-aged may have forgotten their names and the young never knew them. Amy Johnson could not have flown to Australia, Virginia Woolf would not have been generally accepted as the greatest British novelist of the period between the wars, and India would not have appointed Mrs Vijayalakshmi Pandit to her highest ambassadorial post, if the right to vote had never been won.

The Welfare State itself is a product of the women's revolution. During the past decade the Beveridge Report, and the legislation which followed it, have embodied the change in social values which that revolution accomplished.

It is therefore inevitable that the feminist movement should first have impressed itself on the public mind as a series of claims to equal citizenship—in politics, education, professional and industrial employment, legal status, social respect. But these practical claims add up, at a deeper level, to one demand: the recognition of woman's full share in a common humanity.

Accept us, women say, as complete human beings, and we will be content. Freed from false identification with angels or with children, we will find our level as men have always found theirs, and develop with pride our own interests and values. Release us only from irrelevant handicaps based on superstition, outmoded custom, and jealous fear, and each of us as individuals will seek and occupy the place for which she is best fitted. We ask for no favours, but only for the elimination of unreal obstacles which penalise our abilities and shackle our feet. The logical consequence of political and legal equality is the disappearance of artificial restrictions on our range of decision and choice.

Though this range, especially for married women, is still narrower than that of men, the 20th century has already brought to middle-class women the supreme gift of work. After more than a hundred years of imposed unemployment while woman's traditional occupations vanished one after another from the home into the factory, she is no longer sentenced to that enervating parasitism against which Olive Schreiner declaimed so eloquently in *Woman and Labour*.

To the woman in industry or agriculture, who has always worked, the past fifty years have brought relative security, and the acknowledged right to a leisure which no longer exists in theory alone. This leisure, once of use only to the wealthy and highly-educated, has been made enjoyable for the wage-earner by broadcasting, television, cinemas, cheap newspapers, and paper-backed books. Even that economic Cinderella, the hard-working British wife and mother who runs the wage-earner's home with outdated tools and a bare minimum of domestic conveniences, receives for her children a modest family allowance paid direct to her by the State, and can listen to the radio while she cooks or washes up.

Moreover, especially if she is under thirty, she has not quite so often to cook and wash up alone. She still inhabits a man-dominated world, but thanks to the past half-century of revolution the men belong to a different type from that of her grandfather and even her father.

The change in women is constantly emphasised by literature and the Press, but the change in men, which is seldom discussed, has been equally remarkable. At different levels of consciousness modern man is beginning to perceive that, since modern woman has taken over so many of the functions that used to be exclusively his, the balance must be redressed by his willing and intelligent entry into the 'sphere' that once was hers alone.

In the 19th century and the opening years of the 20th, it was commonly assumed (by men) that only men were liable to intellectual frustration. They flattered themselves—as some do still—that one of their number was, in himself, sufficient compensation to a gifted woman for the renunciation of independent work, material reward, worldly success, and spiritual achievement.

> 'And that one talent, which is death to hide,
> Lodged with me useless . . .'

was regarded as a proper expression of despair for Milton, but not for Emily Brontë or Florence Nightingale (though it was Florence, confined to the stuffy tedium of a Victorian drawing-room, who penned the desperate phrase 'Death from Starvation!').

Deprived of natural outlets for their energies, our mothers and grandmothers monopolised their husbands, sought to dominate their sons and possess their daughters, made fetishes of their kitchens, and gods of their homes. Most men, having every apparent advantage by doing so, encouraged this narrowing of a wife's mind and activities. Only the thoughtful few perceived that a voluntary partner is more flattering to self-esteem than a compulsory slave.

Victorian masculinity survives sporadically in the elderly non-adult male who, refusing to adapt himself to the 20th century, still expects to be spoiled and waited on by a dependent female entourage. His realistic junior accepts and welcomes the transition from empty-headed parasite or unpaid domestic servant to the intelligent, independent companion who chooses his society for its own sake, and not for the material benefits which it confers. The price he pays for the great privilege of lasting love and mutual respect is small. It amounts to no more than help with the housework and occasional shopping, in addition to the more constant society of his children and an understanding of their care which benefits both him and them.

A community which has doubled the number of its well-trained and socially-conscious citizens has nothing to regret. It is reaching the stage at which the ancient antagonism between the masculine principle of power and tyranny, and the feminine principle of love and co-operation, will be redeemed and transformed.

Hitherto the majority of women, moulded by tradition and conventional education, have accepted masculine values as a matter of course. A conspicuous few, such as Catherine of Russia and Maria Theresa of Austria (of whom it was said during the 18th-century Partitions of Poland that the more she wept, the more territory she demanded) have outstripped men of comparable status in the application of those values. Conversely a minority of great men, whose ranks include Buddha, Socrates, Jesus Christ, St Francis of Assisi, Erasmus, and Gandhi, have been guided by the feminine principle which seeks harmony and peace.

During the recent past, we have seen an exaggerated development of the masculine principle in that form of moral and spiritual bankruptcy which we know as Fascism. In the destructive Fascist world of power-politics, it was inevitable that women—like Jews and other 'subject' classes—should be relegated to an auxiliary role. In the creative world of individual human values, it is just as inevitable that women should occupy an equal place as citizens.

The history of men and women in the past fifty years suggests that the old conflict between male and female will ultimately reach reconciliation in a new synthesis which is already in sight. The organic type of human being which will emerge from that synthesis may well be the constructive achievement of the next half-century.

2

THE WOMAN OF 1901

NINETEEN-HUNDRED-AND-ONE. The end of an old reign and the beginning of a new century. It was variously described as the Age of the New Realism, the New Theology, the New Politics—and the New Woman. Some enthusiasts, with an optimism which modern students might consider excessive, even called it the Century of Hope.

Yet, for all its wars and barbaric retrogressions, the dawning epoch was not altogether misnamed. It was to prove a century not only of hope but of relative fulfilment for more than half the human race.

What was happening, in 1901, to those men and women who had been, or were to be, the pioneers to whom 20th-century women would owe so deep a debt? Who, and where, were their opponents?

Mary Wollstonecraft, the beautiful woman derided by Horace Walpole as 'a hyena in petticoats' whose book started the women's revolution, had been dead for over a century. Twenty-one years earlier, George Eliot had died in the decade which saw the birth of Virginia Woolf. Three famous pioneers were now growing old. In 1901 Florence Nightingale was eighty-one and Josephine Butler seventy-three. Sophia Jex-Blake, who had fought so brave a battle for medical women, was sixty-one, with eleven years of life before her.

In the United States Susan B. Anthony, the exact contemporary of Florence Nightingale who from 1854 had pleaded for women's emancipation before hostile crowds, was to live five years longer. Mrs Chapman Catt had succeeded her in 1900 as President of the American National Suffrage Association.

Among the younger women carrying on the suffrage campaign in Britain, Millicent Garrett Fawcett was fifty-four, Emmeline

Pankhurst forty-three, Emmeline Pethick-Lawrence thirty-four, and Eleanor Rathbone twenty-eight. Beyond Europe and America women were still shrouded in the night of immemorial custom, though occasionally a woman's voice sounded from afar with a new note to which the future would respond.

One such challenge, the *Story of an African Farm*, had been issued from South Africa in 1883 by Olive Schreiner, who was to send forth another with *Woman and Labour* in 1911. Amid the primitive masses of Eastern women, Sarojini Naidu, the 'Nightingale of India' who ended her life as Governor of the United Provinces, was already writing her poems.

The men associated with this gathering revolution were naturally fewer, since the readiness to work against one's apparent interests for the welfare of others is an uncommon human quality. In 1901 John Stuart Mill, who had initiated the first Parliamentary debate on Women's Suffrage in 1867, had been dead for twenty-eight years. Two other conspicuous thinkers, Sigmund Freud and Bertrand Russell, who were to have their related effect upon the popular attitude towards women, were aged respectively forty-five and twenty-nine.

Amongst the younger politicians David Lloyd George, destined after much adroit evasion to be responsible for the first British instalment of woman suffrage in 1918, was in 1901 the thirty-eight-year-old Member for Cærnarvon Boroughs. Four years his junior was Stanley Baldwin, who was to complete the democratic franchise in Britain by conferring votes on women under thirty in 1928 and to drop a cartload of bricks in the attempt to do it gracefully. ('I would rather trust a woman's instinct than a man's reason.')

Other junior political figures were to prove themselves fence-sitters as expert as Lloyd George, and to support the women's cause only when to oppose it would jeopardise their own political standing. In 1901 a twenty-seven-year-old journalist named Winston Churchill had the previous year become Conservative M.P. for Oldham after serving in South Africa as war correspondent for the *Morning Post*.

As Member for North-west Manchester he was to be present at the historic meeting in Manchester Free Trade Hall on October

13th, 1905, when Christabel Pankhurst and Annie Kenney interrupted Sir Edward Grey with the cry 'Votes for Women!' and started the militant suffragette campaign. Thereafter, as successively President of the Board of Trade, Home Secretary, and First Lord of the Admiralty, Churchill, now openly hostile to the women's cause, was to become a prominent member of the compass-boxing Liberal Government which the Women's Social and Political Union made the special object of their attack.

Between the reigns of Victoria and Elizabeth II, women throughout the world advanced from subjection to a position, in many countries, of comparative equality. The 'New Woman' who had shocked the later 19th century symbolised the most revolutionary change in human relationships which history had known, but the year 1901 registered no sudden transformation in her status. It heralded less a beginning than an end—the end of the period described by Charlotte Luetkens as 'The Hundred Years War for Women's Self-Determination' which concluded with the outbreak of another War in 1914. After that cataclysm the continuing struggle was to become a different type of movement conducted by a different type of woman, far 'newer' than the New Woman of 1901.

The process of emancipation which began midway through the 19th century had moved very slowly. As early as 1840, when female delegates from the United States were denied admission to a World Anti-Slavery Convention in London, the American women had indignantly started an organised militant crusade for their rights. British women launched a similar campaign in 1866, but this made less progress than the founding of schools and colleges, associated with the names of Dorothea Beale, Frances Buss, and Emily Davies, between 1840 and 1880. Charles Kingsley, in spite of putting on record that men must work and women must weep, had helped to initiate in 1847 the series of Lectures for Ladies which in the following year became Queen's College for Women.

By 1901 a few legal concessions had been made to married women, who were still the chief sufferers from female subjection. These included the introduction of an unequal divorce law in

1857, and the recognition of a wife's right to own property by the Married Women's Property Acts of 1870 and 1882.

As citizens, the progress of women had been municipal rather than national; the first female Poor Law Guardians were elected in 1875, and women had been granted a local government vote. The London Government Act of 1899, which created Metropolitan Borough Councils, at first excluded married women from membership, but removed this disability in 1900.

For women the preceding half-century, disappointing as it had seemed to the more ardent revolutionaries, registered the first decisive steps from the anonymity of a class towards the freedom of a person. Some medieval theologians had doubted whether women had souls, but, more disastrously, the scientific developments of the 18th and 19th centuries denied them the former exercise of their faculties in work. As the Industrial Revolution proceeded, a minority of women had begun to realise that they were not qualified to use the hours of leisure left on their hands.

A few male Radicals and philanthropists realised it too; their attitude at its most enlightened was expressed in John Stuart Mill's *The Subjection of Women*, published in 1869. But current conventional ideas about woman's function in society hampered, as always, the development of these new values more than overt opposition.

The emotional domination of daughters by their parents, the prevailing narrow conception of women's place in the family, and the Victorian fear of immodesty which left conspicuous social evils timidly unpublicised, were embodied in a general tendency to discount the personalities of individual women and relegate them to a female class with common characteristics. Fashion endorsed this emphasis on femininity by cumbering adult women with unhygienic clothing and top-heavy hats, and by wrapping up the comely bodies of adolescent girls in stifling layers of woollen underwear.

'There were . . . very large numbers of otherwise intelligent persons', wrote Mary Agnes Hamilton in the symposium entitled *Our Freedom and its Results*, 'who did sincerely endorse the view that members of the female sex were not human, as members of the male sex were. For some they were sub-human, for others superhuman.' Bertrand Russell subsequently recorded the same attitude towards women in his *Unpopular Essays*. 'The belief in their "spiritual" superiority was part and parcel of the determination to keep them inferior politically and economically.'

Many other writers, such as Winifred Holtby in *Women and a Changing Civilisation*, have shown how closely this attitude of fear and exaggerated reverence was related to primitive taboos concerning sexual functions, familiar to any Old Testament student in the Books of Leviticus and Deuteronomy. Absurd superstitions associated with these functions survived owing to the perpetual cycle of pregnancy and childbearing imposed upon 19th-century women by the high rate of infant mortality, combined with their ignorance of contraception which made them the victims of physical chance.

Even in the childhood of women now no more than middle-aged, periodicity was still regarded as a species of feminine illness which provided one of many excuses for excluding women workers from lucrative positions. Strangely enough, it was not considered an objection to charwomen carrying buckets of coal up several flights of stairs, or to hospital nurses standing for hours on duty.

Prejudice, taboo, and the rigid 19th-century conception of woman's obligations added up to an attitude of contempt and distrust which the more progressive women rightly perceived as the chief obstacle to social and political change. An interesting revelation of enlightened Victorian values comes from a course of lectures on 'The Duties of Women', delivered at the age of fifty-nine by Frances Power Cobbe in 1881, and posthumously republished by the American firm of Swan Sonnenschein & Co. in 1905.

Like many social instructors of this period, Miss Cobbe—whose lectures were described by a male contemporary as 'a veritable handbook of noble living'—tended to confuse the important with the trivial, and Christian morality with the severe contemporary attitude towards sexual misdemeanours if committed by women. But she went to the root of much existing evil in her complaint that men had treated women 'uniformly as *minors*'.

'With all their kindly feelings', she added in another passage, 'men give us most rarely that which we really want, not favour, but—Justice. . . . That a woman should really possess *public spirit*, and that its exercise should be as ennobling to her as it is to a man —this is a lesson which it takes most men half a life-time to learn.'

Even by the opening decades of the 20th century, the majority had not learned it. The outlook of many young fathers was summed up during the First World War by an Oxford acquaintance who announced the birth of a daughter by inquiring miserably: 'Have you heard of our fiasco?' This feeling probably still lingers, especially in the aristocratic circles where male primogeniture retains its anachronistic importance. But the fact that public opinion would now be shocked by so frank an expression of sex prejudice is a 'straw' which indicates the changing winds of human values.

More outdated seems the once obstinate belief that all women were unreliable and could not keep secrets. As a girl I suffered a sharp setback to youthful confidence when a business friend of my father visited our provincial home during my schooldays. Mistaking his patronising interest in my progress for real benevolence, I was discoursing eagerly to the visitor about my plan to qualify for a profession when one devastating sentence quenched my effervescence.

'You surely don't imagine', he exclaimed, 'that men would ever put real confidence in one of your sex?'

I have often wished that this elderly accountant could have lived to see the day when innumerable business negotiations would depend upon the trustworthiness of confidential women secretaries, who were to prove more capable than men in a profession so soon to offer women a vast field of choice. Even in 1892 seven Government Departments ventured to introduce female typists, and by 1906 Mrs Hoster's Bureau was advertising 'Secretarial Training for Gentlewomen'. The illusion that women could not be trusted with private information was finally exploded between 1939 and 1945, when the women of the Auxiliary Air Force, acting as front-line sentries in the air defence of Britain, used radar for two years before the British people became aware of its existence.

In 1901, the relegation of women to second-class citizenship still impaired public life. It was not least conspicuous in the all-male House of Commons, where the great social problems recently embodied in the Beveridge Report were contemptuously dismissed as 'women's questions'. Contempt frequently became derision; in her biography (1927) of Josephine Butler, Dame Millicent Fawcett stated that in 1871 'and for many years after, it was the general habit of Members of Parliament to receive any mention of women, or of childbirth, with roars of laughter'. She added: 'It is worth something to have stopped this. That sort of laughter is out of fashion now.'

In *Our Freedom and Its Results*, Eleanor Rathbone described the attempt made by a small group of men and inconspicuous women to rid Britain of its drunken 'Sairey Gamps' by a little Bill requiring that midwives should be trained and registered.

'The very word "midwife",' she recorded, 'in those days was apt to make Members titter and dig each other furtively in the ribs.'

Bernard Shaw, writing in an American newspaper some years ago, recalled similar hilarity among the members of a London Health Committee discussing maternity and child welfare. It is perhaps not surprising that a serious onslaught on maternal mortality had to wait for the second quarter of the 20th century.

'Truly', wrote Frances Power Cobbe of such jocund discussions, 'it is a gallant and gentlemanly sport, and one of which it appears these Members of Parliament will not soon tire.' Going on to lament women's 'terrible want of *esprit de corps*', she deplored the servility of those who flattered men 'by pretending to agree with them in their contempt for the claims of women'.

She would perhaps have been astonished to learn that sixty years later this servility would still exist. It can be found, for example, in Middleton Murry's essay *Adam and Eve* (1944), to which 'Eve' writes a Postscript rapturously accepting the auxiliary position allocated to her by the author. But by the nineteen-forties this emotional submissiveness was only sporadic, and but for the retrogressive period of Fascism in Germany and Italy, would probably have disappeared. In 1901 contempt and servility, with all their tragic social consequences, were still almost universal.

* * *

The International Congress of Women which met in London in 1899 discussed these consequences in relation to contemporary society. Despite persistent constitutional propaganda and such occasional concessions as the right to vote at Borough Council elections given to British spinsters in 1869, the lack of a Parliamentary vote still meant political ineffectiveness for organised women.

A paper read at the Congress by Madame Avril de St Croix, the Josephine Butler of France, insisted that the great obstacle to women's enfranchisement had been woman herself. For so many years she had looked at all questions through the eyes of the opposite sex that until recently she had been blind to her own interests.

One such 'interest' was education, in which at least women could now record an advance. By the British Education Act of 1870 they had been made eligible to serve on School Boards, and in 1873 Mrs Nassau Senior had been appointed a Poor Law Inspector with the special duty of investigating the education given to pauper girls. Three women had served on the Royal Commission on Secondary Education in 1895, and by the end of Victoria's reign, Queen's College for Women and Bedford College had existed for half a century.

At Oxford and Cambridge, colleges had been founded for women, who were now admitted to the University examinations though they were not allowed to take Degrees. London University, bolder than the ancient foundations which were still erring on the side of caution forty years later, had granted Degrees and full membership to women in 1879, and provincial universities had followed their lead.

Since 1870, both sexes equally had received elementary education, and a number of modern secondary schools for girls had been founded.* By 1901 girls therefore had, at least in theory, facilities for secondary education comparable with those of their brothers. In her paper at the International Congress, Mrs Woodhouse, Chairman of the School Section, even inquired whether the education of girls did not follow too exclusively the lines of the leading boys' schools.

* See chapter 6.

'Woman is not undeveloped man, but diverse', she said, expressing an opinion which thoughtful women, though probably for different reasons, were to sustain fifty years later.

The secondary schoolgirl of 1901, with her bicycle which first foreshadowed the Baby Austin type of freedom precipitated by the 1914 War, still represented only a small minority drawn from a few progressive families. Among the majority, especially in the provinces, girls who desired to educate themselves were known as 'bluestockings' and 'strong-minded women'.

These terms were of course disparaging, since strong minds and marriageability were thought to be mutually exclusive, and the 'clinging vine' type of woman still evoked men's moral approval. Education and social custom alike centred on marriage, though sex technique and mothercraft played no part in a girl's curriculum.

Apart from a small number of pioneers, the feminine fear of permanent spinsterhood meant that only women compelled to earn a living entered business and the professions. The types of work then available to them offered little interest or variety and virtually no opportunity of self-advancement, but they were better off than their predecessors half a century earlier.

In 1850 the women obliged to be self-supporting had the choice only of becoming governesses or dressmakers. Both these occupations were pitifully crowded and egregiously underpaid. The 24,770 governesses of 1851 received a salary averaging £25 a year, while dressmakers worked for sixteen hours a day and for 10d. apiece made garments which sold at £5. Occasionally a woman ventured into teaching, only to find herself so ludicrously underrewarded as virtually to be denied professional status. Miss Agnes Maitland, then Principal of Somerville College, Oxford, told the International Congress of Women that at Bedford School in 1800 the salary of the headmaster had been £1,000 a year, but that of 'the mistress' only £80.

The growing number of women who took advantage of the new educational opportunities to become teachers—124,000 according to the Census of 1901—were better off than this, though in a long-established and hence tradition-ridden women's profession they were still to be fighting for equal pay in 1953.

Nursing had acquired prestige from Florence Nightingale's adventures in the Crimean War, and by 1901, 68,000 nurses were at work.

Between 1870 and 1914 the number of women clerks in the Civil Service, aided by the invention of the typewriter which they operated with deftness and speed, multiplied twenty times while that of men only doubled. The Post Office especially employed them—of course at low salaries. But apart from the decorative exception of authorship, the more colourful and responsible professions were still masculine monopolies. Though a few determined pioneers had forced their way, with Sophia Jex-Blake, into the medical profession during the eighteen-sixties and seventies, the Census of 1901 showed only 212 women doctors. Two architects, a few law clerks, and a limited number of secretarial assistants in banks and insurance companies closed the list of adventurous occupations, though nearly 60,000 women were now employed in commerce.

In industry and domestic service the numbers were far greater, but working conditions and rates of pay were still, by modern standards, appalling. The employers of the 1,740,800 domestic servants—representing half the women shown by the Census of 1901 to be employed—expected them even in spacious houses to live in attics and basements. Large numbers of women had worked in factories from the Industrial Revolution onwards; textiles alone accounted for 663,200. But their wages were low, averaging less than £1 a week for a skilled worker, and contemporary factory legislation did not touch this problem.

In *The Cause*, her history of the woman suffrage movement, Ray Strachey noted that as Trades Unionism strengthened, 'women's position as the underdogs of industry came to seem a part of the order of the universe'. An investigation of women's employment in Birmingham by Edward Cadbury and others, published in 1906 under the title *Women's Work and Wages*, showed that in some branches of the metal industries women were paid as little as 6/- a week, and never received more than 24/-. The weekly wages of young girls in these industries ranged from 3/6 to 14/6.

Throughout the working world the very young and the very old encountered much cruelty, both deliberate and unconscious.

In her autobiography, *My Own Story*, Mrs Pankhurst recorded that as a Poor Law Guardian in Manchester during the eighteen-nineties she saw little girls of seven and eight on their knees scrubbing the cold stone floors of workhouse corridors, while the elderly unpensioned woman who had grown too old for work was obliged to become a pauper.

The address given to the 1899 International Congress of Women by Mrs James Ramsay Macdonald drew attention to these evils, which were not confined to Britain.

'From country after country', she said, 'from industry after industry comes the sad tale of long hours, insanitary conditions, wretched pay, poor food and dwellings.... With working women the conditions are even worse than with working men.'

In the ensuing discussion, Miss Margaret Bondfield deplored the 'living-in' system which she held responsible for the ill-health suffered by women in shops: hurried meals were served in badly ventilated underground dining-rooms where the close proximity of drains meant loss of appetite. Most large businesses then allowed their workers only thirty minutes for dinner, and twenty for breakfast and tea.

Four other delegates, Fräulein Saloman of Germany, Baroness Alexandra Gripenberg of Finland, Mrs Stanton Black of the United States, and Mrs Sidney Webb of Britain, foreshadowed some acute future controversies when they enquired how far the widespread exploitation of women workers could be remedied by special legislation. Mrs Webb advocated such measures as an 'instalment of reform' eventually to be applied to all workers, but Baroness Gripenberg believed that they would destroy women's hopes for equal rights.

'Women', she insisted, 'cannot demand both sex privileges and recognition as men's equals.'

The relative helplessness of these appointed representatives in their attempts to raise the position of their sex arose from three major causes, of which the lack of a political status was only the first. To the absence of a vote, the poverty of women and their legal and social disabilities added the implacable conundrum of a vicious circle.

Middle-class women, who had received at least enough education to work for the betterment of their exploited sisters, still depended financially upon their husbands or fathers, and had not the means to endow educational bodies and altruistic societies. The down-trodden workers, exhausted by poor food, low pay, and fatiguing travel, lacked the knowledge and energy to organise themselves, while their self-respect was undermined by the shabby attire which poverty forced upon them.

Even in the posts which ranked as professions, the 'typical' governess or teacher, like the lady's maid, wore a virtual uniform in neutral tints which suggested subservience. No one understood in 1901 that the woman who earns her living cannot afford the dead-weight of an inferiority-complex. Women had still to learn that self-confidence is the keynote of success, and that to be beautiful is less important than to feel beautiful.

Although their poverty made them socially helpless, the legal position of women had somewhat advanced by 1901 from the 'all-time low' of 1800–1850. But the numbers affected by the new right of wives to own property, whether acquired or inherited, were still small. Few married women earned incomes, and few fathers left money unencumbered by restrictions to their daughters.

As parents, women now possessed a legal though unequal status which they had lacked altogether in 1800. Thanks to the almost unaided efforts of Mrs Caroline Norton, whose husband deserted her and removed their three children, a Judge had been enabled since 1839 to grant a mother access to her infant offspring. Fifteen years before 1901, a new Act provided that on a father's death the mother should be guardian, either alone or with a partner of the father's choice.

Compared with the 'superfluous' spinster a wife was legally penalised, for during the first half of the 19th century the law regarded her as virtually her husband's property. Until 1857, marriages could be dissolved only by the costly process of a special Act of Parliament. Mrs Strachey recorded that when at last a Marriage and Divorce Bill came before the House, Mr Gladstone made twenty-nine speeches against a single clause.

The Court for Divorce and Matrimonial Causes finally set up under this Act provided, as everyone expected, only for unequal divorce regulations; the husband could sue by reason of his wife's adultery alone, but the wife had to prove cruelty or desertion as well. This unsensational advance was offset by a retreat of which the results became conspicuous only in the 1914-1918 War; in 1870 British-born women lost their common-law right to retain British nationality on marriage to an alien.

In 1878 and 1895, further Acts had enabled wives whose husbands ill-treated them to obtain separation orders. But married women had to wait until 1923 for equal divorce, since in 1901, despite the respectable surface-morality of Victorian England, a double moral standard was as callously accepted there as in many communities with fewer advantages which the British people regarded as backward.

'There is at present no country in the world, certainly no civilised country', wrote Havelock Ellis in *Man and Woman* in 1897, 'in which a woman may safely state openly her wishes and desires, and proceed openly to seek their satisfaction.'

Many men, on the other hand, sought such satisfaction openly, tyrannically, and sometimes brutally. Marriage was not an equal partnership but too often a master-servant relationship, in which conjugal obedience—described by Frances Power Cobbe as 'slavery' and 'moral suicide'—was expected to include the acceptance of almost unlimited maltreatment. In her lectures Miss Cobbe quoted contemporary figures which showed that, counting only the cases brought before magistrates, an average of four 'aggravated assaults' by husbands on wives occurred in Britain every day of the year. An aggravated assault meant far more than a simple blow; it involved knocking out a wife's eye, setting her on fire, or attacking her with a paraffin lamp.

The law of England (Regina v. Clarence, 1899) then maintained that a husband could not be held guilty of committing rape on a wife who tried to refuse intercourse, even if he was suffering from a disease of which he was aware though she was not. This form of moral subjection had been modified only by the Matrimonial Causes Act, which laid down that a wife who refused to obey a decree for the restitution of conjugal rights would not be imprisoned by the Court, and by a decision of 1891 (Regina v. Jackson) which established that a husband could not seize his wife and restrain her liberty if she refused to live with him. So long as she remained under his roof, the law in all its primitive brutality took effect.

'I denounce this infamy', exclaimed Mrs Wolstenholme Elmy to the Women's International Congress, 'in the name of the wife, the mother, the child, the race, and the higher humanity to which we aspire!'

In the upper and middle classes the wife thus legally penalised was often richly dressed and bejewelled, conveniently advertising her husband's affluence to customers and neighbours. But she was powerless owing not only to financial subjection and the cruelty of the law, but to the still widespread ignorance which made pregnancy an ever-threatening outcome of marital relations, and withheld from her the right to decide the number of her children.*

If a child resulted from illicit intercourse by a married woman, the penalty for both mother and child constituted a form of moral revenge out of all proportion to the offence. Even the enlightenment of Frances Power Cobbe broke down at the point of adultery.

'When a woman', she wrote, 'has committed the enormous double crime, personal and social, of violating the law of chastity, and doing her husband the mortal wrong of breaking her marriage oath, it is fit and right that the society which she has outraged should close its doors to her.'

Would the virtuous and progressive Miss Cobbe, one wonders, have advocated that the backslider should adopt prostitution as a profession? And why had she nothing to say about the numerous Victorian husbands who, with socially approved discretion, broke their own marriage vows? Perhaps, even for her, mercy could not attain its full height until justice had been won.

In spite of society's remorseless penalties, moral mishaps were made difficult to avoid by the total lack of sexual instruction which handicapped 'respectable' girls right up to marriage. Among the overcrowded poor some knowledge of life's realities was inescapable, but for the middle-class girl an atmosphere of perturbing mystery surrounded the many limitations which shackled that social parasite, the leisured woman.

* See chapter 11.

This iniquitous form of 'protection' continued long after 1901. A private school which I attended just before the First World War was exceptional in allowing its pampered pupils to read the newspapers, but before these were handed over, all sexually informative paragraphs had been carefully extracted. Even *The Times*, which was available unimpaired during the holidays, referred to venereal disease with baffling obliquity as 'the hidden plague'.

Dangerous knowledge, like 'strong-mindedness', reduced the marriage-market value of the well-to-do-girl brought up to expect a life of permanent inescapable tutelage. This life too often turned her into a frustrated valetudinarian, and deprived her even of intimacy with her children who were handed over to nursemaids, but her elders and contemporaries considered her a failure if she had not achieved it by thirty. Outside the limited ranks of the professions, marriage still represented the only justification of a middle-class woman's existence, yet training for wifehood and motherhood was the last asset with which her epoch thought it necessary to provide her.

Evidence of the psychological effects of this social attitude and the disabilities which accompanied it has now been gathered from many sources. The writings of famous 19th-century women show that a hampering sense of inferiority was not confined to the shabby governess or impoverished ladies' maid; it penalised every woman, however gifted, who found herself habitually classed with children, and had constantly to throw aside her work because the most trivial masculine need was considered more important.

'Probably only women who have laboured under it', wrote Barbara Stephen in *Emily Davies and Girton College*, 'can understand the weight of discouragement produced by being perpetually told that, as women, nothing much is ever expected of them.'

The compilers of the Report entitled *The Feminine Point of View* (1952) quote George Eliot, some years before she became a novelist, as writing resignedly that her only remaining 'ardent hope' was to be given 'some woman's duty—some possibility of devoting myself where I may see a daily result of pure calm blessedness in the life of another'. Mary Kingsley, the pioneer explorer of West Africa, similarly described herself as being 'the doer of odd jobs', and as living only 'in the joys and sorrows and worries of other people'—a vicarious burden not excluded even in the nineteen-thirties from the short life of Winifred Holtby, who was racing with death to finish her novel, *South Riding*.

'When a woman believes enough in her mission to be ruthless —a Mrs Siddons, a Florence Nightingale, a Mrs Pankhurst—' Winifred wrote with feeling, for she could never cultivate that necessary ruthlessness herself, 'then, indeed, something happens. But most women dread before everything to "cause an upset" or inconvenience a family; and their work suffers.'

In her *Life of Charlotte Brontë*, Elizabeth Gaskell quoted one of Charlotte's letters.

'Life wears away. I shall soon be thirty, and I have done nothing yet. Sometimes I get melancholy at the prospect before and behind me. . . . I feel as if we were all buried here. I long to travel, to work, to have a life of action.'

So Charlotte stayed at home and produced only three great books when she might have written twenty, though her years of weary martyrdom at Haworth saved neither her father from sorrow, her brother from sin, nor herself and her talented sisters from premature death.

'Gifted women . . . cannot get rid of their relations', wrote Mrs Gaskell, herself the wife of a Unitarian minister and the mother of seven children. 'A woman cannot get away from her family even in its absence.'

But it was left to the powerful and bitter pen of Florence Nightingale to express the full anguish of her frustrated contemporaries in the passionate words of her youthful diary.

'Why, oh, my God, cannot I be satisfied with the life that satisfies so many people? Why am I starving, desperate, diseased upon it? . . . Oh, how I have longed for a trial to give me food, to be something real. A nourishing life—that is the happiness, whatever it be. A starving life, that is the real trial. My God, what am I to do? Teach me, tell me.'

When an occasional woman, like Florence herself, surmounted her lack of confidence, training, money and status, she usually had still to overcome that family tyrant, the self-styled lord of creation. Though the law gave disproportionate rights to husbands, it was not husbands only in whom the subordinate position of women produced spiritual pride, self-indulgence, and domineering habits combined with a lack of self-knowledge.

'It is all very well', indignantly wrote Frances Power Cobbe, 'to teach a boy in his catechism to "honour his mother", as well as his father. But when he comes to find that his mother is classified by the constitution of his country along with Criminals, Idiots, Lunatics, and Minors, is it likely he will honour her. . .? Boys receive from women themselves . . . a regular education in selfishness.'

Throughout a man's life, this training in selfishness was apt to reveal itself in trivial but significant actions. One contemporary of my father, taking his family away for their summer holiday, habitually travelled First himself but sent his wife and children Third. The wife's humble acceptance of these inferior facilities belittled, like the meekness of so many women, the status of motherhood itself.

Men's minds, as much as women's, laboured under the dead-weight of prejudice and tradition, originating in primitive assumptions of which the very mention would have shocked Victorian fathers. When men told women what they ought to want, only the few recognised a spiritual impertinence which expressed the crude self-esteem of the holders of power. Such impertinence is unfashionable today, but books written by men who feared women's advance, and believed that a society which perpetuated female subordination would be more comfortable for themselves, persisted into the 20th century. The works of Sir Almroth Wright, and other subsequent defenders of the *status quo*, clearly reveal a determination to protect their vested interests on the part of the sex long proclaimed superior.

But change, though slow, was coming. A new type of male, foreshadowed in the careers of John Stuart Mill and Richard Marsden Pankhurst, and later represented by such civilised personalities as Henry W. Nevinson, H. N. Brailsford, and F. W. Pethick-Lawrence, recognised that society was losing the services of half its members through the exaggeration of sex at the expense of common humanity. At last women found reason to hope that some day the relationship between the sexes would no longer be based upon the conception so forcibly expressed by Milton in *Samson Agonistes:*

> 'Therefore God's universal law
> Gave to the man despotic power
> Over his female in due awe,
> Nor from that right to part an hour,
> Smile she or lour.'

In 1901 the science of psychology was still young, but already a few students of human nature understood why this 17th-century version of 'Life with Father', in which Milton's three daughters dodged his demands and undermined his authority, had become a literary byword. If the claim to freedom so sonorously expressed in the magnificent invective of *Areopagitica* had been extended to all mankind, Milton would have been a better husband and father, and a happier human being. Many a Victorian paterfamilias, adopting his views, repeated his experience, and as the new century came in, pitched battles developed in numerous households between the older and younger generations.

'By 1900', wrote Ray Strachey in 1936, 'women were, in the main, free both in their persons and their properties, their money and their consciences, their bodies and their souls.'

The freedom which she applauded seemed encouraging only in relation to past restrictions, for the woman of 1901, as she admitted, was still 'politically outcast and economically oppressed; under-educated and over-flattered; too much despised and too much admired'. Her position would not suggest freedom to the young woman of today, for the next fifty years were to bring changes, both in and beyond the United Kingdom, far more rapid and extensive than those which occurred between 1850 and 1901.

From a country where politics were controlled exclusively by men, Britain was to become a land in which the government was elected by a preponderance of female voters, and women's values achieved concrete form through the realisation of the Welfare State.

3

THE STRUGGLE FOR POLITICAL EQUALITY

In 1867, an amendment submitted to the Constitution of the American State of Kansas to enfranchise the newly liberated Negro had been accompanied by a parallel amendment to give votes to women.

Slowly the 19th century was feeling its way to the realisation that no subject class, whether composed of wealthy white women or penniless coloured slaves, could achieve full humanity without responsibility and freedom. This conviction inspired the work of Olive Schreiner, who in *Trooper Peter Halket of Mashonaland* (1897) expressed in passionate words her belief that the cause of women, workers, and Negroes was the same.

Eventually it was the Far Western State of Wyoming, and not the mid-Western State of Kansas, which in 1869 gave women the vote. The first country to adopt this American example was New Zealand, in 1893. One last survivor of the New Zealand women who won that early victory, Mrs Clara Alley, died in 1952 at the age of eighty-six.

South Australia followed New Zealand in 1894. Six other countries—Australia (1902),* Finland (1907), Norway (1913), Iceland (1914), Denmark (1915), and the U.S.S.R. (1917)—were to enfranchise their women in advance of Britain.

Eighteen years after the opening of the century, British women received the first instalment of woman suffrage; the final instalment came ten years later. But in 1901 this future victory was far from apparent. A long stalemate had accompanied the hostility to female enfranchisement of Mr Gladstone, who appeared unaware that, in the reigns of Henry III and Edward I, Lady Abbesses had been summoned to Parliament as landowners. In a

* 1902 was the date of the Australian Federal vote. The Australian States enfranchised women at different dates between 1894 and 1905.

letter to Mr S. Smith, M.P., on August 21st, 1892, he had explained his objection to Sir Albert Rollit's Bill to extend the Parliamentary franchise to women.

'I have no fear lest the woman should encroach upon the power of the man. The fear I have is lest we should invite her unwittingly to trespass upon the delicacy, the purity, the refinement, the elevation of her own nature, which are the present sources of its power.'

Another Woman Suffrage Bill, introduced by Mr Faithfull Begg in 1897 and supported by a monster appeal carrying 257,796 signatures, had gone as far as a second reading, only to be defeated by seventy-one votes. The virtual Press boycott on news of the women's struggle continued, a prototype of the similar boycott to be imposed fifty years later on genuine seekers for a road to world peace. Even Mrs Pankhurst, right up to the publication of *My Own Story* in 1914, believed that universal suffrage would not come in the lifetime of any person then living.

The opposition which she and other suffragists had to face took several forms, usually ingenious and often contradictory. Most ordinary citizens still thought a woman too foolish to vote, but a few, like Mr Gladstone, believed—or said they believed—that she was too noble. More difficult to resist, because pseudo-scientific, was the opinion of such medical opponents as Sir Almroth Wright (*The Unexpurgated Case Against Woman Suffrage*, 1913) that the demand for political equality sprang from the sexual embitterment of warped and abnormal female minds.

Exponents of this view persisted into the nineteen-twenties, and were not limited to England. The British weekly journal which described the demand for equal voting rights as 'a clamour raised by women of a masculine or intermediate sex type', found an echo in an article on 'The Female Franchise in Australia' by 'An Australian Politician' in the *National Review* for December 1928.

'It cannot be too strongly urged and reiterated', argued this writer, 'that it is only women of abnormal type, approximating to the mentality and not infrequently to the physical appearance of the male, who enter with zest into the new order of things. To the woman of true type it has no attraction. . . . In Australia a sigh of relief will go up when it is decided to withdraw women from the rough, ruthless game of politics.'

One must charitably assume that this type of argument prevailed with women who opposed the enfranchisement of their own sex, but later did not carry the logic of their conviction to the length of declining to vote, or even of refusing high office. More bitter for the suffrage leaders than the evasive ruses and derisive criticism of their enemies was this illogical contempt for womanhood sometimes displayed by the very individuals who were showing what women could do.

Whatever their own capabilities, they appeared to regard other women as suited only to quiet unspectacular positions. When the female anti-suffragists formed their organisation in 1908, they put forward the growing opportunities for women in local government as a reason for rejecting national equality.

Some of the anti-suffrage women were highly intelligent and even famous; they included the writer, Mrs Humphry Ward, and Gertrude Bell, the distinguished unofficial diplomat who helped to found the State of Iraq. Those paragraphs in *The Letters of Gertrude Bell* which describe her anti-suffrage activities fall on the reader like unexpected blows after the liberal far-sightedness of her diplomacy; it is as though a close friend were discovered in an ungenerous act of betrayal.

Strangest of all was the record of Mrs Sidney Webb, who in 1889 signed a protest in the *Nineteenth Century* magazine by prominent women against woman suffrage, and at the International Congress of Women ten years later argued in favour of restrictive legislation for industrial women. Yet in 1919, as the author of the famous Minority Report issued by the War Cabinet Committee on Women in Industry, she strongly opposed such legislation on the ground that male Trade Unionists themselves no longer objected to the regulation of their working conditions by law.

As though history itself decided to applaud this unusual move from one side of the fence to the other, Beatrice Webb became in 1947 the first woman, apart from royalty, to be buried in Westminster Abbey on account of her own achievements.

* * *

Between 1901 and 1910 the woman suffrage movement divided; both in Britain and the United States a group of 'militants' broke away from the constitutionalists who for half a century had patiently propagated the women's cause. At this time Mrs Henry Fawcett was the recognised leader of the British constitutionalists, and Mrs Carrie Chapman Catt of the American.

The fundamental disagreement between the two wings of the movement is now an old but not a pointless controversy; reforms will be needed so long as humanity endures, and the makers of revolutions, whether spiritual or material, have always to decide by what means they can best undermine the vested interests of the *status quo*. Eleanor Rathbone, herself a convinced constitutionalist who in 1919 succeeded Millicent Fawcett as President of the National Union of Societies for Equal Citizenship (the former National Union of Women's Suffrage Societies), generously recorded in *Our Freedom and Its Results* her belief that both types of campaign were necessary.

She added that the militant movement had deeply impressed Mahatma Gandhi. In spite of its brief period of positive violence, he was said to have studied its technique with care before launching his own campaigns of non-violent resistance in South Africa and India.

At the beginning of the 20th century, after fifty years of persistent agitation, the constitutional suffrage movement had failed to capture the support of any political party. The Liberal leaders opposed woman suffrage, though the Liberal rank and file tended to uphold it; the Conservative leaders, 'playing politics', proclaimed friendliness, but their followers remained implacably hostile. The rising Labour Party proved even more disappointing; its leaders, while professing abstract approval, fought shy of practical pledges. By 1908, when Mr Asquith became Prime Minister, he was refusing to see or hear the suffrage leaders at all, and in the eyes of the Press the women's agitation had become so stale that their claims had ceased to be 'news'.

The women who belonged to this older and larger wing of the suffrage movement were mainly interested in progressive reforms. They saw the vote, in Eleanor Rathbone's words, as 'a key to the house of citizenship', and the numerous activities which this house contained tended to divert their minds from the concentration required to open the door.

In 1911, when the dramatic Conspiracy Trial of Mrs Pankhurst and the Pethick-Lawrences filled the columns of the newspapers, the National Union of Women's Suffrage Societies consisted of 411 self-supporting groups, each of which had to be consulted on every major decision. The fifty meetings that these groups held each night in the years preceding the First World War naturally attracted less attention than the deliberate self-martyrdom of Emily Wilding Davison, who tried to stop the King's horse at the 1913 Derby as a protest against non-enfranchisement.

Such histories as Ray Strachey's *The Cause*, and such biographies as Mary Stocks's study of Eleanor Rathbone, make clear that the machinery so painfully evolved from feminine inexperience had become too cumbersome. By the early 20th century, in spite of some well-organised mass demonstrations, this slow constitutional procedure was actually hampering the very ends which it was designed to serve. In shocked sentences Mrs Strachey records of the militant suffragists that they did not care what impression they made on other people, and with huge sums pouring in from their supporters were actually careless about their accounts. Such indifference was deplorable, no doubt; but it was less deadly to the women's cause than the creaking weight of glamourless organisation which delayed action and postponed decision.

The constitutionalist leader, later Dame Millicent Fawcett, was born in 1847 and lived until August 1929. Both she and Mrs Pankhurst, eleven years her junior, strangely illustrated the axiom that 'Man is immortal till his work is done', for both died within the eighteen months which followed the final instalment of woman suffrage.

Compared with the meteoric brilliance of Emmeline Pankhurst, one of history's shooting stars, Dame Millicent's eighty-two years of patient consolidation seem a somewhat pedestrian affair. Though capable of hard-hitting and shrewd diagnosis, she was invariably sensible, courteous, and judicial; and indispensable as these worthy qualities are to revolutions which without them would run amok, popular enthusiasm is seldom inspired by those who possess them. The revealing vignette of Dame Millicent by

Mrs Strachey, her admiring biographer, probably explains why the constitutional suffrage movement has never quite received its due from the British public.

Dame Millicent, Mrs Strachey tells us, 'was the central figure in scenes of passionate enthusiasm and equally passionate despair. But in the midst of it all she remained unaltered. She showed the same even judgment, the same quiet conviction and the same humorous breadth of outlook from beginning to end, and there were no dramatic developments in her character and none in her history. An unshaken reasonableness was evident in everything she did, whether great or small, and consequently her biography contains nothing sensational. She knew how to work and how to wait, but she did not know how to give way.'

Even the ruthless young for whom the suffrage movement appears *vieux jeu* know that the militants were led by Mrs Pankhurst, the fragile woman with the lovely face of a tired saint in whose sex there was nothing 'intermediate'. As the devoted wife of Richard Marsden Pankhurst, who died in 1898, and the mother of five children, she testified in *My Own Story* that her home life and relationships had been 'as nearly ideal as possible in this imperfect world'.

The militant movement began in 1903 with the decision of some Manchester working women to form their own suffrage society, the Women's Social and Political Union, with Mrs Pankhurst as leader. In 1895 she had been elected to the Manchester Board of Guardians, and after her husband's death was appointed Registrar —one of the first women to hold such a position—of Births, Marriages, and Deaths in Manchester.

'I thought I had been a suffragist before I became a Poor Law Guardian', she wrote years afterwards, 'but now I began to think about the vote in women's hands as not only a right but as a desperate necessity. Those poor unprotected mothers and their babies I am sure were potent factors in my education as a militant.'

Out of her vehement compassion for the poor and helpless, Mrs Pankhurst developed an imaginative and dramatic initiative which would probably have astonished her earlier self. As leader of Britain's most colourful revolution, she displayed remarkable qualities seldom combined. Enthusiastically supported by her brilliant eldest daughter Christabel, and less uncritically by her artistic second daughter Sylvia, she marshalled her forces with the remorseless precision of a military dictator. Yet she sought and accepted the martyr's crown of suffering, and exacted from her followers no more than she was willing to endure herself.

Like her husband, Mrs Pankhurst had been an active Liberal, but with many other women Liberals she experienced disillusionment owing to the obstructionist tactics of Mr Gladstone. From the beginning of the militant movement, her politics were determined solely by the interests of women. After losing faith also in the Labour Party she finished her life as Conservative candidate for Whitechapel, since the Conservative Party had given women the final instalment of the vote.

When the Unionist Government collapsed in the autumn of 1905, the militants seized their opportunity. The resounding tale of monster demonstrations, street contests, imprisonments, hunger-strikes, trials and martyrdoms which then began is now a vivid page of British history. Mrs Pankhurst's policy sprang partly from her contempt for the decorous failure of the constitutionalists to make any significant impact on public opinion, but it was rooted more deeply in the influence of books, such as *The Pilgrim's Progress* and *Uncle Tom's Cabin*, read aloud in her childhood by her idealistic parents.

These books, she related, 'awakened in me the two sets of sensations to which all my life I have most readily responded: first, admiration for that spirit of fighting and heroic sacrifice by which alone the soul of civilisation is saved; and next after that, appreciation of the gentler spirit which is moved to mend and repair the ravages of war'.

Civilisation still awaits the effective leavening of that 'gentler spirit', but numbers amongst its heroines many voluntary victims of the 'fighting and heroic sacrifice' which the militant movement demanded. Their names include Mrs Mary Clarke, a sister of Mrs Pankhurst, and Cecilia Wolseley Haig, both of whom died after their experiences on 'Black Friday' (November 18th, 1910). A better-known victim was Lady Constance Lytton, who suffered from valvular disease of the heart. After arrest she described herself as 'Jane Warton', a seamstress, and endured the forcible feeding which her rank and health would certainly have spared her.

Numerous other militants experienced rough treatment, combined with a peculiar type of humiliation which arose from the incompatibility of women's clothes with women's claims. Its very possibility has vanished today with flannel petticoats, ostrich feather boas, and hats adorned by birds of paradise reposing amid luscious nursery gardens of flowers and fruit. The Press attitude of contemptuous ridicule, always so much harder to fight than fierce political opposition, can still be gauged from the old posters preserved by the Suffragette Museum, now part of the London Museum at Kensington Palace.

It is through suffering and ecstasy that those who lead great campaigns appeal to the constructive instincts of mankind; words and actions, to inspire others, must spring from the heights and depths of human experience. The most effective crusader for peace has known at first hand the pity and terror of war; the surest saviour of a starving people from subjection is he who has endured both fasting and prison. Woman suffrage did not stir the sympathy of millions until women had proved their readiness to buy freedom and equality at the cost of torture and death.

For all their impatient violence, the brief spectacular years of militancy achieved more for the advancement of women than the preceding half-century of patient organisation, wearisome committees, and meritorious resolutions. The militants captured public imagination, and to the few who possess the rare ability to accomplish this miracle, everything is forgiven.

Because she had it, Emmeline Pankhurst rightly stands on her lonely pedestal in Victoria Tower Gardens at Westminster. She could not have scaled the heights of national eminence without the patient spade-work of her predecessors, and many measures of inestimable value, such as the provision for Family Allowances demanded by Eleanor Rathbone, are associated with the names of pioneer women who could not follow her and deplored her methods. Nevertheless she remains, for all time, the symbol of their achievement as well as her own.

The suffrage movement in the United States bore some resemblance to the agitation in Britain. Both revolutions owed their first inspiration to Mary Wollstonecraft, and both looked back to the Seneca Falls Convention of 1848 as their starting point. Each divided into a constitutional and a militant group, though in the United States the division came late, and the militant methods, compared with those of Britain, were as cider to champagne.

Here, however, the parallels cease. In the U.S.A. the constitutionalists thought it necessary to win over the leading States before attempting to obtain woman suffrage for the whole country. Though several States, mainly in the West, had given votes to women before the First World War, the constitutional leaders supported the demand for a Federal Amendment to the American Constitution only after woman suffrage had been carried in the key State of New York on November 6th, 1917.

In Britain also the issue was never confused, as in the United States, with that of a great humanitarian cause. American feminism suffered a long setback because the leaders of the anti-slavery campaign first made use of the women's propaganda, and then shamelessly repudiated them after the Civil War. Nor had Britain, in spite of the final symbolic triumph of Mrs Pankhurst, any one woman who could be regarded as the mother of the feminist movement in all its aspects, political, legal, economic, and social. In the U.S.A. this pioneer was Susan B. Anthony, 'the woman who changed the mind of a nation'. Though she did not live, unlike the British leaders, to see her work accomplished, she was both the founder of the constitutional movement led in the 20th century by Dr Anna Howard and Mrs Chapman Catt, and the originator of militancy.

Six years after her death, when the National American Woman Suffrage Association was working for State-by-State legislation instead of the Federal Amendment on which she had always insisted, Alice Paul and Lucy Burns, two young women fresh from their experience of British militancy, revived the Susan B. Anthony policy. In 1912 they broke away from the Association and formed the Congressional Union, later known as the National Woman's Party.

When the Nineteenth (Woman Suffrage) Amendment became part of the American Constitution in 1920, 'it was the soul of Susan B. Anthony that went marching on', wrote her biographer,

Rheta Childe Dorr. In November 1952, thirty-two years after the Nineteenth Amendment became law, twenty-nine million American women voted in the election which sent President Eisenhower to the White House, as against fewer than twenty-seven million men.

In other countries the suffrage movement followed a variety of patterns dictated by history and national psychology. The men of the liberty-loving Scandinavian countries seemed readier than most males to treat women as equals; though full political rights did not come in Sweden till 1921, the 19th-century agitation led by Frederika Bremer achieved some success as early as 1862. Her contemporary, Frederika Runeberg, played a similar part in Finland, and Norwegian women formed their first suffrage association in 1885 under the leadership of Gina Krog. Finland, Norway, Iceland, and Denmark had all given political equality to women before partial suffrage reached the Statute Book in Britain.

Among feminist campaigns in other civilised countries, the most stubborn and ultimately the most tragic was that of Germany. Here the struggle had not only to overcome complications caused, as in the U.S.A., by the division of the country into States, but also encountered peculiar difficulties owing to the *Hausfrau* tradition which assumed the intellectual superiority and absolute predominance of men. In spite of this conventional dead-weight, the movement begun by Louise Otto after the Revolution of 1848, and later linked with the names of Frau Minna Cauer and Dr Anita Augspurg, so far made progress that equal rights were written into the short-lived Weimar Constitution.

Thirty to forty women sat in each of the Reichstags between 1919 and 1933, and in 1926, when Germany was admitted to the League of Nations, she appointed a woman, Dr Gertrud Bäumer, as technical adviser. But after the advent of Hitler, with his reactionary theories of the auxiliary female, the previous prolonged submissiveness of German women made all too easy the period of retrogression which followed.

The similar reign of reaction in Mussolini's Italy seemed less disastrous, since women in countries under the legal system of the Code Napoléon had made little political progress even by 1933. The women of France and Italy had in fact to wait until 1944 and 1945 for equal suffrage, though it had been a French woman, Olympe de Gouges, a contemporary of Mary Wollstonecraft, who laid a 'Declaration of the Rights of Woman' before the Convention after the first French Revolution.

In Russia, the violent repudiation of the past gave votes to the women of a retarded country before the end of the First World War. Other backward nations were less fortunate. Throughout Asia and Africa the unenfranchised millions of illiterate wives and mothers awaited a new day which then seemed unlikely to dawn during the course of the century.

Between 1914 and 1916 the suffrage cause in Britain, unlike the American movement, remained in abeyance. Mrs Pankhurst herself called a truce to militancy on the outbreak of war, and the National Union of Women's Suffrage Societies revived the claims of women only in 1916, when changes of population had rendered useless the existing register of male voters. At last they were given a respectful hearing. Lord Robert Cecil, Mr Lloyd George, and Mr Arthur Henderson supported woman suffrage within the Cabinet, and even the Press became friendly.

In August 1916, converted by women's wartime achievements, Mr Asquith himself abandoned his resistance. After the fall of the Asquith Cabinet Mr Lloyd George, the new Premier, agreed that votes for women should be included in the coming Franchise Bill. But the preponderance of British women had always appeared an obstacle to equal rights, and some disqualification was sought which would reduce the number of women voters to a safe minority. Finally the suffrage societies accepted the illogical suggestion of votes at thirty for fear of again finding women totally disfranchised.

When the woman suffrage clause was debated on June 19th, 1917, favourable speeches were many and opponents few; it was carried by an overwhelming majority. My own future mother-in-law, a vigorous suffragist continually thwarted by her disapproving clerical husband, heard that historic debate; the subsequent entry in her diary must have been typical of many similar records:

'Tuesday, June 19th. Managed to get into Ladies' Gallery at H. of Commons. Suffrage Clause in Reform Bill passed by majority of 330. Only 55 against. *Sursum corda.*'

On February 6th, 1918, the first instalment of woman suffrage became part of the British Constitution. Few spectacular and colourful revolutions can have triumphed so inconspicuously as that long-contested measure, which reached the Statute Book in the deep night of wartime depression.

'Gone was the mirage of a society regenerated by enfranchised womanhood as by a magic wand', wrote Sylvia Pankhurst in *The Suffragette Movement*. 'Men and women had been drawn closer together by the suffering and sacrifice of the war. Awed and humbled by the great catastrophe . . . the women of the Suffrage Movement had learnt that social regeneration is a long and mighty work.'

When the First World War ended, women had increased their power to advance that mighty work in quite a few countries; they could now vote in the greater part of the British Commonwealth, the United States, Germany, Scandinavia, Czechoslovakia, Holland, Luxembourg, and Poland. Ten years later more than thirty countries had accepted woman suffrage; these included Burma and six Indian States. The only English-speaking territories which still refused to enfranchise women were the Province of Quebec and Newfoundland in North America, and South Africa, where the colour problem introduced additional complications. Other countries which continued to withhold political rights from women were the Latin States of Europe and South America, Turkey, Bulgaria, Serbia, and Switzerland.

Between 1918 and 1928, the continuing British struggle was enlivened rather than hampered by a number of masculine anti-feminists, whose published lamentations against changes which were 'unfair to male interests' (as one of them put it with engaging simplicity) were accustomed to maintain somewhat contradictory propositions. Women, in addition to an inferiority obvious to these literary Jeremiahs, were represented as embittered, domineering, inefficient, irresponsible, and materialistic; no modern psychologist would have contemplated entrusting children to the evil influence of such perverse monsters. Yet, oddly enough, their critics still regarded child-bearing and child-rearing as the main function of married women.

Undeterred by these ludicrous arguments, a minority of women gave practical expression to their cause as defined by Professor George Catlin in his Introduction to the *Everyman* edition of Mary Wollstonecraft's *Vindication* and John Stuart Mill's essay on *The Subjection of Women*: 'Feminism, properly understood, does not consist in an assertion of the abstract equality of all women with all men, but it does insist that each human being shall find his or her level apart from pre-determined status.'

Women were entering Parliament, and one, Margaret Bondfield, had even been appointed a Cabinet Minister. In growing numbers, though the total was still very small, they found themselves elected to local government committees, chosen to serve on Royal Commissions, and appointed magistrates. Out of approximately 23,000 unpaid magistrates, 2,000 women had served by 1930.

Though the percentage of women in public life then was, and still is, totally disproportionate, the vote itself had changed beyond recognition the attitude of Members of Parliament and Borough Councillors towards the problems of women and their children. Access to Members was now easy, and measures once consigned to limbo as 'women's questions' multiplied on the Statute Book. In the first eighteen years of the 20th century, only four Acts were passed which affected the position of women. Between 1918 and 1929 no less than sixteen went through Parliament, and created a revolution in their status.

Before her death, Dame Millicent Fawcett was able to write in *What the Vote Has Done*: 'Having had opportunities of observing manners in the House of Commons, and comparing them over a period of nearly sixty years, I see an enormous, almost an incredible improvement in this respect in recent years. Democracy is a great teacher of manners. Women felt the difference and the improvement almost immediately after February, 1918.'

Ten years of enfranchisement clearly showed that women would not vote as a Party; the old bogey of a great feminine phalanx uniting to defeat men on every major issue now appeared as the hallucination which it had always been. So on March 8th, 1928, in the presence of Dame Millicent Fawcett and Mrs Pankhurst, who sat on the platform, and of Eleanor Rathbone, who took the chair, Mr Baldwin announced to a United Franchise Demonstration in the Queen's Hall that a Bill to enfranchise women at twenty-one would be presented in Parliament the following Monday. The final stage in the struggle for political emancipation had been accomplished in Britain.

Three weeks after the Equal Franchise Bill passed the House of Commons on May 23rd, 1928, Mrs Pankhurst died. Even in death, her instinct for drama was unerring. She quit the scene of her triumph at the height of the political and social season; her body lay in state at St John's, Smith Square, a church which stands in the heart of political London; and her funeral took place on the very day that the Franchise Bill received its final reading in the House of Lords. When the funeral cortège left the church for Brompton Cemetery, spectators of every age and class thronged the byways of Westminster.

That same year, reviewing Mrs Strachey's book *The Cause*, I ventured, as one of the young women who had held midnight vigil beside Mrs Pankhurst's coffin, to embark upon a prophecy concerning the women's revolution. 'Should a representative of that movement be summoned to Valhalla to join the always inspired but not always judicious company of humanity's liberators—Oliver Cromwell and George Washington, Danton and Mazzini and Lenin—it is Mrs Pankhurst and no other who would appropriately play the part.'

The magnificent memorial service held for Dame Millicent Fawcett in Westminster Abbey fifteen months later might have appeared to falsify that prediction, but in 1930 it was fulfilled by a moving and spectacular little ceremony in Victoria Tower Gardens beneath the shadow of St Stephen's.

There the statue of Mrs Pankhurst—only the fourteenth British woman to be thus honoured throughout history—was unveiled by Mr Baldwin himself. Another colourful and unorthodox rebel, Dame Ethel Smyth the composer, resplendent in the grey and scarlet robes of a Doctor of Music, conducted the accompanying orchestra of the London police by whom both women had so often been battered and imprisoned.

Once again the British people, by canonising a heretic, had closed the door on the uncomfortable past, and purged from their conscience those errors of judgment which had caused them to miscalculate the verdict of future generations.

Since the political injustices which remained to be remedied were now fewer and less drastic, the rate of women's progress in the next two decades became inevitably slower. One or two civilised countries went through searching experiences of war and revolution which changed the attitude of their governments and peoples towards many basic problems. Germany under Hitler returned to the dark ages of womanhood, and after his downfall had to retrace her backward steps with the help of such outstanding women as Frau Regierungspräsident Theanolte Behnisch of Hanover, and Dr Louise Schroeder, Mayor of Berlin at the time of the Allied air-lift. Italy, similarly shaken, enfranchised her women as France already had done.

Though enlightened Switzerland, whose Constitution had served as a model to both the United States and Canada, still incongruously rejected equal rights, twenty-one countries—including China, Israel, and Thailand in Asia, and Albania, Bulgaria, Roumania, and Greece* in Europe—were added after 1945 to those which accepted woman suffrage.

In December 1946, before the Commission on the Status of Women had been established, the General Assembly of the United Nations passed a resolution, sponsored by Denmark, calling on all Member States which had not already done so 'to adopt measures necessary to fulfil the purposes and aims of the Charter . . . by granting to women the same political rights as to men'. When the Status of Women Commission met at Beirut in 1949, it reaffirmed an earlier recommendation of the Economic and Social Council 'that Member Governments consider women equally with men when appointing their delegations to organs and agencies of the United Nations'.

Among Member States change was perhaps most dramatic in India, where women had been brought into politics through Gandhi's Civil Disobedience campaign. Though the Hindu Code

* Greece and Bolivia gave women the Parliamentary franchise only in 1952.

Bill, endorsed by Premier Nehru and designed to improve the legal position of women by removing many anachronisms, failed to become law in 1951, Indian women voted on the same terms as men in the General Election of 1952. Since the custom of 'purdah', or seclusion, forbade Muslim women to stand in line with men, double voting booths were arranged with separate entrances, and animal symbols provided to help the many illiterate voters of both sexes.

In 1950, the American *Worker Magazine* reported in characteristic left-wing phraseology that 'women's participation in political life in China is a part of the construction of the people's political democracy'. Chinese women entered politics during the ten years of civil war, and an average of eighty per cent are said to take part in elections. An All-China Women's Federation was formed about 1949.

By 1953, only fourteen countries still denied equal voting rights to women. Apart from Switzerland, those having Parliamentary institutions but only a male franchise included Afghanistan, Egypt, Ethiopia, Honduras, Iran, Iraq, Nicaragua and Paraguay. Women had only municipal votes in Mexico, Monaco, and Peru. In three others, El Salvador, Guatemala, and Portugal, special qualifications limited the number of enfranchised women.

Women now enjoy equal voting rights with men in fifty-four sovereign States. Although the British Government professed its intention of establishing a 'democratic' Sudanese Government, the Draft Constitution for the Sudan provided for male suffrage only. A protest on the exclusion of women appeared in *The Times* on October 10th, 1952, signed by Dame Vera Laughton Matthews, the Chairman of the British Status of Women Committee which co-ordinates the work of sixteen national women's organisations.

In Britain, women voted on the same terms as men in the General Elections of 1929, 1931, 1935, 1945, 1950, and 1951, yet many rights and opportunities symbolised by the vote remain to be fully achieved. It gave women, for the first time, the means to express their wishes, but it did not thereby fulfil their demands. Most women in public life still occupy positions as substitute-delegates, vice-chairmen, sub-editors, and assistant-secretaries; they are human beings with a hyphen, never quite complete.

The swift realisation of political and educational rights has been offset by a slower impetus towards equal opportunities and equal pay, and by the scarcely shifted dead-weight of convention in marriage. Homes in which change lags far behind the altered status of women as such still confine the majority of wives and mothers within four walls, and the pattern of living laid down even for new towns and housing estates presupposes the sacrifice of one woman's whole existence to the needs of each small family.

Equal franchise, now accepted by so many countries, marked the end of the beginning, but its implications await realisation in every field of endeavour—political, professional, economic, and social—where inequalities continue. The rest of the story remains to be told, and before it can be told it must first be lived.

4

WOMEN IN POLITICS

WOMEN, wrote the late Eleanor Rathbone, became politicians through the struggle to enter politics. But this does not mean that the women who led the struggle were rewarded by prominent political positions. Amongst the first women in British politics, only Eleanor Rathbone herself and Ellen Wilkinson had been conspicuously associated with the suffrage movement.

The generation which became adult after the suffragists had done their work sought in vain for their names in the Cabinet, in Parliament, on County Councils, and in the once-closed professions that they opened for their successors. Political eminence seemed too often to be reserved for women who had been hostile to 'the cause', or to be accepted, with a pretty show of reluctance, by others who had not even been sufficiently interested to oppose the feminist movement.

An allegory in *The Story of an African Farm* describes the death of a hunter who died holding only one feather of the bird of Truth which he had pursued through mountains and deserts for a lifetime. A passage spoken by the hunter suggests that, despite the baffling irony of life which often reserves its best prizes for those who do not compete, the fighters who seem to have won so little receive their own reward.

'Where I lie down other men will stand, young and fresh. By the steps that I have cut they will climb; by the stairs that I have built they will mount. They will never know the name of the man who made them. At the clumsy work they will laugh; when the stones roll they will curse me. But they will mount, and on *my* work; they will climb, and by *my* stair!'

But even the successors of the suffragettes did not, and do not, compete in politics on equal terms or in equal numbers with men. Of the 625 British Members of Parliament elected in 1951 only seventeen were women, and Mr Churchill's Cabinet contained no woman Minister. When the late Ellen Wilkinson became Minister of Education in Mr Attlee's 1945 Government his Cabinet included her, but when Miss Florence Horsbrugh received the same appointment her Ministry was 'demoted'.

Three explanations for this procedure have been suggested. Either Mr Churchill did not consider Education an important Department; or he did not want a woman in the Cabinet; or the contrast between the abilities of Ellen Wilkinson and Florence Horsbrugh was overwhelming. The last suggestion can hardly be taken seriously, since in that event it seems unlikely that Miss Horsbrugh would have become a Minister at all.*

The same story is true of local government. In September 1952, Dr Horace King, M.P. for the Test Division of Southampton, gave to a women's conference some significant figures from his own borough, which had proved exceptionally progressive in electing women to official positions. Of sixty-eight Southampton Councillors thirteen were then women, in favourable contrast to the Hampshire County Council which had twelve women Councillors and ninety-three men, two women Aldermen and twenty-three men, and a man as Chairman of every Committee except the Children's. Even in Southampton, with a woman as Chairman of the Hospital Management Committee, not one woman was chosen to represent the professional members of the Health Executive Committee which administered the Mental, Dental, and Optical Departments of the National Health Service.

In 1951-52 the London County Council, which had a woman Chairman, Mrs Eveline Lowe, in its Jubilee year, included forty-six women members, or nearly one-third of the whole. But the larger Urban District Councils appointed only fifteen women Chairmen (about fourteen per cent of the total) and a fair number of women Councillors. No woman in that year was a Lord Mayor or Lord Provost, though women had previously served as Lord Mayors of Liverpool, Manchester, Norwich, and Stoke-on-Trent. In England thirty women (about seven per cent of the total) were Mayors, and in Scotland three out of 106 were Provosts.

Such a modest representation of women outside London

* Miss Horsbrugh was promoted to the Cabinet in September 1953.

ELEANOR RATHBONE
English Politician

DAME MILLICENT FAWCETT
Feminist and Social Reformer

BRITAIN'S FOUR WOMEN MINISTERS

Ellen Wilkinson
Florence Horsbrugh

Margaret Bondfield
Dr Edith Summerskill

naturally means that on the bodies which they serve they cannot do everything expected of them by other women. Mrs Strachey quotes the 19th-century feminist, Emily Davies, as saying on her retirement from one local authority: 'When it is remembered that the Board has consisted of forty-seven gentlemen and two ladies, it will not be a matter of surprise that the two ladies have proved incapable of doing their half of the work'.

The reasons for this disproportion between the sexes—which is typical of national and local government not only in Britain but abroad—can best be sought after the history of women in politics since the first instalment of the vote has been recorded.

The British General Election of 1918 followed by less than a year the new Representation of the People Act, which conferred the vote on women householders and the wives of householders of thirty years of age and over. Sixteen women, including Christabel Pankhurst, stood for Parliament at this election. All were defeated except an Irish Republican, the Countess Markevicz, who in protest against the Government's Irish policy never took her seat.

On a Private Members' Day in April 1919, the Labour Party introduced an Emancipation Bill designed to remove women's remaining disabilities, and thus created a precedent for the Equal Citizenship (Blanket) Bill proposed by a British feminist, Dorothy Evans, after the Second World War. The Emancipation Bill, though carried against the Government, was defeated in the House of Lords. Instead the Government introduced the Sex Disqualification (Removal) Bill, which opened with a praiseworthy pronouncement: 'A person shall not be disqualified by sex or marriage from the exercise of any public function, or from being appointed to or holding any civil or judicial office or post, or from entering or assuming or carrying on any civil profession or vocation, or from admission to any incorporated society'.

The various women's organisations, even when they were interested in social reform rather than in politics, now almost all included Equal Rights and Equal Pay amongst their objectives. After the Sex Disqualification (Removal) Bill became law in 1919, they combined in a nation-wide attempt to ensure that the word 'Removal' escaped from its brackets.

Before the end of that year the first British woman M.P.—though ironically enough she was American-born—took her seat in the House of Commons. On November 28th, 1919, Lady Astor was elected for the Sutton Division of Plymouth at a by-election made necessary by her husband's accession to the peerage.

Nancy Astor was then an attractive woman on the early side of middle-age. Like Mrs Pankhurst she was the mother of several children, and her spirited femininity suggested nothing 'dubious' to the critics of women's advancement. But here, apart from the high courage which they shared, the resemblance between the two women ceased. Where Mrs Pankhurst had been judicial Lady Astor was impulsive, and for the older woman's remarkable capacity for organised leadership she substituted a technique of light-weight but irrepressible attacks on the entrenched citadels of masculine privilege.

Writing in the *Australian Women's Digest* for January 1945, Mrs Edith Howe-Martin, one of the older suffragists, recalled that a powerful group of men in the House of Commons so keenly resented Lady Astor's presence that they did everything possible to dissuade her from seeking re-election. When she resisted their arguments, they showed her an open hostility which dismayed even her gay and spontaneous temperament. That temperament was in itself a gift to women; a more melancholy and less resilient woman might well have abandoned the experiment which chance had made possible.

'Men whom I had known for years', she recorded long afterwards, 'would not speak to me if they passed me in the corridors. They said I would not last six months. But I stuck it out.'

She 'stuck it out' for a quarter of a century, retiring in December 1944 after twenty-five years of uninterrupted Membership in which she showed that women had their place in Parliament not only as citizens but as women. Throughout her career Lady Astor championed their interests, undaunted by the cries of 'Sit down, Nancy!' which invariably arose when she supported such causes as the Criminal Law Amendment Bill and legislation for Nursery Schools. At the luncheon given by twenty-eight past and present women M.P.s to celebrate her Silver Jubilee, her loyal husband, who died in 1952, paid her a characteristic tribute.

'When I married Nancy, I hitched my wagon to a star. And then when I got into the House of Commons in 1910, I found that I had hitched my wagon to a shooting star. In 1919 when she got into the House, I found I had hitched my wagon to a sort of V2 rocket. But the star which is represented by Nancy Astor will, I am sure, remain a beacon light for all with high ideals.'

Between 1919 and 1928 Lady Astor had only ten successors, though these included such outstanding women as Margaret Bondfield, subsequently Minister of Labour; the Duchess of Atholl, once an anti-suffragist, who became Parliamentary Secretary to the (then) Board of Education; Ellen Wilkinson, afterwards Under-Secretary at the Home Office and later Minister of Education; and Susan Lawrence, who was to be Parliamentary Secretary to the Ministry of Health in the Labour Government of 1929.

The earliest General Elections clearly showed that most political women entered public life as 'Party' politicians in exactly the same way as men. In the Election of 1929 which brought a Labour victory, fourteen women went to the House of whom nine were Socialists. In 1931, when the Conservatives swept the board, the electorate chose fifteen women, of whom all but two were Conservative-Nationals. These women, like their male colleagues, were and still are elected by a preponderance of enfranchised women who vote, as most men vote, on a Party ticket. The 1951 Census showed that British women of all ages exceeded men by about two million (approximately 25,423,900 women to 23,416,800 men), though up to the age of fourteen the male population was greater than the female.

The number of women in Parliament never rose to more than fifteen until the General Election of 1945, when eighty-seven women stood for Parliament and twenty-four were chosen—twenty-one Labour, one Conservative, one Liberal, and one Independent. In 1950, the number of women Members fell to twenty-one, and in 1951, when they became four fewer, they represented under three per cent of the total Membership.

Of these small numbers two women, Margaret Bondfield from 1929 to 1931, and Ellen Wilkinson from 1945 until her death in 1947, attained Cabinet rank. Two others, Dr Edith Summerskill, who became Minister of National Insurance in 1950, and Florence Horsbrugh, were Ministers outside the Cabinet.

As personalities, these four widely-known politicians showed that leading women present the same contrasts as leading men. Margaret Bondfield, hard-working, experienced, neat and austere, typified the Trade Union organiser. Ellen Wilkinson will be long remembered as one of the most vital individuals produced by the Labour movement; small, red-haired and dynamic, she suggested the more colourful type of journalist. Dr Edith Summerskill, tall, handsome, and dignified, carried into politics the controlled calm of the Harley Street consultant. Miss Horsbrugh was the veteran Party politician whose life had been spent on speech-making and administration.

A few other women held junior Ministerial positions. Nearly all those elected entered freely into the debates and committees of Parliamentary life, and promoted legislation which usually concerned, directly or indirectly, the interests of woman. In May 1948, Mrs Florence Paton became the first women to occupy the Chair in the House of Commons when it was in Committee of Supply on Scottish Estimates. Outside the House twelve women, seven Conservative, four Labour, and one Liberal, were Chairmen of their Parties, and presided at the Annual Party Conference.

After 1918 British women in public life were supported by a number of small voluntary political groups which added their dynamic activities to the more deliberate work of such older and larger bodies as the International Alliance for Suffrage and Equal Citizenship, the International Council of Women (which in 1952 had a Swiss Chairman, Dr Jeanne Eder-Schwyzer), the National Union of Societies for Equal Citizenship, and the British Commonwealth League.

The Women's Freedom League, associated during the final years of the militant campaign with the work of Mrs (later Lady) Pethick-Lawrence, concerned itself especially with the election of women to Parliament and public bodies. St Joan's Social and Political Alliance, a Catholic organisation, endeavoured to lead them towards the more elusive goal of social and economic equality. The very name of the Six Point Group suggested preoccupation with a series of thorny problems, each replaced after solution by new 'points' which became more comprehensive as the years went by.

Another progressive body, the Open Door Council, campaigned especially for the removal of restrictions on industrial women. Soon after the establishment of the International Labour Organisation, they sent their Chairman, Mrs Elizabeth Abbott, to represent several women's societies at Geneva during the discussion of a Draft Convention on Wage-Fixing Machinery.

Early in the Second World War, a number of women started a voluntary group to provide overseas news of British women's war-work. They soon realised that a bigger task awaited them, and formed the Women's Publicity Planning Association which aimed at educating women to take their democratic responsibilities more seriously. After publicising a campaign to secure equal compensation for war injuries, the W.P.P.A. concluded that its progress required a stronger body of women in Parliament. They therefore founded a movement known as Women for Westminster, which tried to persuade able and experienced women to offer themselves as candidates for national and local government.

Women for Westminster did not long survive the death of its organiser, Dorothy Evans, in August 1944. But during its brief existence it made a useful impact upon the lethargy and deficient confidence which still prevent women from freely offering themselves for public service.

Over a hundred women's organisations exist in Britain today. Most of these devote their energies to some form of social service, such as child welfare, the care of the old, and a better standard of domestic arts and handicrafts. Others concern themselves with sport, and yet others with the interests of women in business and the professions. The more political have tried to promote the admission of women to the House of Lords, where their absence appeared the more conspicuous when the right to sit in the Canadian Senate was conceded to women in 1929.

After the Sex Disqualification (Removal) Act had been added to the Statute Book, Viscountess Rhondda, a Peeress in her own right, lodged a petition in 1922 praying for a writ of summons to

Parliament. The Lords' Committee for Privileges twice considered this petition. On the second occasion its opponents mustered a large body of reactionary peers, which rejected it on the ground that the Sex Disqualification (Removal) Act had not been intended to create new rights, but only to remove existing disqualifications.

During the next few years a series of Bills introduced in the Upper House by Lord Astor endeavoured to bring the Lords into line with the Commons, but no significant change occurred until 1949. A motion to admit peeresses in their own right to the House of Lords was then proposed by Lord Reading, supported by Viscount Cecil of Chelwood, Lord Pethick-Lawrence, and Lord Balfour of Burleigh, and carried on a free vote by forty-seven Peers against twenty-seven.

'The real objection to the acknowledgement of full equality between the sexes', Lord Pethick-Lawrence then said, 'is not now, and never was, merely a matter of reason; it was an instinctive objection of men, who for the most part in their dealings with women are on an emotional plane, to admit that they could be coadjutors in an intellectual and administrative capacity.'

In spite of this amiable retreat from hostility by the Lords, British peeresses still do not sit in the Upper House. No opposition now exists on the part of public opinion or amongst the majority of peers, but the Labour Party, in power from 1945 to 1951, objected to the hereditary principle. There was, they maintained, no purpose in extending it, though they frequently added to the number of male peers, and after going out of office approached the Conservative Party to suggest a larger Labour representation in the Upper House.

The admission of women peers thus came to be conveniently tied up with the reform of the House of Lords, always supposed to be imminent, but never actually accomplished. On November 1st, 1952, the leading letter published by *The Times*, from Mr Edward F. Iwi, Chairman of the Executive Committee, Petition to Admit Women into the House of Lords, maintained that 'the continued exclusion of women peers . . . violates justice, logic, and sex equality'.

* * *

In twenty-one other countries—where national complications, if not fewer, are different—women have made their way to the Upper House. These countries include Australia, Canada, New Zealand, India, and Ceylon from the British Commonwealth, and outside it the United States, France, Italy, Norway, Sweden, Poland, Jugoslavia, and Japan. In some of them women's influence is not confined to the Second Chamber; they have forged far ahead of Britain in selecting women for important political positions.

The United States, where forty of the forty-eight State Legislatures had appointed a total of 237 women by 1951, was long represented on the United Nations Organisation by Mrs Eleanor Roosevelt, who became Chairman of the Commission on Human Rights until her retirement after the Presidential Election of 1952. Mrs Edith Sampson, a gifted Negress, acted as an alternative U.S.A. delegate. Other American political women well known abroad have been Miss Frances Perkins, Minister of Labour in the Roosevelt administration; Congresswoman Ruth Baker Pratt, the first woman elected for New York State; Ruth Bryan Owen, sent to Congress by Florida; and Clare Boothe Luce, Republican Congresswoman from Connecticut. Mrs Luce, who also tried to stand as candidate for the Senate but failed to secure nomination, made history by her appointment as American Ambassador to Italy in February 1953.

Mrs India Edwards, known as the Washington Queen-Maker, reputedly declined the Chairmanship of the Democratic Party when President Truman gratefully offered it as a reward for her successful campaigning in 1948. Instead she became the £100-a-week Vice-Chairman, and a Federal Judge. 'If the U.S.A. ever elects a woman President', wrote Frederick Cook in the *Evening Standard* for April 10th, 1951, 'the historians of the time will put it down to the work of Mrs India Edwards, who operated in Washington, mostly behind the scenes, in the middle of the 20th century.'

Soon after his election as President, General Eisenhower nominated two Republican women to important political posts. One, Mrs Oveta Culp Hobby, became 'Minister of Health' as administrator of the Federal Security Agency, and the other, Mrs Ivy Baker Priest, was made United States Treasurer. The Press regarded these appointments as a tribute to the power of the women's vote in giving General Eisenhower his 'landslide' victory.

In Canada the first woman elected to the Senate was Karin Wilson in 1930. The widow of a former Prime Minister, Dame Enid Lyons, served for a time in the Australian Cabinet as Vice-President of the Executive Council. The stormy House of Assembly at Cape Town has long been adorned by the eloquent South-African-born politician, Margaret Ballinger, who was elected by the Natives of the Cape Eastern Circle in 1937, and received the tribute of a 'Clerihew' in the *South African Sunday Times:*

> 'Knowing the erudition of Mrs Ballinger,
> I'm afraid to challenge her
> On the status of the Bantu.
> Aren't you?'

Amongst Commonwealth countries no change of status has been so remarkable as that gained by the women of India. Their leaders have leapt the gulf between conflict and achievement through which many women with a larger share in the political history of their nations are still struggling.

'It is a startling fact', wrote Mrs Ela Sen in *Indian Opinion*, the weekly paper published from Natal by Manilal Gandhi for the Indian community in South Africa, 'that more women hold public positions of executive authority in India than anywhere else in the world, except in the Soviet Union. This is in spite of eighty-five per cent mass illiteracy, and that women form the larger percentage of adult illiterates.'

Following the example of Mahatma Gandhi, who treated as equals the women supporters of his Civil Disobedience campaign and thought women morally superior to men, the Indian Government has been able to find efficient women for prominent positions from the minority which forms part of its literate fifteen per cent. The best known outside India are Mrs Vijayalakshmi Pandit, Mr Nehru's sister, who was appointed Indian Ambassador first in Moscow and then in Washington; Rajkumari Amrit Kaur, once Gandhi's secretary, who was put in charge of the Ministry of Health, and is also conspicuous for her work with the World Health Organisation; and Mrs Sarojini Naidu, the inspired poet who became Governor of the United Provinces. Equally respected within India is Begum Abdullah, the wife of Sheikh Abdullah, Kashmir's former Prime Minister, who as a leader in her own right held the banner of communal peace above the frenzied riots which tore Kashmir asunder in 1947.

The new State of Pakistan, a Muslim country with a deeply-rooted tradition of female subjection, owes much of its rapid progress to two women. One, Miss Fatima Jinnah, the constant companion of her brother, Mohammed Ali Jinnah, who founded the State, now lives a secluded but highly respected life as virtual Queen Dowager in Karachi. The other, Begum Liaquat Ali Khan, the widow of Pakistan's first Prime Minister, brought the women of her country out of their homes during the communal riots which accompanied partition, taught them to overcome their most cherished inhibitions, and rallied them to aid the millions of refugees who poured into Pakistan from India.

Another Muslim country, the new Egypt created by General Neguib, possesses in a young and beautiful woman, Doria Shafik, one of the most attractive contemporary fighters for women's rights. Educated at the Sorbonne but denied a post in Cairo University by the Faculty of Letters, Doria Shafik, launched two periodic reviews after the War, and founded a feminist movement named after one of them, *Bint El Nil* (Daughter of the Nile).

'In the land where thousands of years ago men humbly submitted to the yoke of Queens like Nefertiti and Cleopatra women are today denied the vote', wrote William Forrest in a Press article in December 1952. 'And every day of Doria Shafik's life will continue to be a storm until they get it.'

Outside the British and American orbit, the work of women pushing their way into public life can best be studied in the numerous publications of U.N.O., U.N.E.S.C.O., and the I.L.O. Other reports of varying reliability state that between ten and forty per cent of the people's representatives in Chinese local government are women. In China's national government one conspicuous woman, Madame Li Te-Chuan, widow of the

Christian General Feng, serves as Minister of Health, and is also President of the Chinese Red Cross.

Books by several authors have already been devoted to the women of the Soviet Union, which has given equal rights not only in theory but in practice since the Revolution of 1917. The women of Russia and its satellites—such as Dr Anna Pauker, the former Roumanian Foreign Minister—share with their men the advantages and disadvantages of Soviet high office, of which the holders so often go up like a rocket but descend with the speed of the stick.

In her contribution to *Our Freedom and Its Results*, Eleanor Rathbone described what she believed at that time (1936) to have been the special assets of women in public life.

They had brought into politics, she affirmed, the fruit of their personal knowledge, an 'expertise' never used in the days of subjection. This difference of outlook had shown itself in the greater attention now given to health, housing, child welfare, and kindred social questions; and above all, perhaps, in the overwhelming desire, expressed even before the attainment of political rights, to relieve some neglected area of suffering to which women's minds were especially responsive.

She might have added that women, being biologically creative, tend when uninhibited to be mentally and morally constructive. Men on the whole appear to be concerned with *things*—property, wealth, the accumulation of armaments—and often to regard persons as merely the means to an end, while women interest themselves in human beings, whom they look upon as ends in themselves.

At least one male Member of Parliament has expressed the opinion that if women had dominated governments in this century, there might well have been no wars.

Yet the scales are still weighted against political women, especially in the Parliamentary constituencies where women Conservatives are chosen to contest industrial areas, and women Socialists struggle to make an impact upon the unchanging serenity of the cathedral close. This tipping of the scales to women's disadvantage has altered little since 1929, when fully enfranchised women voted for the first time in a British election.* Women candidates, whether successful or not, have brought new life, new purpose, and new standards into many constituencies, yet the dice continue to be loaded, and the elected women a very small minority. We can only ask why.

The slogans once used against women in politics are no longer believed by more than a few diehards. Two wars have found even governments campaigning against the idea that woman's place is the home, while election after election has dispelled the illusion that men will vote only for men. Increasingly, too, all voting, whether national or local, tends to follow a Party line. It has been unkindly said that Socialists would vote for a cauliflower if it were ticketed 'Labour'.

Why, then, have women failed to achieve a fifty-fifty share in public life?

The answer appears to lie in the conclusions which inspired that short-lived organisation, Women for Westminster. At the foot of the ladder, where the initiative of women, as of men, must always begin, female social awareness is still too limited. The one-third representation of women on the London County Council suggests that in places where they are politically and socially conscious they can command their own opportunities, despite the survival of some hostility and a comfortable preference for time-honoured practice.

The old antagonists of sex-equality remain, but they are less formidable today than the apathy, diffidence, and inhibitions which still handicap women after centuries of subjection. Only when a great band of women have learned to accept the challenge of responsibility, and from every class and neighbourhood demand a share in policy-making as they once demanded the vote, is the proportion of men and women in politics likely to reach a reasonable equality.

* The choice of three women for safe Parliamentary constituences which fell vacant in 1953 (Mrs Patricia Ford, Ulster Unionist, North Down, unopposed; Mrs Harriet Slater, Labour, Stoke North; Miss Edith Pitt, Conservative, Edgbaston, Birmingham) suggests that this discrimination is at last beginning to modify.

5

THE STRUGGLE FOR EQUAL RIGHTS

'As long as law and custom treat women as one race and men as another there will remain a woman question, and not until men and women, equal and united side by side, work together free and untrammelled, will the woman's movement be a thing of the past.'

These words occurred at the end of a pamphlet on the Status of Women issued by the Equal Rights International, a voluntary association, shortly before the Second World War. The women who published it understood that laws do not create change, which originates in the mental perception of need and the spiritual urge to fulfil it. As the Scottish poet, William Soutar, wrote in *But the Earth Abideth:*

> 'Men are more gentle than their laws
> Which doom and justify;
> And are more righteous than the cause
> For which they kill or die.'

But women know that laws announce and perpetuate change, and thus contribute by definition to the process of history. For this reason, through more than a decade, organised women in India have simultaneously agitated for a higher status, and for its legal recognition by the revised codification of Hindu law.

So far they have been less successful than the women of Turkey, another country with a long record of female subjection. As long ago as 1923, Turkish women under the leadership of Madame Halidé Edib persuaded the Angora Government to change the family law of Turkey, abolish polygamy, and institute divorce reform.

Unlike the campaign for the vote, which had to be won nationally and in some countries State by State, the struggle for the equal rights and status of women has been shown to progress more effectively at the international level. The most important events of this century in the history of women have been the Universal Declaration of Human Rights adopted by the General Assembly of the United Nations in Paris on December 10th, 1948, and the Draft Convention on the Political Rights of Women adopted at the Seventh Regular Session of the General Assembly on December 20th, 1952.

The Declaration symbolises the fact that women, having won a large measure of rights for themselves, are now able to regard that victory as one aspect of the struggle for human rights as a whole. The first paragraph of Article 2 runs as follows:

'Everyone is entitled to all the rights and freedoms set forth in this Declaration, without distinction of any kind, such as race, colour, sex, language, religion, political or other opinion, national or social origin, property, birth, or other status.'

No person is excluded by this statement from these rights, which are looked upon as essentials of human existence. The final Article (No. 30) affirms: 'Nothing in this Declaration may be interpreted as implying for any State, group or person any right to engage in any activity or to perform any act aimed at the destruction of any of the rights and freedoms set forth herein.'

At a Press Conference on May 18th, 1950, Mrs Eleanor Roosevelt, then Chairman of the Human Rights Commission, spoke of the Declaration's value as a starting point:

'The importance of this document is the fact that it constitutes a beginning and not an ending ... it is a good beginning.'

In the Preamble to the Charter of the United Nations, the Member States reaffirmed their 'faith in fundamental human rights, in the dignity and worth of the human person, in the legal rights of men and women, and of nations large and small'. Both the Preamble and the Declaration thus lay upon the United Nations an obligation to investigate and seek to remove those discriminations which still penalise women on account of their sex.

At an Inter-American Conference on the Problems of War and Peace held in Mexico City in 1945, it was stated that women's war services 'proved beyond question their capacity to meet all the responsibilities of citizenship and of professional and vocational life'. In spite of this amiable tribute, inequalities and anomalies affecting women's position remained in many countries. Early in 1946, the Economic and Social Council of the United Nations therefore established a Sub-Commission (which later became a full Commission reporting directly to the Council) on the Status of Women.

Its task was to make recommendations 'on the promotion of women's rights in political, economic, civil, social and educational fields', and to prepare a detailed study of legislation affecting the status of women, with its implications for men, children, and family life.

Under its Chairman, Madame Marie Hélène Lefaucheux, this Commission held several sessions at Lake Success, one at Beirut, Lebanon, and one, in March 1952, at Geneva. During the Geneva session the Commission considered a resolution referring to women's right 'of physical integrity and moral dignity', a protest against female circumcision. On this motion the British delegate, Miss Mary Sutherland, abstained from voting, on the ground that the resolution as drafted did not fully meet the problem with which it had to deal. Disappointment among organised women at this lack of British support was reinforced by the loss to the Commission of Miss Minerva Bernardino of the Dominican Republic, one of its most active members, who had been replaced by a more docile delegate.*

Earlier in the history of the Commission, Australian women had protested against their Government's failure to appoint a representative. The reason officially alleged for this omission was that women lacked 'qualifications' of a kind seldom demanded from newly appointed men.

'Only experience', urged the *Australian Women's Digest*, 'can give the qualifications which the Government, in the case of women, demand as a first essential.'

Apart from its work for political rights and equal pay—subjects discussed in other chapters—the Status of Women Commission has exhaustively studied the Nationality and Property Rights of married women. All over the world, wives are still victims of con-

* Miss Bernardino subsequently became the Dominican Republic's first woman Minister.

flicting nationality laws. Only five countries (the United States, Salvador, Uruguay, Venezuela, and Jugoslavia) give a woman the right to transmit her nationality to a child born of her marriage with a foreigner. In all countries a man's nationality is unaltered by his marriage to a foreign woman, while that of the woman who marries a foreign man is affected in varying degrees both during the marriage and after its dissolution.

In some countries where the laws conflict, a woman may lose her citizenship without acquiring the nationality of her husband, and hence becomes stateless. Until 1933 British women, amongst others, were liable to this dilemma.* In September 1928, the London *Evening News* published a letter which described the fate of a young Englishwoman married during the First World War to a Canadian soldier whose parents, both British subjects, had emigrated to the United States where he was born.

'He crossed to Canada and enlisted long before America came into the war, and was killed in France a few months after his marriage. He was then found to be technically an American citizen, and, although a pension is paid by the Canadian Government to the widow, she has lost her British nationality, and, never having been in America, is not recognised as a citizen of the United States. As a result she is compelled to report herself regularly to the police in her native village, where she has lived for over thirty years, and where her mother, brothers, and sisters live.'

In 1948 British women, after years of campaigning, reacquired the right lost in 1870 to retain their nationality on marriage to an alien. The women of some other countries are less fortunate, and, like the subject of the *Evening News* letter, are liable to be regarded in one country as citizens of a particular State, and in another country as citizens of a different State. The Status of Women Commission aimed at a general Convention on the Nationality of Married Women which would assure wives equality with husbands, and replace the 1930 Hague Convention on Nationality

* The British Nationality and Status of Aliens Act, 1933, laid down that a woman who did not acquire her husband's nationality could keep her own, and thus avoid statelessness. The Nationality Act of 1948 enabled a woman marrying an alien to retain her British nationality unless she took steps to change it.

which wrote sex inequality into international law.

Throughout the world, women as wives, mothers and home-makers still suffer many forms of legal incapacity apart from those caused by confused nationality legislation. Various countries impose limitations upon the property rights of married women, restricting their power to control their own possessions and earnings, and to undertake independent business ventures. In some States wives have definite duties to perform without being entitled to salary or wages; in others it is possible for a husband, even when wealthy, to leave his wife destitute and without redress at his death.

Since Article 16 of the Declaration of Human Rights states that 'men and women . . . are entitled to equal rights as to marriage, during marriage, and at its dissolution', the United Nations Secretariat, at the request of the Status of Women Commission, sent out in September 1949 a questionnaire on the world-wide property rights of married women.

In 1939 the International Labour Organisation published an extensive survey of the legal status of employed women in a document entitled *The Law and Women's Work*. The Women's Service Library at Westminster contains a summary of the chapter by Madame Thibert on women in professions, made for the British Federation of Business and Professional Women by Miss Vera Douie in 1946 with an Appendix bringing the material up to date.

This survey showed that all professions—sometimes owing only to the absence of regulations to the contrary—were open to women in twenty-six countries. Holland was included among these, since only the profession of notary public was closed to Dutch women. Most countries excluded women from the armed forces and the State Church, but under the stress of the Second World War a number developed auxiliary Women's Services. In Britain these Services amounted to nearly three per cent of the total force.

Norway had long admitted women to the State Church, and the U.S.S.R. sent them into the forces many years before 1939. They were barred from some professions in thirteen countries, which included Canada, France, Germany, India, Italy, and, unexpectedly, Sweden.

Some of the most liberal laws on Equal Rights were written into the Constitutions of the Latin American States, where

Mrs ELEANOR ROOSEVELT

First Chairman of the U.N.O. Commission of Human Rights

BEGUM LIAQUA
ALI KHAN

Full delegate to U.N.
from Pakistan

Mrs VIJAYALAKSHMI
PANDIT

Indian Ambassador to
Moscow and Washington

President of United Nations
General Assembly, 1953

relatively few women were then competent to take advantage of them. In Brazil the Constitution of 1934 not only gave equality, but in Article 121 actually forbade the payment of different rates for the same work on account of age, sex, nationality, or marital status. Similar regulations existed in Cuba, where Article 12 of the Constitutional Act of 1935 recognised no privilege of person, class, or sex, and legislative Decree No. 598 forbade private employers to dismiss women on marriage.

The present international status of women—favourable in theory and steadily improving in practice—has not come without a long struggle, much of it carried on by voluntary societies.

The Covenant of the League of Nations, as conceived by its authors in 1919, at first contained no word referring to the rights and interests of women. Where the equal citizenship of men and women can be taken for granted the omission of specific documentary reference to women is natural, but no such assumption could be made in the years immediately following the First World War. The failure to mention women in the Treaties meant that their share in the remaking of a world torn by war, which had shattered their homes and hurried their fathers, brothers, husbands, and sons into premature death, was regarded as negligible by the politicians.

Only when Dame Millicent Fawcett arrived in Paris with a deputation to President Wilson organised by the International Council of Women and the International Women's Suffrage Alliance, did the Treaty-makers belatedly realise that the organisation of peace affected one half of humanity quite as much as the other.

President Wilson's reception of the women was characteristic; he met them with the terse statement that three minutes must suffice for the expression of their views. In response to their natural protests he added: 'Anything which cannot be said intelligently in three minutes is not worth the trouble of saying at all.'

The women accepted his challenge, and the three minutes had not expired before Paragraph 3 of Article 7 was drawn up for addition to the Covenant: 'All positions under or in connection with the League, including the Secretariat, shall be open equally to men and women.' A similar paragraph, Principle 7, was added to Part XIII of the Treaty of Versailles, which contained the Charter of Labour drawn up to guide the International Labour Organisation: 'That men and women should receive equal remuneration for work of equal value'.

In the earlier years of the League, women's representation was perhaps as good as any realistic woman could have expected. Though no women were selected to sit either on the League Council or on the Permanent Court of International Justice at The Hague, quite a number held positions of varying responsibility in the Assembly and on the Secretariat.

From the beginning the Scandinavian countries included women in their delegations, though never as full delegates. Roumania followed in 1921, and Great Britain and Australia in 1922. At the Secretariat a well-known Red Cross administrator, Dame Rachel Crowdy, became head, though not Director, of the Social Section. An American woman, Miss Florence Wilson, held the post of Chief Librarian for a time, though America was not a Member of the League. Eight of the various League Commissions appointed women members, including the Commission of Intellectual Co-operation which invited two women, Madame Curie of France and Dr Kristine Bonnevie of Norway.

Disappointment followed this encouraging start. During the next decade the women substitute-delegates continued to be substitutes, and only once, when the British Labour Government delegation of 1924 included Mrs H. M. Swanwick, did a keen feminist appear at Geneva in an official position. In 1930 Dame Rachel Crowdy's term of service ended after one renewal for two years only, though the contracts of two men Directors and a male Chief of Section had been extended for further seven-year periods.

Even greater disillusionment gathered in the wake of the I.L.O., which tended from the first to treat women as 'a controlled annexe to industry'. This body was responsible for many discriminations against women in fields where male competition was keen, but suggested no legislation to improve such backward occupations as nursing and domestic service, which affected few men. Yet upon the foundation-stone of the International Labour Office had been inscribed the words: 'If you desire peace, practise justice'.

It was now becoming clear to the international women's societies which met annually at the Geneva Maison Internationale in the Rue de Vieux Collège that the unequal status of men and women not only refuted the ideal of abstract justice, but affected adversely the relationship of States seeking international solutions for social problems. Countries which used female sweated labour could enter into harmful competition with more enlightened nations, while the confused nationality laws which complicated the lives of married women led to friction in peace-time and potential danger in war.

The traffic in women, already the subject of a League Convention, illustrated the degradation to which women were reduced by economic subjection. Finally, the exchange of teachers and students, continually recommended by the Commission of Intellectual Co-operation as a means of establishing friendly relations between countries, proved impracticable for the majority owing to substantial variations in women's status and education.

A move on the other side of the world created a precedent to which the present Status of Women Commission owes a debt probably recognised by few of its members. At the Pan-American Conference held at Havana in 1928, an intrepid feminist from the United States, Doris Stevens, appeared with a delegation from the National Woman's Party. There she launched upon the astonished delegates a proposal for a comprehensive Treaty of Equal Rights between men and women which had been born in the mind of her legalistic colleague, Alice Paul. The first and major article of this Treaty ran as follows:

'The Contracting States agree that, upon the ratification of the Treaty, men and women shall have equal rights throughout the territory subject to their respective jurisdictions.'

The idea of international action grew rapidly during the next few years. An early step was the establishment by the Havana Conference of an Inter-American Commission of Women, with Miss Stevens as its first Chairman and one representative appointed by the government of each American State, to study the position of women throughout the Americas. Later in the year an 'incident' reminiscent of the militant days occurred at Rambouillet, near

Paris, where six feminists were arrested for attempting to present an Equal Rights Treaty to the signatories of the Kellogg Pact assembled in France.

An idea so startling, so simple, and yet so exhaustive as this Treaty was not likely to appeal so readily to the more rigid minds of the Old World as to the elastic intelligences of the New. In 1933 an Equal Rights Treaty was actually signed at Montevideo by representatives from the Governments of Cuba, Equador, Paraguay, and Uruguay. An Equal Nationality Treaty drawn up at the same time received much more support, being signed by the representatives of nineteen American Governments.

Meanwhile an Equal Rights International to work for the Treaty had been formed in 1930 by several groups of women in and outside Europe. Its officers included an Australian Chairman, Mrs Linda Littlejohn, and a Swiss Treasurer, and its Vice-Chairmen were drawn from England, France, Czechoslovakia, Persia, and Poland. During the next twelve months, the leaders of the theoretically feminist British Labour Government suffered considerable embarrassment from questions in the House demanding support for an Equal Rights Treaty.

Owing to the persistent voluntary work of women, the nineteen-thirties saw increasing support from League of Nations delegates for treaties which dealt with Equal Rights and Equal Nationality. In 1934, ten States asked the 15th Assembly to put the Equal Rights Treaty on its Agenda for 1935. The status of women was duly discussed at Geneva for the first time as an international concern, and a Resolution was passed asking the Governments of Member States for 'observations' and 'information as to the existing political and civil status of women under their respective national laws'.

In February 1936, a body of organised women containing members from the British Six Point Group and the American National Woman's Party attended a meeting of the Governing Board of the International Labour Organisation, and endeavoured to obtain from it a declaration supporting the principle of women's right to earn on the same terms as men. The Director of the I.L.O. submitted this proposal to his Governing Body.

'I feel', he said, 'that it is not sufficient to deal simply with the legislative aspects, but the effects of the legislation in practice must also be studied. . . . I recommend that the International Labour Organisation occupy itself with this question as laid before it by the Assembly.'

The steady darkening of the political horizon and the coming of war in 1939 ended, for the time being, these attempts to find an international remedy for inequality. But even during the war, they were not wholly forgotten. In 1943-44, for instance, Women for Westminster protested against the absence of women from the meetings of the I.L.O., and suggested an amendment to its Constitution by which the Government, Worker, and Employer blocks should each be represented by one man and one woman instead of by one (usually male) delegate only.

With the establishment of the United Nations Organisation, the work of twenty-five years began to show results in the Status of Women Commission and the Declaration of Human Rights. The recognition that such rights were suitable subjects for international action had at last been won, but the Equal Rights Treaty or Convention to which this recognition would logically lead still awaited general acceptance.

At the San Francisco Conference, the delegations from Brazil, Mexico and the Dominican Republic, supported by the Chilean delegation, presented amendments designed to include specific mention in the Charter of equal rights for men and women. From that time onwards, the Latin American countries pursued the idea with determination. At Bogota in 1948 the Ninth Inter-American Conference approved a convention on the political rights of women, and inspired the Status of Women Commission at its 1949 session in Beirut to ask the Secretary-General of the United Nations to submit a similar draft convention at its next session.

Subsequent events were described by Madame Ana Figueroa, Deputy Representative of Chile, in the *United Nations Bulletin*, Vol. XIII, No. 1, for July 1st, 1952.

'The Convention on the Political Rights of Women', she wrote, 'has been like a play in three acts. In the first it threatened to develop into a drama. In the second, it looked as if the play would have innumerable acts and would take a long time to reach the last scene. In the third, however, a happy ending was achieved.'

At the twelfth session of the Economic and Social Council at Geneva in 1950, the majority of Council members attacked the principle of a Convention on women's political rights, but the Status of Women Commission remained firm. At the thirteenth session in 1951, a less direct type of obstruction developed when the Council decided that the Member States of the United Nations must all be consulted and provide comments before the Draft Convention could be submitted to the General Assembly.

With the comments of the governments before it, the Sixth Session of the Status of Women Commission approved the Draft Convention by a majority of thirteen, with three abstentions. Again they submitted it to the Economic and Social Council, which finally adopted it in 1952 by eleven favourable votes and six abstentions. According to Madame Figueroa, the representatives of countries where women already enjoyed political rights mostly supported the Convention, but among the abstentions, in unusual alliance for reasons best known to themselves, were the United Kingdom and the Soviet Union.

On December 20th, 1952, this Draft Convention came before the Assembly in New York, and was adopted by a vote of forty-six in favour, none against, and eleven abstentions. The key clauses of the Convention run as follows:

'*Article* 1. Women shall be entitled to vote in all elections on equal terms with men, without any discrimination.

'*Article* 2. Women shall be eligible for election to all publicly elected bodies established by national law, on equal terms with men, without any discrimination.

'*Article* 3. Women shall be entitled to hold public office and to exercise all public functions, established by national law, on equal terms with men, without any discrimination.'

In her article, Madame Figueroa made a preliminary assessment of the Convention's value.

'Many still have doubts as to the possible effects of this convention. How useful will it prove in such countries as already grant women political rights? Will the other countries ratify such a convention without changing their legislation accordingly? But these doubts and arguments could be applied equally to all conventions. If the international commitments of countries mean so little as not to lead them to adjust their domestic legislation to the pattern of the San Francisco Charter, we could well ask for what the United Nations exists.'

A convention, as Madame Figueroa indicated, becomes part of international law. The concession of rights to women has kept pace with the economic and social evolution of countries; to refuse to ratify such a convention would be a sign of social backwardness that no country would wish to acknowledge in the face of international public opinion.

'This', she concluded, 'is the culmination of a great effort, the success of which is largely owing to the Latin American countries.'*

However theoretically successful the establishment of international principles may be, they remain, as Madame Figueroa insisted, practically ineffective until they are implemented by national action. Too often, in too many countries, the status of women remains far below the noble level defined by international legislators.

The struggle for Equal Rights in Britain has been typical of similar struggles in civilised states with old and recalcitrant traditions. More swiftly dramatic results are sometimes obtainable in so-called backward States, such as Turkey, India, and Indonesia, which suddenly find it possible to release themselves from their past and write the changed status of women into a new Constitution. It then becomes an accepted ideal towards which national leaders have an obligation to press, instead—as in old countries with continuous histories—of a revolutionary idea which the representatives of vested interests continue to resist.

When the new British voters began to exercise their political rights after 1918 and 1928, they soon realised that legal reforms affecting women did not represent the sole interests of women as Parliamentary electors. Women in professions and industries were

* After 34 years of endeavour by the I.L.O. and seven by the U.N. Status of Women Commission, a comparable Equal Pay Convention came into force on May 23rd, 1953, after ratification by Jugoslavia and Belgium.

Subsequent ratifications included Mexico and France but not Britain, which pays lip-service to the principle but refuses to practise it. See Chapter 9.

equally interested with men in legislation promoting the welfare of their group; a woman writer, for instance, was as much concerned about the reform of the libel laws as a married woman with the laws regulating nationality. The fact remained that laws affecting both sexes received the support of both, whereas the redress of inequalities and anomalies in the position of women still largely depended, as it always had done, upon women themselves.

In September 1943, a letter signed by Emmeline Pethick-Lawrence and Dorothy Evans, describing a new campaign for the adoption of an Equal Citizenship (Blanket) Bill by the Government, appeared in the *New Statesman and Nation*. Its first two paragraphs ran thus:

'We all want our democracy to be made perfect after the War. It cannot be if the nation contains subservient classes. It is not generally realised that women are in a second-class category in over thirty laws upon the Statute Book. They are not allowed to assume their full status as citizens, being subordinate in the matter of their British nationality, their liability to income tax, their claim to their savings, voluntary or compulsory, their position under national insurance and their opportunities, conditions, and pay as employed persons.

'It is essential that the principle should be established, once for all, that every citizen should be upon the same footing before the law, irrespective not only of creed, class or colour, but irrespective also of sex.'

The writers of this letter, both conspicuous in the militant suffrage movement, had lived long enough to know that women's still unequal status represented an enormous advance upon their legal position a hundred and even fifty years earlier. In 1850, when Millicent Garrett Fawcett was three years old, women had been of no account except in so far as they were related to male persons. They received little education and owned no property; if married they had no right to their own earnings, no legal control of their children above seven years old, and no power to divorce the worst of husbands. Whether married or unmarried they possessed no standing in industry, could enter no profession save that of governess, and in middle-class families had usually no occupation whatsoever.

But even by 1922, four years after the first instalment of the vote, the women who listened from the Strangers' Gallery of the House of Commons to the curious late-night debate on the Third Reading of the Criminal Law Amendment Bill designed to improve the legal protection of adolescent girls, had realised from the facetious gibes about 'pig-tails' and 'effeminate men' that the old 'roars of laughter' over 'women's questions' were still round the corner. How far was Britain, after 1918, able to introduce that 'controversial legislation' of which Mr Henderson and Mr Dalton, parrying questions on an Equal Rights Treaty in 1930-31, were to appear so much afraid?

One major change, due largely though not entirely to the first suffrage victory, had been the establishment in 1919 of the Ministry of Health. This Ministry, with the Ministry of Pensions and the later Ministry of National Insurance, assumed responsibility for many of those problems, once ventilated mainly by women, which were now seen equally to concern both men and children. By means of petitions and deputations to these and other Ministers, by Parliamentary questions and unofficial lobbying in the corridors of St Stephen's, women and their male supporters succeeded in getting no less than 101 Acts concerning their special interests on to the Statute Book between 1918 and 1950.

These measures naturally varied in importance. Not all were wholly advantageous, or carried out in the best possible way. But between them they created a revolution in the legal position of women—as juveniles, adolescents, adult citizens, salary and wage-earners, wives, mothers, widows, old persons, property-owners and legatees, taxpayers, employers, and law-breakers. In the last of these categories, women throughout their history as citizens have been less troublesome to the State than men. In February 1951, the Home Secretary disclosed that there were 16,867 men in prison but only 877 women, while the Borstal institutions contained 2,871 boys and 222 girls.

A few examples will illustrate the legal changes of the past thirty years and the extent to which some of these were overdue. In 1923 the Matrimonial Causes Act, originally introduced by Major Entwistle as a Private Member's Bill, for the first time established equal rights of divorce. But though it gave equality it did not attempt to remedy other anomalies in the divorce laws, and twenty-eight years afterwards a women Member, Mrs Eirene White, introduced a Bill admitting marital failure in itself as a ground for divorce. Its consequence was the appointment of a new Royal Commission on Marriage.*

The Guardianship of Infants Act, 1925, gave mothers equal rights as guardians with fathers, though Mr Justice Lawrence, giving evidence on the Bill before a Joint Committee of both Houses in 1922, protested that it offered an insult to God Almighty and the father whom He had appointed. By the Legitimacy Act, which became law in January 1927, the stigma of illegitimacy was lifted from a child whose parents subsequently married if neither had been married to another partner at the time of its birth. This Act led to the issue of no fewer than 4,000 certificates of legitimation by the Registrar-General.

In 1925 the first of several Widows, Orphans and Old Age Contributory Pensions Acts was passed. Ten years later the Law Reform (Married Women and Tortfeasors) Act removed an outdated privilege, and placed married women bankrupts and debtors in the same position as single women and men. The Inheritance (Family Provision) Act of 1938 prevented the total disinheritance of either spouse and of dependent children. In 1945 the Family Allowances Act recognised women's maternal responsibility by providing for the payment of children's allowances to the mother. Three years afterwards, the Nationality Act at last restored to British women their previous right to retain their nationality on marriage.

Thirty-two of these Acts, including the important Nationality measure, had still to be achieved in 1943 when Dorothy Evans, supported by the Women's Publicity Planning Association, drew up and published the text of the Equal Citizenship (Blanket) Bill, 'designed to free our laws and regulations, present and future, of all inequalities between men and women'. One injustice especially, in 1943, caused indignation amongst the usually inarticulate mass of housewives; the Co-operative Society was ordered by the Court to pay to a certain Mr Blackwell the £103 which his wife

* See Chapter 10, p. 157.

had saved in seventeen years from her earnings, house-keeping, and profits on lodgers.

During that year ten women's societies organised a deputation to the Board of Inland Revenue, asking that taxation should be the same for married as for single persons. They also requested that the Post-War Credits deducted from a married woman's wages should be paid after the war to her, and not to her husband. In spite of a few concessions, the British Income Tax Law of 1918 still regards a woman living with her husband as an incapacitated person who ranks with infants, idiots, and imbeciles.

Other inequalities remain under the National Insurance Acts, of which the first was passed in 1911 and the latest in 1946. By a later regulation which became operative in August 1952, a married woman in business with her husband could be insured as a self-employed person provided that she gave twenty-four or more hours weekly to the business, and earned from it not less than £1 a week. Before this regulation was accepted, a woman so occupied had been classed as a non-employed person. Under previous Insurance Acts contributions, like sickness and unemployment benefits, were lower for women than for men, and remain lower for married women. The 1946 Act at least recognised that the basic needs of men and women were the same, and to this extent was an advance towards equality.

Another type of legal discrimination has long been directed against women described as 'common prostitutes' or 'of known immoral character'. In 1951 the law which refused protection to such women against procurers was repealed, but they could still be convicted of 'loitering for the purpose of prostitution', or of 'solicitation to the annoyance of some unnamed person', on the uncorroborated evidence of the police.

A strong body of opinion seeks the amendment of this law, which does not similarly penalise the men who use the services of prostitutes. Responsible women also desire to abolish the few remaining legal 'privileges' which have especially hampered the struggle for equal pay.

In ordinary married life, for example, a British husband carries the legal obligation to support his wife and children, with no reciprocal obligation on her part to support him even if she is wealthy. When Mr Philip Piratin, the former Communist M.P. for Mile End, London, appeared in the Bankruptcy Court in 1951, the following interchange was reported in the Press:

Mr Newman (the Official Receiver). 'We have heard in this Court today that your wife has substantial means though you yourself appear to have no assets. Have you approached your wife to see if she will help you?'

Mr Piratin. 'Yes.'

Mr Newman. 'What is the result?'

Mr Piratin. 'She refuses.'

A number of women have publicly done their best to amend this one-sided legislation. At the Annual Conference of the National Council of Women held at Eastbourne in November 1952, Mrs Florence Earengey, a barrister, moved a resolution that wives should be legally entitled to a proportion of their husbands' incomes which concluded with a Clause C:

'That where the husband through age, incapacity, disablement or other misfortune, including bankruptcy, becomes necessitous, and his wife has separate resources, she shall be liable to maintain her husband to such an extent as the Court may consider reasonable and just in the circumstances.'

A husband has a further liability to pay his wife's income tax if she fails to meet it herself, though she may be rich and he poor. She has also the 'presumed' authority to pledge his credit, but this obligation can be repudiated by a Press announcement.

Many people believe that the damages often demanded in breach of promise cases are a feminine monopoly, but such an action is equally open to either party in a marriage contract. In practice the woman usually brings it, but the large damages sometimes awarded tend to be reduced on appeal if the recipient is young and vigorous. Marriage is no longer assumed to be her only available form of livelihood, and some juries take the view that genuine grief for a broken love-affair is more likely to assuage itself in work than to seek compensation in money.

In addition to these few museum pieces bequeathed by past legislation, British women occasionally find themselves placed in special categories by their sex. Peace-time conscription is not imposed on women, and they may be exempted from jury service for several reasons which include pregnancy. The old dependent status still tends to be reflected in legal documents where a married women is a signatory; in the assignment, for instance, of a house-lease jointly held by a married couple, the husband is described by his profession but the wife merely as his wife.

In spite of such minor time-lags in legal practice, the status of British men and women is now in effect identical; like the vote, it offered a well-defined objective which has been reached within the short period of thirty years.

Today many women take these achievements for granted with a complacency unlikely to be shared by those who recall, however dimly, the suffrage campaign. Their attitude was typified by Marghanita Laski, critic and journalist, in a *News Chronicle* article on 'Women' published in October 1952:

'I was born too late for the battle. Older and nobler women struggled that I should be free, and did their work so well that I've never even bothered about being bound. Rights for women, so far as my generation is concerned, is a dead issue.'

Many young German women probably thought the same until they lost, in 1933, everything that their feminist movement had gained. For them the issue of equal rights returned disastrously to life, but for millions of women in Asia and Africa it has not yet existed. Rights once won cannot be guaranteed against loss until the equal status achieved by some has become the possession of all.

'Nowadays the social and political emancipation of women is discussed much less than it was fifty years ago', wrote Georges Fradier in the *Unesco Courier* for December 1951, 'and because it is rarely mentioned there is a tendency to consider the problems as solved—or nearly so. Facts demonstrate the contrary, for while in many countries women have the right to go to law and to vote, over half of the world's women are still deprived of these rights.... The Englishwoman or the Swede, for example, may with good reason point to the successful evolution of her legal status, but she should not forget that millions of other women are still no better off in this respect than their female ancestors of the Middle Ages.... The need for personal action was stressed recently by a member of the (Status of Women) Commission who said: "It is up to all woman to make equality a reality".'

6

BECOMING EDUCATED

THE last chapter ended with a reference to an article by Marghanita Laski, who thought women's rights a 'dead issue' because she had never been compelled to fight for her own. This gifted modern woman became more constructive when she discussed education, for equal education was a benefit which she had enjoyed and appreciated. It made her especially critical of the second-rate material served up to women by the contemporary Press and radio.

'Consider the prototype woman of today as she appears in almost every article, advertisement, radio feature and pep-talk by politicians . . . something of a peculiar and special order of idiocy, the so-called Women's Angle, has to be prepared and presented to *us*. . . . Men cannot really like constantly coming up against the impression that all women, wives, mothers, daughters, sweethearts, their own included, are gullible imbeciles. . . . And women, in their turn, are beginning to get angry at the pap that's fed to them. After all—a fact too often forgotten—today we are as well-educated as men.'

We have indeed reached this happy position in Britain, but for more than half the world's women it is not yet in sight. And even in Britain and other comparable countries, the period in which equal education has been available is less than a watch in the night. In the second half of the last century, when a number of new publications for women began (*The Queen* was founded in 1861, *The Woman's Magazine* in 1880, *The Lady* in 1885, and *Home Chat* in 1895),* the idea that women readers alone would provide enough support for commercial publications was modern and daring.

* These magazines had a predecessor, *The Lady's Magazine*, started in 1759. In some ways it was superior to the Victorian publications, and even had a section devoted to 'Foreign News'.

The pages and columns headed 'For Women Especially' which appeared much later in high-standard newspapers represented yet a further advance. However insulting they might appear to the still small minority of highly educated women, they were in themselves a recognition that women in substantial numbers read papers which covered such once exclusively 'masculine' topics as foreign affairs, politics, business, the arts, economics and finance. The realisation by editors that women have any use for knowledge at all is, historically speaking, an innovation.

Yet history, especially in periods when the level of scholarship was high, has always supplied instances of women's yearning for knowledge. At the beginning of the Renaissance in Europe a young woman, Christine de Pisan, daughter of the physician-astrologer to Charles V of France, actually supported herself by writing, and put into words her belief in education for women:

'If it were the custom to send girls to school and teach them as boys are taught, women would understand the subtleties of art and science, as well as men do.'

She was followed by other rebels against the established order; Mary Astell in 17th-century England, and in France the women who supported the revolutionary philosophers of 1789. After the Revolution of 1848, their successors organised lectures in the hope of obtaining educational equality.

During the second half of the 19th century, the impulse towards knowledge spread like a forest fire among the women of civilised countries. In Holland the University of Gröningen, followed by all the other Dutch universities, opened its doors to women; it was the first woman student, Aletta Jacobs, who started the campaign for the vote in 1883.

Two German women, Augusta Schmidt and Helene Lange, formed in 1890 the German 'General Association of Governesses' which sought to obtain for women the same education, degrees, and posts as men. A Finnish writer, Sarah Wacklin, founded boarding-schools for girls in Helsinki and elsewhere, while her feminist colleague, Frederika Runeberg, demanded improved education and better opportunities for work. And in Britain, after the foundation of Queen's College and Bedford College 'to train governesses' in 1848 and 1849, the movement for new facilities had steadily grown outside those Quaker and Nonconformist groups which alone educated both sexes.

A regret at the lack of real education for British women first expressed itself in evidence before the Schools Inquiry Commission of 1865, when the first modern secondary schools for girls already existed. The North London Collegiate School had been founded by Frances Buss in 1850 and the Cheltenham Ladies College by Dorothea Beale in 1854, and girls were first informally examined in the Cambridge Local Examinations as early as 1863. Unhappily only a minority of citizens then shared the concern shown at the Schools Inquiry Commission, and the recalcitrant majority included many of the parents for whose daughters the new opportunities were intended. One typical mother complained to Miss Buss: 'You can't send a girl into the drawing-room repeating the multiplication table, so why should she trouble to learn it?'

Why indeed? For the next seventy years pioneer women were to be faced with that fundamental question, and to seek an answer which would satisfy the devotees of tradition who asked it. To teachers especially fell the task of explaining that spheres of usefulness for women could be found outside the drawing-room; that marriage was not the sole purpose of a girl's existence, and even if it had been, she did not become a less desirable life-partner by learning to be an intelligent companion. As Mrs Sidney Webb later remarked of another group confronted with a kindred problem: 'A woman does not make a more efficient wife and mother by having been an inefficient factory hand.'

The insidious pressure of home influence and tradition increased for would-be educators the difficulties already created by the poor training given to women teachers. 'They have not themselves been taught', stated the Report of the School Inquiry Commission, 'and they do not know how to teach.' But the new colleges and training schools gradually created an educated minority which cared enough for women's opportunities to disregard the gibes that belittled them as 'unsexed' and 'strong-minded'. Within the next generation, the number of girls' secondary schools rapidly increased.

One important landmark came in 1870, when the Act which

established national elementary education included girls as well as boys. Another soon followed with the foundation of the Girls' Public Day School Trust by Maria Grey and her sister in 1872.

By 1891 the Trust had started thirty-six schools, an achievement commended in March 1951 by an editorial in *The Times* on the suggested establishment of 'the Friends of the Girls' Public Day School Trust' to support the twenty-three surviving institutions. These schools, commented *The Times*, 'gave girls the same scholastic opportunities as their brothers, rescuing them from "the plain work, pudding-making and pickling" which Miss Buss rightly judged to be too narrow a curriculum'.

The Ministry of Education now gives substantial help to the Day School Trust foundations. They are known as 'direct grant Grammar Schools', and their status is that of the greater grammar schools in Britain. The relevant local authorities appoint representatives to sit on their governing bodies, but do not control them.

The battle for equal elementary and secondary education had thus virtually been won by the end of the 19th century. The 20th has seen the development and expansion of girls' schools rather than their pioneer stages, but these schools still have their special problems. They find, for instance, a greater difficulty than boys' schools in staffing their science sixth forms, a deficiency which handicaps girls who wish to enter the scientific departments of universities. Such staffing problems, which endanger school standards, are closely related to the inadequate and unequal salaries which women teachers still receive.*

The struggle for equality in the Universities was longer and sterner owing to the entrenched resistance of Oxford and Cambridge, though the first was to yield to the time-spirit many years before the second. Girton College had been founded at Cambridge in 1869, exactly twenty years after George Eliot attended Bedford College, and met, in Barbara Leigh-Smith, the model for her *Romola*. A decade later the foundation of Somerville College and Lady Margaret Hall at Oxford occurred in the same twelve months as the liberal gesture from London University which admitted women students to Degrees and full Membership,

* See Chapters 7, 8, and 9.

though the majority of London Medical Schools were not open to women until after the War of 1939-45.

The provincial and Scottish Universities adopted the same progressive policy as London. St Andrews had instituted a Diploma for women with the title of L.L.A. as early as 1876, and in 1892 the Universities of Edinburgh, Glasgow, St Andrews, and Aberdeen admitted them to Membership and Degrees. But the older foundations, 'unchanging . . . beneath the hand of the centuries', had no intention of following such a precedent. Unmoved even when Mrs Fawcett's daughter Philippa was placed above the Senior Wrangler at Cambridge in 1890, they proceeded majestically for many more years along the old man-dominated paths. Though women had been permitted, first informally and then formally, to sit for the University examinations, Degrees for Women was still a subject of passionate controversy at both Oxford and Cambridge when these Universities resumed their normal life after the First World War.

The revolution in women's education between 1850 and 1920 had been accompanied by another which was steadily transforming both their health and leisure.

One of the first criticisms launched against the new opportunities emphasised the adverse effect of study upon women's physique. To counter this objection, Mrs Garrett Anderson (formerly Dr Elizabeth Garrett) had suggested that the curricula at girls' schools and colleges should include games and gymnastics, already practised in Germany, Sweden, and Denmark. Even by the eighteen-eighties, this idea had met with sufficient sympathy for Frances Power Cobbe to write in *The Duties of Women:* 'Of recent years, I am thankful to note, many young English ladies are beginning to take pride in physical activity and vigour. They ride across country, take long walking tours, swim, run, play lawn tennis.'

In August 1929, a letter to *The Times* from a former Honorary Secretary of the Simla Cricket Club in India recalled a 'match for ladies', played about 1885, in which the heroine who made fifty runs was Mary Tribe, the daughter of Archdeacon W. H. Tribe of Lahore. This young woman, consistently developing her physical vigour, later became the 'flying Duchess' of Bedford, who ultimately disappeared on an aeroplane expedition in 1937.

A decade or two of experience soon showed that traditional notions about feminine fragility were due, not to inherent weakness, but to the indoor confinement, voluminous unhygienic clothing, and (in the middle classes) lack of stimulating occupation, which had afflicted 19th-century women. By the time that Elizabeth II ascended the throne, the female sex had come to be recognised as tougher and longer-lived than the male. The British 1951 Census showed approximately 305,300 women aged between 80 and 84, 111,600 between 85 and 89, and 27,300 between 90 and 94, while men at the same ages numbered 177,000, 55,600, and 9,400 respectively. Even at the now comparatively early ages of 65-69, the total number of British women exceeded that of men by nearly four hundred thousand.

The position of women in sport nevertheless remained a subject of anxious discussion for fifty years after the question whether a lady should ride a bicycle had been hotly debated. Inventiveness in the cycling trade finally disposed of the argument that a good woman could not wear bloomers. 'A bishop's wife clothed in seemly skirts rode a bicycle through the streets of Leamington', Jerome K. Jerome recorded of this controversy in *My Life and Times*.

While women in the first quarter of the 20th century were forming polo, cricket, hockey and basket-ball teams, entering for mixed tennis or golf championships, and even trying to swim the Channel, newspapers still found a ready public for articles discussing the probable effect of these activities upon feminine health. Was sport beneficial or dangerous for women? Above all, did it interfere with their functions as wives and mothers?

These questions became especially acute in the United States owing to America's greater interest in commercialised sport for both sexes. As early as 1830, the importance of 'suitable bodily exercises for young women' had been emphasised by Dr John Collins Warren, who helped to start the men's gymnasium at Harvard. Nearly a hundred years later, an article entitled 'Women and the Sport Business' by John R. Tunis in *Harper's Magazine* for July 1929, described the special dangers threatening American women athletes.

The author admitted some undeniable facts which by that time were recognised in all the countries where physical exercise had become as customary for women as for men. The nation's health had improved 'immeasurably' since women began to take up outdoor sports. Their interest in games had led to the greater freedom and convenience of feminine dress, and they had learned in sport as well as in business the advantages of fair play, co-operation, and self-reliance. But, he complained, 'the tendency in recent years has been to over-stress competition as opposed to play', and 'in competitive sport women are far more in need of medical supervision than men'.

To redeem the mistakes, not confined to women's sports, which caused energetic American organisers to concentrate upon champions and Olympic teams instead of devising athletic programmes suited to the health and leisure of less exceptional citizens, Mrs Herbert Hoover called a Conference of educational leaders and others interested in 'sane athletics for women'.

This Conference, which met at Washington in 1923, started the Women's Division of the National Amateur Athletic Federation. Its purpose was to mitigate commercialism by promoting 'wholesome athletic competition for the greatest number of girls and women', and in co-operation with medical authorities to encourage investigations seeking answers to the questions now publicly asked about the effect of sports on women's health.

The Forum Magazine conducted one typical inquiry amongst the graduates of Smith College for Women at Northampton, Massachusetts, and invited Dr Linda Gage Roth to summarise the results in an article which appeared in May 1929. The 1,209 answers received to a questionnaire circulated to all Smith graduates in Classes 1910 to 1922 showed that no complications had occurred during pregnancy and childbirth amongst the keener athletes.

On the contrary, declared Dr Roth, 'it does seem that the women whose participation in athletics was enthusiastic, and who probably, therefore, took exercise most frequently, appear to have a slight advantage, at least in health during pregnancy, over those with whom it was casual or negative. While this advantage may not be large enough to be statistically significant, it is at least a convincing repudiation of the argument that athletics are detrimental or disastrous to women.'

Such harm as a few women may have suffered from their part in sports twenty and more years ago probably arose from their determination to prove themselves 'as good as a man' in feats requiring strength rather than skill. Today that type of inferiority-complex has become unfashionable; in sport, as in business, the arts, and the professions, women care less to compete with men than to make the utmost use of their special abilities and aptitudes as women.

One of the youngest competitors, Pat Smythe, Britain's leading horse-woman at twenty-three, stressed this point in the *News Chronicle's* series of 'World Beyond Tomorrow' articles, published in October 1952. Answering the question 'Will Women Beat Men at Sport?', she emphasised the gracefulness of women skaters, and the outstanding success of women riders owing to the sympathy established between the horse, which provides the strength, and the girl who rides him.

The next half-century, she concluded, 'need not give rise to a race of Amazons. It could presage a race of truly feminine sportswomen, to equal and outstrip men simply by applying to the utmost their peculiarly feminine qualities of grace and accuracy.... By A.D. 2002 there could well be many another Blankers-Koen or Dyson. For in this, as in other sports, women will make astonishing progress by their patience and persistence throughout long laborious training.... Their victory will be one of mind rather than physique.'

A balanced development of body and mind, with the health of the one contributing to the keenness of the other, became the ideal of the 20th-century schools and colleges which all included games and gymnastics in their curricula. But the rowing, skating, tennis and hockey-playing girls who went up to Oxford and Cambridge after the First World War to take Degree courses without the promise of a Degree, recognised like their tutors that the most perfect co-operation of mind and body would not enable women to realise their full powers without equal opportunity.

The Oxford of that day produced, in a well-known classical tutor and a remarkable college Principal, the women to match the hour.

Miss Annie M. A. H. Rogers, born in 1856, spent her long life of over eighty years entirely in Oxford, where as tutor for St Hugh's College and the Society of Home Students she worked quietly in the background for Degrees for women. Her memoir, *Degrees By Degrees*, published posthumously in 1938, described her part in that struggle.

Miss Penrose (later Dame Emily), two years Miss Rogers' junior, had been Principal of Somerville College since 1907. Not only was she an outstanding classical scholar who had been the first woman to take a First in 'Greats'; she was also a born stateswoman. In the interest of Degrees she found it desirable to curtail even the limited freedom of post-war women students, and urged them 'to avoid conspicuousness and exercise self-restraint'. Degrees for Women were held over them like a bunch of carrots suspended above the head of a would-be tempestuous donkey as an inducement to good behaviour.

It was largely owing to the work and influence of Annie Rogers and Emily Penrose that Oxford was ready, more than a quarter of a century before Cambridge, to take advantage of the Sex Disqualification (Removal) Act passed in 1919. The 'permissive' Clause III of this Act stated that nothing in the Statutes or Charter of any University should be deemed to preclude the authorities of such University from admitting women to its membership.

After some exuberant pen-wielding by literary women students and much discreet background propaganda in Senior Common Rooms, the Statute granting Degrees to Oxford women was passed on May 11th, 1920. When it came into force the following Michaelmas term, one of the Vice-Chancellor's first duties was the matriculation of nearly 1,000 women students. Taking my place amongst them with my contemporary, Winifred Holtby, I remained to watch the Degree-giving ceremony in which long-qualified women, wearing caps and gowns for the first time in Oxford history, passed through quadrangles brilliant with ampelopsis into the Sheldonian Theatre.

Two years earlier Emily Davies, the founder of Girton College,

Cambridge, had recorded her first Parliamentary vote at the age of eighty-nine. Her long life of almost a century had seen the whole struggle for women's education from its despised beginnings to the Sex Disqualification (Removal) Act, but when she died in 1921 her own University was still refusing equal status to women students.

Cambridge did not actually admit women to full Membership until 1947, though the backwoodsmen with voting powers amongst its Members, and not the University itself, were responsible for this long resistance. Where progress rested exclusively with the Senior Common Rooms, it sometimes overtook the changes at Oxford; Dr Dorothy Garrod, for instance, became Disney Professor of Archeology at Cambridge in 1939, whereas Oxford's first woman Professor, Dr Ida Mann, was not appointed Professor of Ophthalmology until 1945.

Even at Oxford, Degrees for Women were not synonymous with full equality, either within the University or under college regulations. Both at Oxford and Cambridge the number of women undergraduates was limited by statute, in the proportion of one woman to six men at Oxford, and one woman to ten men at Cambridge.* This restriction provoked Miss Margery Fry, who followed Miss Penrose as Principal of Somerville, to a characteristic pronouncement: 'Women do their best work when they are allowed to do it, not as women, but as human beings'.

Within the colleges, the tradition that women as a sex needed protection against men died a slow and painful death. The ancient 'chap. rules' which compelled the presence of a woman chaperone at every mixed Oxford tea-party disappeared after the First World War, only to be temporarily replaced by a regulation which insisted that in all such social functions the number of women should exceed by at least one the number of men. No explanation was vouchsafed for this peculiar arrangement. The students thus penalised always supposed that, if any pairing-off

* In 1952 Cambridge began to discuss a project for a new women's college, to provide for at least 100 additional students, while in Congregation at Oxford on May 19th, 1953, a statute was promulgated to increase by ten the quota of undergraduate students permitted to be in residence at each of the women's colleges.

tendency should display itself in the tea-party, the extra woman was counted on by the authorities to oppose it tooth and nail.

Not until after the Second World War did Oxford women realise what complete freedom could mean in richness of intellectual life and social experience. Even then, some anomalies remained. In 1950 Somerville became the first Oxford women's college to change its charter and elect its governing body from its own Senior Common Room and official Fellows, instead of partially depending upon the benevolent patronage of University men. Still more recently the University itself introduced a small change in its conduct of Viva-Voce examinations. Custom had previously ordained that all the men candidates should be questioned before the women, who believed that fatigue or irritation in their examiners sometimes accounted for the loss of a good Class. Today the candidates for Viva-Voce examinations appear in alphabetical order, whether they are women or men.

In 1951 over 19,000 full-time women students were registered in the Universities of Great Britain. This number still represented less than one-third of the male student population, but the proportion has been large enough to contribute distinguished women to most of the leading professions. Political women, of whom Eleanor Rathbone from Oxford and Mrs H. M. Swanwick from Cambridge were among the first, have visited their old Universities as Members of Parliament or delegates to international assemblies. Others have returned as social pioneers, scientists, doctors, head mistresses, broadcasting administrators and television experts. Oxford has produced so many women writers that one group, which included Rose Macaulay, Dorothy L. Sayers, Margaret Kennedy, and Winifred Holtby, became popularly known in the nineteen-thirties as 'the Somerville School of Novelists'. During the same period England's best-known woman preacher, Dr Maude Royden, once a student at Lady Margaret Hall, reached the peak of her fame.

From all the Universities, women scholars and research-workers have made honourable names. In 1949 Professor Lillian

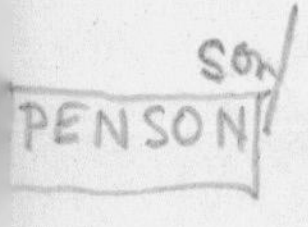

Penrose, of Bedford College, was elected Vice-Chancellor of London University. Three years later about thirty women Professors were holding Chairs. A group of scholars responsible for

the development of historical studies at London included Dr Caroline Skeel, a student of Girton from 1891 to 1895 who took a Double First in Classics and History and survived till 1951. At Oxford Dr Janet Vaughan, appointed Principal of Somerville College in 1945, brought to the University a distinguished reputation as the pathologist in charge of the North-West London Blood Supply Depôt during the Second World War. She also made history by holding, as a married woman with two daughters, a post hitherto reserved for spinsters.

Today all the British learned societies accept women as members. The last to be converted was the Royal Society founded in the reign of Charles II, when women were more conspicuous as Royal Duchesses than as scientists. Seven women, including the Quaker crystallographer, Dr Kathleen Lonsdale of Bedford College, can now write the letters F.R.S. after their names.

Dr Lonsdale, a wife and mother like Dr Vaughan, can count herself more fortunate than the first 20th-century woman whose admirers approached the Royal Society. In 1902, when an attempt was made to elect Mrs Hertha Ayrton, the scientific mother of the late Mrs Barbara Ayrton Gould M.P., Counsel's opinion decided that though Mrs Ayrton might be eligible for the Royal Society as a woman, as a married woman she was excluded altogether.

The women of civilised countries who now play a normal part in University life have more work to do for their sisters in backward states than for their own rights and privileges. With the idea of raising the world level of women's education, the International Federation of University Women was founded in 1919. By 1927 its members included the women graduates of twenty-seven nations, for whose benefit Crosby Hall on Chelsea Embankment was opened as a London centre. In 1952 the Federation had a membership of thirty-one affiliated National Associations of University women, and was in contact with groups or individuals in Bermuda, Chile, Hong-Kong, Japan, Korea, Turkey, Liberia, Pakistan, and Spain.

Throughout its thirty-four years of life the Federation has encouraged scholarly research, and up to May 31st, 1950, had awarded over £65,000 in international fellowships and grants.

Between 1928 and 1950, sixty-two fellowships and fourteen grants were given to scholars of twenty-four countries and twenty-six nationalities. The six awards made in 1951–52 went to anthropologists from England and Australia, two Canadians respectively studying zoology and economics, a Dutch student of Indology, and a Scottish chemist. In 1950–51 the Federation appropriately published a book entitled *Human Rights: The Task Before Us*.

Their research-workers, like the international students sponsored by the Fulbright Committee of the United States, act as cultural ambassadors from their own countries to the scenes of their studies. They represent an advance guard of the educated women whose numbers the United Nations Organisation plans to increase through the work of its Status of Women Commission.

In January 1948, the Commission recommended that the right of education be guaranteed to all women 'by general compulsory education, a system of State bursaries for outstanding students in high schools, school instruction in the indigenous language of the country, and the organisation in enterprises and rural areas of free industrial, technical and agricultural instruction for women'.

Several Member States and some non-self-governing territories submitted a detailed report on existing disabilities in education to the Beirut session of the Commission in March 1949. A second study to ascertain the causes and extent of educational discrimination against women then began with the help of the United Nations Educational, Scientific and Cultural Organisation. Their report was published in 1952 by the International Bureau of Education in Geneva under the title *Access of Women to Education*, and contained information supplied by Ministries of Education from forty-seven countries.

In Britain education is now free but compulsory between the ages of five and fifteen for boys and girls alike. Though most non-State schools still accept either boys only or girls only, the two sexes are usually taught the same subjects to the same standards. The needs of a future career, rather than sex discrimination, determine any variation in the normal programme.

Up to the age of eleven, co-education is customary in State

schools. After that age it continues in Scotland, but not in England or Wales, until the University period, in which it is usual throughout the country. Britain thus reverses the practice of the United States, where co-education is normal in schools but infrequent in Universities.

Official grants and scholarships to British Universities are equally available for boys and girls, and the Ministry of Education allocates University Scholarships to each sex in proportion to the number of candidates. But boys have greater access to scholarships from private funds, and gifted girls worthy of endowment are handicapped by the poverty of women as a sex.*

On paper, at least, the picture now suggests a reasonable equality. But women, far more than men, are still the victims of hidden handicaps, arising from long-established habits of thought and the slow dying of domestic prejudice. How far have such concealed obstacles postponed real educational equality for 20th-century women?

During the first quarter of the century, the middle-class girls who largely supplied the scholars and professional pioneers suffered from two contrary disadvantages. In some secondary and nearly all private schools, pupils with no special aptitude or ambition in these subjects wasted many hours of valuable time in learning 'accomplishments'—a little drawing and music, some harmless handicrafts, and a good deal of fancy dancing. But they were not expected to become proficient enough to earn money, or even to entertain their friends.

Reacting against this genteel dilettantism, the girls' public schools developed a harsh preoccupation with school and college examinations, which narrowed the minds of able girls just as 'accomplishments' made dabblers of their less talented contemporaries. The driving intensity of many women tutors at the older Universities also arose from the sharp competition for college vacancies imposed on women students by the statutory limitation of their numbers. An excessive concentration on examination work tended to restrict women's opportunities, and deprived them of a liberal education as distinct from a technical training.

Both these handicaps have virtually disappeared. An impove-

* See Chapter 8.

rished society has little use for the dilettante, whatever her background, and a college student is now valued for her total contribution to the University. A conspicuous part in its journalism, politics, games, debates, and theatrical ventures may influence the student's future as directly as success in examinations.

A third type of liability which affected girls of every age and educational level has also diminished since the publication, in 1926, of a Board of Education Report on the Differentiation of the Curriculum for Boys and Girls in Secondary Schools. This Report stressed the interruption of schoolgirls' studies by domestic work; 'in general the home always weighed more heavily on girls than on boys, and in cases of family illness, additional strain and anxiety fell on them'.

The custom of using even the most brilliant daughter as domestic servant, nurse, or hostess persisted until about 1930. It started to die when a large enough number of women who had themselves struggled to work against interruption began to educate daughters on whom they determined to impose no special claims. By 1950, in spite of a steady decrease in domestic help, many families were beginning to tackle household duties as a unit, and fathers and sons to share in the 'chores' which in old-fashioned homes are still loaded on to the long-suffering backs of mothers and daughters.

Such hindrances as women still face in education are even more imponderable than these former obstructions. The *Report of a Conference on the Feminine Point of View*, drafted by Olwen W. Campbell and published in 1952, showed that the training of women for higher-paid posts is still restricted, as in Medical Schools, on the ground of its 'wastefulness'. Women, it is assumed, will quit their professions on marriage—though few women doctors do.

'The validity of this objection', adds the Report, 'would be reduced if part-time work and re-training were available as a matter of course for married women.' The compilers make the further point that women's achievements are habitually underestimated in history teaching, which still tends to pay undue attention to wars, battles, and the competitive policies pursued by statesmen of questionable merit. Yet whenever a women has made a dent on history, an extensive literature grows up around her;

books, plays, and films abound on the lives of Joan of Arc, Elizabeth I, Queen Victoria, Florence Nightingale, the Brontës, and Madame Curie.

In education as in politics, the scope of women's influence has been disproportionate to their numbers and usually inadequate. Yet even in countries where women habitually take second place, a few remarkable women have shown the power of their initiative.

An Italian woman, Maria Montessori, revolutionised the teaching of children, and extended throughout the world a child-consciousness which did not exist until women claimed their share in education. An Egyptian woman, Madame Hoda Charaoui Pasha, spent much of her great wealth in starting technical schools for girls. In Pakistan, Begum Liaquat Ali Khan—herself a pupil at the Isabella Thoburn College founded by American missionaries in Lucknow—used her political influence to create a revolution in women's education and training.

When Winifred Holtby reviewed the Board of Education Report in 1926, she raised another question which is still debated.

'Should education', she inquired, 'be directed towards emphasising or eliminating the differences that exist between the sexes? In spite of the Hadow Report, opinion still wavers.'

Three years later Dr William Allan Neilson, then President of Smith College, Massachusetts, repeated this question in the American *Forum Magazine*. 'Should Women Be Educated Like Men?' And he gave an answer which came close to the reply that intelligent women—and men—would give today.

'For women no less than men it is desirable to sharpen their sensibilities, to develop their faculties, to broaden their outlook, to provide themselves with means of self-expression, to store up those resources that make life rich and full and give the soul immunity from the changes of fortune and the shocks of fate.'

Differences of emphasis there must always be, both within and between the sexes. Our ideas are changing on what constitutes knowledge, and on what kinds of knowledge are important. We recognise at last that a grasp of technique is at least as important to the young mother bringing up her first baby, as to the machine-minder in a factory.

The 'Woman's Page' may disappear from national newspapers

with the realisation that international affairs, Parliamentary debates, literary controversies, and the latest scientific discoveries are, or ought to be, of equal interest to both sexes. But we are unlikely to see the end of the women's magazine; nor, though there is room for a vast improvement in its quality, does there appear to be any reason why we should.

Women have a special though not an exclusive interest in rearing children and managing homes, and they wear different clothes from men. The quality of their magazines is not alone in its need for reform. Publications which specialise in such male preoccupations as cars, aeroplanes and field sports seldom discuss topics of general interest more intelligently than journals designed for women.

Though it is now accepted that men and women have different outlooks and a number of different interests, the need for a different education has ceased to be thought necessary except in so far as some special training is required for every function, including motherhood. The contrast between men and women today expresses itself rather in their interpretation of their knowledge and the manner in which their skill is applied.

The history of 20th-century womanhood has shown that becoming educated is a process which must begin with the opportunity; where that is denied, only the impassioned pioneer will advance. But education, for women as for men, clearly does not end with examinations and Degrees, or even with the exchange of teachers, Fulbright scholarships, and the opportunity to travel. It has failed unless it develops perspective and awareness, and that respect for truth and justice which we describe as 'integrity'.

The woman with these spiritual and intellectual standards is not yet adequately catered for, as Marghanita Laski complains, by that Press and publicity machine of any country. But the standards themselves provide her own defence. Once she has learned, as women today are learning, to detect the second-rate, she is for ever secure against its insidious influence upon her life and thought, and has become an educated person.

7

THE STRUGGLE FOR EQUAL OPPORTUNITIES

Any historian recording women's struggle for equal opportunities, and later their still less successful attempts to secure equal pay, has to leave the neatly-defined realms of legislation for a complex scene in which custom and prejudice decide the rate of advance.

Where the position of women could be altered by legal measures it has changed with relative speed, for such measures are limited in scope and directed towards the remedy of conspicuous wrongs. Much less responsive to revolutionary pressure are personal and social competition, economic status, moral tradition, and long-accepted habits which Virginia Woolf once called 'tough as roots but intangible as sea-mist'. The stock excuse for inaction—'it's not done'—is offered as frequently by the victims of outdated convention as by those who perpetuate inertia for their own benefit.

In the professions, as in education, some progress is visible because the substantial minority of women affected have been more aware of a purpose, and less blunderingly at the mercy of traditional values, than the mass of the population. They were the conscious pioneers of revolution, the leaders of assaults on masculine citadels, the exploiters of negative or 'permissive' freedoms granted by such 20th-century legislation as the Sex Disqualification (Removal) Act. Because the altered position of all women owes so much to the educated few who question existing situations and perceive fresh opportunities, professional women have an importance out of proportion to their numbers.

Compared with the millions of women employed in factories the world over, those numbers are small. An up-to-date analysis of women workers in Great Britain, where the first Census for twenty years was taken in 1951, shows that 'professional and technical occupations' accounted for only 587,100 women in a total of 6,916,300 'gainfully occupied'.

'Administrators, Directors, Managers' added a further 46,600, and another 24,300 should perhaps be included from the 89,900 persons 'professionally engaged in entertainments and sport'. Professionally qualified women thus amounted to about one-tenth of the whole. Another large group of women, the 1,580,100 employed on 'personal service' in clubs, hostels, restaurants, and other institutions, occupied positions which approximated to commerce and industry rather than the professions.

In countries with civilisations comparable to Britain's, we may assume a similar proportion of professional to industrial women; in backward countries it will be smaller still. A world picture of progress or the reverse, though still difficult to obtain, emerges more clearly from comparative studies which have been made of professional women in many countries, than from the vast and often supine mass of women in industry.

For many industrial women, work is a routine safeguard against starvation, a glamourless necessity untouched by the romance of a 'career'. Because, in comparison with professional women, they are still half-conscious and semi-organised, they have before them an even longer and more formidable struggle for Equal Pay, which is the subject of Chapter 9.

The world survey made by Miss Douie from an I.L.O. publication in 1946* and sponsored by the British Federation of Business and Professional Women, showed a complicated and sometimes unexpected pattern existing just before the 1939 War.

Students of the feminist movement might have foreseen that in long-civilised States with established traditions, women would have a sterner fight for justice than in countries of late social development or recent political revolution. (From this angle, ancient Asian countries such as India and China, and historic European countries such as Russia, rank amongst the 'recent'.) Comparative experience in teaching and nursing, and other traditional professions which some women had entered when all women were regarded as fit subjects for restriction, also showed a resistance to change which did not appear in such modern careers as advertising and broadcasting, or in social and welfare work

* See Chapter 5, p. 64.

which has so recently graduated from voluntary effort to the standing of a profession.

But it was more surprising to find that good records of professional achievement did not always follow a high social and legal status. In some States many occupations were open to women, but the qualified practitioners were few. In others, and especially in Germany, Fascist reaction emerging from economic catastrophe deprived women of their former opportunities, and caused a miasma of psychological repression to spread even to such countries as Britain and the United States, which believed themselves to be fortresses of anti-Fascism.

Throughout the civilised world, women probably come nearest to sex-equality in arts and letters, though these are precarious callings even for the highly gifted and only the few earn more than a pittance. Since writing provided an outlet for a frustrated spirit, some of the best-known women in literature, such as Jane Austen and the Brontës in Britain and Georges Sand in France, made reputations before the feminist struggle began.

On the stage the names of Mrs Siddons, Sarah Bernhardt, and Eleonora Duse are as well remembered as those of Edmund Kean and Henry Irving. In ballet-dancing, Anna Pavlova stands on a pedestal unshadowed by that of Nijinsky. So far women musicians and artists have been less prominent, and even in literature standards of achievement vary from the highest professional levels in some countries to a stage little better than the old-fashioned 'accomplishment' in others.

Wherever women do make a living as writers and artists, they receive equal remuneration with men. Sometimes, especially in films and on the stage, their salaries are higher. Payment in the arts is normally fixed by the demand for an individual's work, and not by sex or any other irrelevant classification. The publisher who offered his female authors a lower royalty because they were women would soon find himself boycotted by literary agents.

In journalism, equal pay is also given for equal work; the 'star' writer, whether man or woman, receives a star's rate. At lower levels, fees are usually determined not by sex but by space. It is the 'equal work', rather than the fair remuneration, which women journalists have still to seek. Apart from some offices of women's magazines, of which many are still edited by men, few women hold leading positions as editors and editorial writers.

A woman, Mrs Ogden Reid, edits the influential *New York Herald-Tribune*. Several American women, such as Anne O'Hare McCormick, Dorothy Thompson, and Eleanor Roosevelt as the indefatigable author of 'My Day', have made conspicuous reputations as 'columnists'. No national or provincial British newspaper has appointed a female editor, though one woman edits *The Church Times*, and another, Viscountess Rhondda, both owns and edits the weekly review, *Time and Tide*. The two best-known film critics on national newspapers are women, and *The Economist* employs a woman as assistant-editor.

According to the 1951 Census, 6,700 women were occupied as 'Authors, Editors, Journalists, Publicists', compared with 22,100 men. But authorship is a profession difficult to assess in statistical terms.

The influence of women upon the arts has long extended beyond the limited ranks of those who practise them. Especially in the United States, where every form of art is highly commercialised, women are greater patrons of libraries, theatres, concerts, cinemas, and art galleries than men. Their tastes decide the directions in which all the arts are developing today.

In the older professions, such as teaching, medicine, and the law, women's progress has been slower. Through the centuries these occupations, so long dominated by men, evolved their typical masculine rituals, and the competition of women appeared as an intrusion which was resisted by the customary weapons of poor salaries, dismissal on marriage, ostracism, and general discouragement. Such penalties led women with no vocational urge for them to leave these well-worn paths, and instead to visualise and try to meet the newer needs of a modern community.

Forty years ago, teachers and nurses accounted for all but 87,000 of the 347,000 professional women shown in the British Census of 1911. Most of the 217,400 women teachers scheduled in 1951 still received lower salaries than men, though those employed in grammar schools were mainly university graduates. In Secondary Mixed Schools, 1,943 men held headships in 1951, and only fifty-three women. Out of 254,000 teachers in schools under local education authorities, sixty-two per cent were women receiving salaries on the Burnham Scale. This scale fixed the 'women's' rate at about four-fifths of the 'men's', though rents, rates, fares, and food-prices were not reduced for women.

Before the Second World War many local authorities expected their women teachers to resign on marriage, but in 1935 the London County Council removed this ban. During the War the prejudice against married women disappeared, owing to the shortage of teachers and a growing recognition that the beneficial influence of wives and mothers in schools was cheaply purchased at the price of some slight reorganisation. In 1944 the Education Act laid down that 'no woman shall be disqualified from employment as teacher in any county school or voluntary school, or be dismissed from such employment, by reason only of marriage'. One battle was over; the struggle for Equal Pay remained.

In both the United States and the U.S.S.R., teaching during the past half-century has fallen largely into the hands of women. Just before the Second World War women represented about four-fifths of all American teachers, though men held most of the supervisory posts.

A report of the National Education Association of the United States, entitled 'Teacher Personnel Practices, 1950-51', shows that discrimination against women teachers by reason of sex or marriage has greatly diminished since 1940. In 1951 only twenty per cent of American cities reported differences of pay based on sex, compared with forty-seven per cent in 1941. Marriage was still a cause of discrimination, but no more than fifty-nine per cent of the cities made it a handicap in 1951, as against ninety-five per cent ten years earlier. Only eight per cent still maintained an unconditional policy against married women's employment.

Recent and accurate figures are more difficult to obtain from the U.S.S.R. A Moscow handbook published by the Central Department for Economic Statistics showed that between 1927 and 1935 the percentage of women teachers rose from 81.3 to 90.2 in urban elementary schools, and from 61.6 to 67.9 in rural areas.

Woman teachers appear to receive the best treatment in Scandinavia, Latin America, India, and unexpectedly, France.

There they are admitted to the teaching staffs of all faculties, receive equal pay throughout the profession, and, if married, have been entitled since 1910 to two months' maternity leave with full salaries.

In Denmark women teachers receive equal pay with special marriage regulations, and since 1916 have been eligible for the headship of mixed schools. Brazil's women teachers—eighty-one per cent of the total staffs of primary schools—receive equal pay, retain their posts on marriage, and can claim three months' leave for childbirth. In India, owing to the scarcity of qualified women teachers, they sometimes receive higher salaries than men.

Today it would be difficult to imagine an all-male medical profession. In most countries, medicine was the first 'masculine' profession to admit women; even in Switzerland, the University of Zürich gave women the right to study medicine in 1864, and France permitted them to practise in 1875. By 1910 some Asiatic women could qualify, though few were able to use the opportunity; Japan, for instance, has recognised women doctors and dentists since 1906.

As doctors women have proved especially successful, though medical women are few in relation to teachers, nurses, secretaries, and Civil Servants. The 1951 Census showed that about 7,200 of Britain's 36,300 physicians and surgeons are women, and the Medical Register now contains 10,000 women's names. In 1947 all medical schools, including the Royal Free Hospital which previously accepted only women, became co-educational. But by 1951 women students were still getting less than one in four of the vacancies available; Guy's Hospital, for instance, had 537 men and only sixty-four women.

A prejudice against women doctors still survives in this restriction of opportunity, though it has rapidly diminished since 1914. In that year the group of medical women who later organised the Scottish Women's Hospitals in France and Serbia were told, on offering their services to the British War Office, that women were required only to go home and keep quiet.

Under the National Health Service, women practitioners have the same salaries and working conditions as men. One woman, Professor (later Dame) Hilda Lloyd made medical history by being elected President of the Royal College of Obstetricians and Gynaecologists in 1950. Another, Miss Diana Beck, became the leading brain surgeon at the Middlesex Hospital.

By 1938 no known bar existed in any country to the practice by women of medicine, dentistry, pharmacy, and the profession of veterinary surgeon. At one time the proportion of women doctors in the U.S.S.R. rose to nearly eighty per cent, and the regulations were revised to ensure a more even balance between the sexes. All the leading belligerent countries made full use of medical women during the Second World War; in Great Britain, the Dominions, and the United States, women doctors and dentists received commissions with the same military rank and pay as men and served on many fronts. After the War, all but four of America's eighty-two medical schools admitted women students.

In practice women have not shown much enthusiasm for dentistry; only about 1,000 of Britain's 12,600 dentists are women, and there are relatively few women pharmacists, opticians, and sanitary inspectors. In the other medical auxiliary professions, such as dietetics, physiotherapy, radiography and occupational therapy, women appear to predominate in all countries where the necessary training is available. In 1951 Britain's four hundred qualified dieticians were all women; so were 8,300 of her 10,000 physiotherapists.

A disconcerting contrast exists between the speed with which women have achieved legislative reforms, and their slow progress in the practice of the law itself. Discrimination against women is here more marked than in any other great civilian profession except the Churches.

In Britain the legal profession was one of several occupations opened to women by the Sex Disqualification (Removal) Act. About thirty years earlier an Indian, Cornelia Sorabji, had been the first woman to be admitted, as a Somerville student, to the Oxford Law School examinations. The Act of 1919 also permitted British women to fill 'judicial offices', such as that of Justice of the Peace. In the same year the professions of barrister and solicitor were opened to Italian women, though they could not become judges or magistrates.

Almost every country now allows women to practise as barristers; this has been possible in France since 1900, and in Denmark since 1906. In 1945 a French woman was sworn in as a Clerk at the Paris Law Courts, the first such appointment ever given to a woman. A few years later another woman, Miss Helga Petersen, became Danish Minister of Justice, and in this capacity visited the British Law Courts in April 1951. In China, where political offices tend to change quickly, a woman, Miss Hsi Liang, was mentioned by *The Times* as Minister of Justice in January 1952.

More restrictions upon women have survived in the profession of notary; the legislation of Quebec, for instance, excludes Canadian women as notaries, though they can take Degrees in Law and became eligible for legal practice in 1947. Judicial offices (including the office of Public Notary in South Australia) were opened to Australian women by various Acts between 1918 and 1928. By 1947, fifty women lawyers were practising in Victoria, and twenty-four in New South Wales.

In both the U.S.A. and the U.S.S.R. women are eligible for high judicial positions, and have held them. According to an American *Survey of Women in Public Life* made by the National League of Women Voters in August 1936, a woman was then a Judge* of the Supreme Court in Ohio. The War created a demand for women with legal training; they found positions in the U.S. Treasury Department, the Surgeon-General's Office, and in some divisions of the War Probation Board.

After the War a leading American lawyer, Judge Dorothy Kenyon, was appointed to the United Nations Status of Women Commission. In 1947 a list issued by the American National Association of Women Lawyers showed fifty-one women Judges in U.S.A., of whom three were Federal Judges, and ten held judicial positions in New York State.

Few other women, whatever their country, have as yet been appointed Judges. Between the Wars, Madame Grabinska became the first woman to sit as Judge for the Children's Courts in Poland under the League of Nations, and in 1950 a woman, Buo Ping, was reported to be Judge of the People's Court at Ting Hsien,

* A Judge in the U.S.A. is not synonymous with a British Judge. Much of the work done by American Judges is carried out in Britain by unpaid magistrates.

Hopei. During the Second World War Canada appointed two women Judges, one to the County Court in Ontario and the other to the Criminal Court of British Columbia. Great Britain, with approximately five hundred women barristers and the same number of women solicitors, did not select a woman Judge until 1953, when Mrs Elizabeth Kathleen Lane became Assistant Recorder at Birmingham. London's Stipendiary Magistrates include Miss Sybil Campbell, and in 1951 the first woman Coroner, Miss Lilian M. Hollowell, was chosen for North Suffolk.

In 1946 the General Council of the British Bar for the first time elected a woman, Mrs Helena Normanton. Two years later Miss Margaret Kidd, of the Scottish Bar, became the first woman K.C. in the British Isles. Two members of the English Bar, Mrs Normanton and Miss Rose Heilbron, joined her in 1950.

Miss Heilbron has appeared in several important cases, including the Old Bailey trial of the seven Merseyside and London dockers accused of inciting dock-workers to take part in illegal strikes. In April 1951 she was briefed for their defence, and eighteen months later for the defence of Harold Winstanley, the footman accused of two murders at Knowsley Hall, who was subsequently found guilty but insane.

Few women as yet practise legal work at this top level, but the salaries that they receive show no sex-discrimination. Among professions auxiliary to the law are the police and prison services. The Police Act of 1919 gave the Home Secretary power to make regulations which would bring women 'within the scope of the Police Acts for all purposes', and the Sex Disqualification (Removal) Act of the same year made it legal for them to be attested as constables.

Countries with women police include Australia, New Zealand, and India, where Bengal women had positions specially reserved for them in the Police Force before the Second World War. In 1952, 1,800 women formed part of the 82,200 Police Force of England and Wales, and in both England and Scotland a woman held the post of Prison Governor. Since the War ended, women police have been recruited again in both Germany and Japan.

Occasionally drama enters a policewoman's life; it was a woman's report which led to the arrest of the Kensington murderer, John Haigh. But her main purpose is the prevention of crime rather than its punishment.

'Women's infiltration into the Civil Service has been phenomenal when judged by most changes in Whitehall', wrote Geoffrey Murray in his review of a book by T. A. Critchley entitled *The Civil Service Today* (1951). According to Mr Critchley, the British Treasury took fifty years to change from candles to electric light.

When the telegraph system was nationalised in 1870, the Post Office brought in about a dozen women. Twenty years later, with the introduction of typewriters, Whitehall found to its alarm that women typists were necessary. But they were carefully locked into their top floor offices, while the one woman in the Board of Agriculture was tucked safely away in a small and dingy basement.

During the last twenty years of the 19th century, the Board of Education appointed a few women inspectors for domestic subjects. The first woman factory inspector followed in 1893. Up to the First World War, when a number of women were temporarily appointed to administrative offices, the male permanent officials regarded their introduction with hostility. The first examination where women in the Administrative Grade competed on equal terms with men did not take place till 1925.

Between 1918 and 1939 the status of British women Civil Servants changed relatively fast, though the Sex Disqualification (Removal) Act had permitted the Civil Service to frame its own rules for their entry and employment. They were declared ineligible for a number of posts, and with a few exceptions received lower salary rates than men; they were also compelled to resign on marriage. Eventually the Administrative Grades of the Colonial, Dominions, and India Offices accepted them, and married women were 'directed' to Civil Service appointments during the Second World War. Women Civil Servants who married at that time were also required to stay in the Service, but were transferred from the permanent to the temporary staff.

In 1946 the regulations demanding resignation on marriage were rescinded, and women also became eligible for the Foreign Service from which they had previously been excluded. The

Royal Commission of that year examined the 'principle' of equal pay, to which lip-service had been given since 1921 though the practice remained in an economic Eldorado.

By October 1951 the Civil Service employed about 233,000 women, or thirty-four per cent of the total numbers engaged, in addition to approximately 50,000 (one-third of the total) in local government. Though 30,500 women Civil Servants were typists, some 14,000 held posts in the Executive Grade and about 400 in the Administrative Grade, which had employed only twenty women when the Royal Commission on the Civil Service sat in 1929.

Two women, Dame Marjorie Cox of the Ministry of Pensions, and Dame Evelyn Sharp of the Ministry of Town and Country Planning, rose to the position of Deputy-Secretary, or second-in-command of their Departments. Dame Evelyn, who became the youngest-ever D.B.E. in 1948 at the age of forty-four, was then almost unknown outside her Ministry. In 1952, with a salary of £3,250, she ranked as the highest-paid woman in the British Civil Service.

Women in the Federal Service of the United States have long been legally eligible for both elective and appointive offices. They can enter for examinations on the same terms as men, and once appointed have in principle the same chances of promotion. Since 1870, payment in this Service has been based on grade, not on sex.

By August 1936, some 162,518 women worked in the Federal Executive Civil Service, and in the State Services a number held high posts which included the organiser of Works Progress Administration in Georgia, the Secretary of State in New Mexico and South Dakota, and the State Treasurer in Idaho. After much agitation against the marriage bar, a clause was added in 1937 to the Civil Service Act of 1883: 'No person shall be discriminated against in any case because of his or her marital status in examination, appointment . . . promotion, transfer . . . removal or retirement. All Acts or parts of Acts inconsistent herewith are repealed.'

Many American women filled highly responsible positions after the United States entered the Second World War in December 1941. One obtained an unusual appointment as Regional Director of the Man-Power Commission in New York. After the War ended, the number of women in high-grade positions increased.

Before 1939 women could claim theoretical equality of Civil Service status in thirty-one countries, three Australian States, four Canadian Provinces, and five North American States. The thirty-one countries included the majority of South American Republics, Austria until 1933, China, the U.S.S.R., Turkey, and Denmark. The Danish public service had employed women since 1865, and after 1921 Denmark gave them equal rights apart from military service and ecclesiastical office.

In Chile, France, India, Italy, Roumania, South Africa, the Commonwealth Service of Australia, and the Dominion Service of Canada, women had less chance of promotion than men. Switzerland barred them from specified posts, and in some Swiss cantons, as in the State of Luxembourg, they were not admitted to the public service at all. Belgium, Bulgaria, Germany, New Zealand, and the Australian Provincial Services of Tasmania, Victoria, and Western Australia then only employed women in lower grades.

In 1935, a British Report of the Inter-Departmental Committee on Women in the Diplomatic Service defended their exclusion on the ground that less advanced nations would find their employment 'odd'. One passage ran thus:

'Even if nothing more than surprise were evinced if a woman were appointed as Third Secretary of His Majesty's Embassy or Legation, there would be a very different feeling if the British Chargé d'Affaires, in the absence of the Ambassador or Minister, happened to be a woman, as well might, indeed, must be the case after a few years' service. It is feared that her position would then be regarded as ridiculous. . . .'

This passage itself appears 'odd' and even 'ridiculous' today, when one woman from a 'less advanced' nation, Mrs Pandit of India, has served as full Ambassador to both Moscow and Washington, and in 1952 led the Indian Delegation to the Assembly of the United Nations.* The oddity now lies in the failure of successive British governments to give women diplomats the same opportunities as the governments of many other States.

Long before India became qualified to choose her own Ambassadors, the U.S.S.R. had appointed Madame Alexandra Kollontai

*Mrs Pandit, in 1953, was elected President of the Eighth General Assembly of the United Nations.

as Minister successively to Norway, Mexico, and Sweden. Earlier still, in 1919, the short-lived Karolyi administration nominated Madame Rosika Schwimmer to be Hungarian Minister to Switzerland, though she never took up the post.

In 1933 the United States sent Mrs Ruth Bryan Owen, later Mrs Rohde, as Minister to Denmark, and in 1937 appointed Mrs Florence Borden Harriman as Minister to Norway, where she experienced and announced the Nazi invasion of 1940. Between these two appointments, the Republican Government of Spain sent Señora Isabel de Palencia as Spanish Minister to Stockholm. On her arrival she faced an unusual diplomatic problem, as her predecessor, a Franco adherent, at first refused to leave. Another woman Minister of that year was Señorita Palma Guillen of Mexico, sent first to Columbia and later to Denmark.

After the Second World War, several outstanding diplomatic appointments fell to women. In 1947 Madame Carmen Vial de Senoret became Chilean Minister to the Netherlands, and the following year Denmark appointed Madame Bodil Begtrup, a member of the Status of Women Commission, as its Minister to Iceland. In 1948 Israel also sent a woman, Mrs Golda Myerson, to represent its government in Moscow, and Bulgaria similarly chose Madame Siella Blagœva as its Ambassador to the Soviet Union. Two years later, New Zealand made Miss Jean McKenzie its Chargé d'Affaires in Paris. In 1950 Mrs Josephine McNeill was appointed by Eire as Minister to Holland, and twelve months later Señora Elida de Crespo became Panama's Ambassador to Mexico.

By 1951 the United States had 2,400 women diplomats serving in 294 overseas missions, with Mrs Eugenie Anderson as Ambassador to Denmark and Mrs Perle Mesta as Minister in Luxembourg. According to reports current two years earlier, Mrs Roosevelt was offered but declined the U.S. Embassy in Paris. After the election of General Eisenhower as President, the United States for the first time appointed a woman as Ambassador to a large nation when Mrs Clare Boothe Luce became American Ambassador to Italy in February 1953. Another woman, Miss Frances E. Willis, was chosen by the President in July 1953 to be U.S. Ambassador to Switzerland.

At least fourteen other countries opened their Diplomatic Services to women after the Second World War. The first woman to qualify as a diplomat in France passed the necessary examinations as early as 1930, and after serving with distinction in the Resistance Movement during the War, appropriately rounded off her career by marrying the Foreign Secretary. Even in Britain a number of women now possess the necessary qualifications to be future Ambassadors.

In the newer professions, such as advertising, broadcasting, television, and recent varieties of scientific research, little discrimination is shown against women because these occupations developed after anti-feminist prejudice had begun to disappear. Of about 11,000 persons employed in British radio and television, nearly half are women. They include writers, producers, programme engineers, the heads of children's programmes in both mediums, and the leading talks controllers, Mary Somerville and Mary Adams. The names of American women who run famous feature programmes, such as Mary Margaret MacBride, have become household words in millions of homes.

Many young women now spend months alone in primitive territories as anthropologists, archeologists, and entomologists, or travel unaccompanied to remote parts of the globe; the struggle for equal opportunities has never been part of their experience. Others have shown a gift for horticulture, which appears to be a profession where women excel. The first International Horticultural Congress held in London after the Second World War was attended by a thirty-year-old Swedish woman, Miss Gunny Larsson, who cultivated a strawberry known as Rubus Arcticus at a State Research laboratory within fifteen miles of the Arctic Circle.

One or two women architects qualified as early as the eighteen-nineties, though the London Architectural Schools were closed to them until after the passing of the Sex Disqualification (Removal) Act. Up to 1953 the most outstanding success by a British woman architect had been Miss Elizabeth Scott's design for the Shakespeare Memorial Theatre at Stratford-on-Avon. In 1943 the first woman architect was appointed to the permanent staff of the Ministry of Health. Throughout the Second World War, many women in various countries worked on the construction of factories, camps, aerodromes, and hostels.

Women entered some once exclusively male occupations, such as engineering, long after they were established in other professions, and found themselves handicapped by the difficulty of obtaining practical experience rather than by regulations based on tradition. In Britain the opportunities now open to women in engineering and electrical work are due to the tireless pioneering of Dame Caroline Haslett, who became Secretary of the newly-founded Women's Engineering Society in 1919, and started the Electrical Association for Women in 1924. Her most original colleague has been Miss Victoria Drummond, a member of the Institute of Marine Engineers, who received her Second Engineer's Certificate in 1926, and was decorated for gallantry during the Second World War.

Closely allied to engineering is aviation, which has furnished the 20th century with such modern-style heroines as Amy Johnson, Amelia Earhart, and Jacqueline Cochrane, the foremost woman pilot of the United States, who in May 1953 became the first woman in the world to fly faster than the speed of sound.*

In three out of the four leading vocational professions, women throughout the world either dominate, or encounter little opposition. Nursing is now a great women's profession in every country apart from one or two Muslim states, where women defy tradition by leaving home at all. Even here a few women have become pioneers and gone abroad for their training; a number from Pakistan began to enter British hospitals soon after the new State was founded. The only two British professions to employ more than 100,000 women are nursing and teaching. In 1951 women amounted to 148,700 of the 171,900 trained nurses and midwives shown by the Census. A further 88,500 women included assistant and student nurses and 25,900 nursery nurses.

Social work, where it exists as a skilled occupation, has also become largely a women's profession, and the educational standards of the 12,100 British women employed are usually higher than those of the men. The status and qualifications now required owe their level to the voluntary work of such pioneer

* In August 1953 Mme Jacqueline Auriol, daughter-in-law of French President Vincent Auriol, became the second woman to break the sound barrier.

women as Mary Hughes, Mrs Cecil Chesterton and the McMillan sisters in Britain, Jane Addams in the United States, and Rajkumari Amrit Kaur, the first Minister of Health in India.

Librarianship now employs mainly women, though prejudice against them has not disappeared from the Public Library Service and the headship of large libraries usually goes to men. Of approximately 15,000 British librarians who may possess a University degree and must have had a specialised training, 11,100 are women.

A very different picture appears in the oldest of all vocational professions, the practice of religion. Apart from such honourable exceptions as the Society of Friends and the Salvation Army, the Churches and other religious bodies the world over are still organised upon a purely masculine basis.

The authors of *The Feminine Point of View* have stressed the fact that far more women than men belong to religious organisations. The attempt, they suggest, made by most wives and mothers to apply Christian principles within their homes might indicate that their influence would be useful in reducing the current disparity between personal moral standards and those which normally prevail in business and politics. Yet women have little share in denominational teaching and even less in religious interpretation, while in some faiths men and boys are still brought up to despise the women of their own communion.

According to custom, a Jewish boy daily thanks God that he was not born a woman—one of those outdated Judaic practices against which the Jewish publisher, Victor Gollancz, launched a vigorous attack in his 'Autobiographical Letter', *My Dear Timothy*. In September 1952 at a convention in Boston, women were refused equal voting rights with laymen in the Protestant Episcopal Church, which is the American equivalent of England's Church Assembly, where women have been able to vote for over thirty years. American women have also been barred from the episcopal legislative body, the House of Deputies, since 1789.

An article in *The Woman's Pulpit* (U.S.A.) for October-December 1948 quoted a Report made that year to the American Association of Women Ministers by Hazel E. Foster, Chairman of the Research Committee on the Ecclesiastical Status of Women.

This Report stated that the foreign field then contained some 5,500 more women missionaries and missionaries' wives than men, yet most women doing the professional work of the older Churches still lacked professional recognition.

Some of the younger American Churches offered better openings to women; the Report quoted the Congregational Christian Year Book for 1946, which gave the names of 163 ordained women (one to every thirty-seven men). The Presbyterian Church had appointed women as deacons and elders for about two decades though it still drew back from ordination, and the Methodist Church included such prominent women Ministers as the Rev. Pearl Spurlock and Dr Georgia Harkness.

Hazel E. Foster also mentioned the ordination of at least seventeen women by the United Church of Canada and the use by its Anglican Church of about twenty women known as Bishop's Messengers, who served especially in isolated areas of the North-west owing to the shortage of rectors. But she showed that in some countries the East, in its attitude to women, was ahead of the West, and quoted statements published by Hindu and Muslim leaders in the *Colombo News* which affirmed that in the past their women had shared equal rights with men in religion and learning. Cairo University, famous for its teachings on the Koran, had added a department for women students, and in Japan the Rev. Mrs Uemura, President of the Japanese Y.W.C.A., had taught Christianity to the Empress and the two royal princesses.

Denmark, so long a leading country in the struggle for equal opportunities, passed a law in the nineteen-forties permitting the ordination of women in the State Lutheran Church. In Britain, women's ordination has been for some years a subject of controversy, with Canon Charles Raven, Dr W. R. Matthews, Dean of St Paul's, and Dame Sybil Thorndike as chief sponsors of the Society for the Equal Ministry of Men and Women. Notwithstanding the prominent religious work of Dr Maude Royden Shaw, Mrs Reinhold Niebuhr, and the Rev. Elsie Chamberlain, women are still officially barred from the priesthoods of the Anglican and Roman Catholic Churches and by the Methodist and Presbyterian Ministries, though they are admitted to the

Ministry of the Presbyterian United Free Church in Scotland.

Books on careers for women seldom give much space to religious vocations; few women are concerned, and those mainly in auxiliary work. But the number affected might be large, and from the inspiration given by women as mothers, teachers, and writers, it seems clear that their influence within the Churches could be great at a dangerous turning-point of civilisation.

'No truly incarnational theology', wrote Canon Raven in an article on *Women in the Churches* published by *Fellowship*, U.S.A., in October 1951, 'no fully Christian way of life can be attained until both male and female can contribute fully and equally to its achievement. . . . It is a tragic fact that whereas in the past half-century all the other great callings have admitted women on equal terms and to their great enrichment, the Church of Christ which ought to have been the first to do so if it had been true to its Founder and to its Scriptures is still hesitant and obscurantist.'*

In countries where a large part of the population remains backward and illiterate, the choice of professions by women tends to follow national needs. Three years after her independence, the new India could contribute only one nurse for every 56,000 individuals and one Health Visitor for every 350,000, and naturally attaches primary importance to the welfare professions.

A pamphlet entitled *Some Careers for Women*, produced for the All India Women's Conference in 1947 by Mrs Avabai B. Wadia, a qualified barrister and the editor of *Roshni*, gave its first and longest chapter to Paid Social Work. Only three pages apiece were devoted to Commercial Arts and Crafts, and to Stenography and Secretaryship (in India still largely a male profession).

Another huge and once equally backward country, the U.S.S.R., has transformed the animal-like woman peasant of Tsarist Russia into a skilled worker on a collective farm. Though it is unlikely that the Soviet Union has become the feminist Eldorado suggested in books by such apologists as G. N. Serebren-

1 Further discussion of this subject may be found in *Should Women be Priests and Ministers?*, by Edith Picton-Turbervill, O.B.E., published by the Society for the Equal Ministry of Men and Women in the Church, 42 Crutched Friars, London, E.C.4. 1953. 2s. 6d.

nikov (*The Position of Women in the U.S.S.R.*, Gollancz, 1937), the most vehement anti-Communist can hardly deny that within the past thirty years many millions of oppressed and illiterate Russian women have been changed into trained and self-respecting citizens.

In strange contrast to India and Russia has been Germany, a civilised country with a strong feminist movement, where women reverted under the Nazi régime to the medieval subjection already experienced by them in Mussolini's Italy.

Hitler had attained power on the strength of a promise to restore German prosperity and end unemployment. One method of dealing with unemployment was to eliminate certain large groups as unemployable, and his idea of women's place made him ready to sacrifice them along with Jews, trade unionists, and pacifists. The subsequent exaltation of woman as a Madonna-like wife and mother provided a useful camouflage for the social degradation which annihilated the German women's movement, substituted male for female workers in industry, and deprived professional women of their posts as teachers, doctors, and lawyers.

When the Second World War ended with the defeat of Nazi Germany, a dozen years of such experience had left German women lost, bewildered and discouraged. During the post-war period several British women were sent to Germany in order to recall the feminist revolution to German women, and help them back to the position of self-respect which they have since recovered. But Germany was not the only country to be influenced by Hitler. Nazi anti-feminism spread across Europe and became one of several adverse influences which independent women had to face in the nineteen-thirties.

A number of young British and American women, growing up at a time when Fascist reaction was rampant, adopted a disdainful attitude towards the women's movement and its leaders who fought for the rights enjoyed by later generations. The causes of yesterday tend to appear more antiquated than those of a century ago; all parents are aware that the period of their own youth represents for their children the dowdiest epoch in history. For some years it was 'modern' to regard women's biological differences from men as a species of inferiority, and scornfully to describe the continuing work of organised women as 'flogging a dead horse'.

Traces of this attitude still linger, though the young women who adopt it now would probably learn of its origin with horror.

Another influence adverse to equal opportunity, and one even deeper and more prolonged than the effects of Hitlerism, arose from the treatment inflicted upon the thousands of women already in industry when trained professional women were still numbered only in hundreds. Three trends especially in the employment of industrial women handicapped the position of women in the professions.

The long-established tradition of 'women's rates' and 'women's processes', like legislative restrictions on women employees, depressed the salaries of professional women and curtailed their opportunities. The industrial woman's habit of giving up her job on marriage owing to domestic burdens imposed by a primitive home* led in its turn to the marriage bar which limited several important professions to spinsters.

The history especially of teaching and the Civil Service in this century has reflected these consequences of industrial precedent. They have been intensified by other social and economic suppositions which have insisted, often in the teeth of direct contrary evidence, that all men have dependants and all women lack them; that work in the home is more 'moral' for a woman than work outside; that the more hampered this work is by old-fashioned equipment, the more moral it becomes; and that all women are basically inferior to all men in brain-power, staying-power, reliability, and physical health.

Myths die slowly, for they are part of the cultural heritage of the race, and their capacity for survival, which is usually quite unrelated to facts, draws its life-impulse from a compound of superstition and habit. They explain the incompleteness of equal opportunities in practice where the right to them has been theoretically conceded.

Justice for women is unlikely to be attained in full so long as the average (though not now the exceptional) woman still lacks self-confidence, is denied an equal training with her brother owing to the expectation of marriage, and is required to be more experienced and better equipped than a male candidate in order to

* See Chapter 11.

obtain a post officially open to either sex on identical terms. The poverty which is still the chief handicap of women will be discussed in the next chapter, and in Chapter 11 the double job, with its unrelieved toil and constantly shifting attention, of maintaining professional standards while running a home.

Yet some of the benefits arising from women's entry into the professional world are today little debated. Experience now seems to have established their superiority in work which requires, like the secretarial profession, attention to detail, deftness of touch, and a delicate co-ordination of hand and eye. Predominance in nursing has long been conceded to women—without envy owing to the under-payment and archaic restrictions which so long prevailed. But more recently the success of women in social welfare and similar occupations requiring insight and sympathy has suggested that they are, as a rule, better suited to work involving the happiness of individuals than to the exploitation of property or the pursuit of power.

In all such human work, the qualities of patience and gentleness have special value in counteracting the social violence and spiritual indifference created by a politically turbulent age. The general diminution of drunkenness and public brawling (despite a recent slight increase in Britain) owes a debt to the influence of women as teachers and welfare workers. In medicine the care of mothers and children, once neglected victims of pain and poverty, has assumed a new importance since the coming of women doctors.

The day of the leisured woman has gone, never to return, and it is doubtful whether the most conservative husband or father would really be happy to see it come back. Two great wars and a series of industrial depressions have made life too expensive and insecure to be burdened by parasites, however elegant. Self-sufficiency, and the power to order their own lives in terms of the unfettered opportunities recognised today as a human right, have become the aims not only of women for themselves, but of those who administer the many occupations now revolutionised by the part which women can play.

8

WOMEN AND MONEY

MIDWAY between the professions and industry lies the kaleidoscopic world of commerce, into which women have penetrated with such determination during the past fifty years that on the lower levels it has become virtually a women's occupation. Here, if anywhere, may eventually be found a means of removing the chief handicap still imposed upon women—their poverty as a sex.

Except in the United States, where women hold a special and privileged position, their control of financial resources, whether earned or inherited, has hitherto been trivial and ineffective. The great social contributions made by the very few exceptions—such as the 19th-century philanthropist, Baroness Burdett Coutts, whose benevolences ranged, says Ray Strachey, 'from the details of slum charities to the endowment of Colonial Bishoprics'—merely show up in humiliating contrast the limited scope of most women for financial initiative.

In the nineteen-twenties an enterprising Surrey fishmonger caused some amused comment by registering his business under the title of 'Marment and Daughter'. Such a variation on the time-honoured style 'and Son' was then still inconceivable to most British fathers, though women had begun to appear in offices and shops towards the end of the 19th century, and the 1891 Census recorded the employment of 17,859 female clerks.

By 1921 the number of women clerks had reached half a million, and their salaries ranged from 45/- to 60/- weekly during the next ten years. The 346,774 shop assistants of 1921 multiplied until, three decades later, they represented fifty-seven per cent of all persons employed in retail trades. Before and after 1950 women secretaries ran every kind of business, and their salaries rose with the cost of living to £8 or £10 a week. The 1951 Census gave 1,415,700 women clerks and typists to 916,500 men.

Most of these business women still held subsidiary positions. A few managed small firms, directed unimportant companies, or ran their own little shops, but women were rarely included among the directors of large enterprises. Though banking was officially open to them, in practice they could seldom obtain the necessary experience. In 1953 however an Oxford graduate, Miss Irene Shrigley, was Librarian to the Institute of Bankers.

The British masculine tradition, which has made the world of high finance into an Eleusinian mystery where only the initiated male may enter, still excludes women from the London Stock Exchange. Though the provincial exchanges are open it is difficult for women to earn a living as stock-brokers, but one resolute woman, the late Miss Gordon Holmes, managed to become both wealthy and successful.

During the present century many prosperous family businesses have passed into the hands of strangers owing to the death in war of only sons whose fathers' prejudices refused responsibility to daughters, often the actual inheritors of the paternal flair. Few fathers have yet realised that a daughter can carry on a prosperous firm as capably as a son if she is similarly endowed with capital, and given the same opportunities for training, travel, and business contacts.

Viscountess Rhondda, an only child trained to follow her father in the directorship of large commercial firms, estimated ten years after the First World War that Britain's 27,000 company directors included only three hundred women, most of whom were associated with small undertakings. Among well-known British women who have graduated more recently to key positions in large companies has been Miss Christina Foyle, the youngest Director of Messrs W. and G. Foyle, the international booksellers. She staked her claim to this position while only in her 'teens by starting the now popular series of Foyles' Literary Luncheons.

Another successful business administrator, Miss Elizabeth Wilkinson, was appointed the only woman among ten directors of a leading group of fashion stores, and received one of the highest salaries paid to women in Britain.

In February 1953, a Press article by Hugh Cleland reported that there are now a few women holding conspicuous posts even in that male preserve, the City of London. His list included Mrs Lucy Borchard, seventy-five-year-old Chairman and Managing Director of Borchard (U.K.) Ltd; Miss Margaret Irving, Managing Director of Brash Brothers, the Rood Lane tea-blenders; Miss Elizabeth Hawes, Director of a Leadenhall Street firm of opticians; and Mrs Katherine Greenaway, Managing Director of a Bishopsgate firm of insurance brokers. A few others of comparable status may be found within the British Federation of Business and Professional Women, of which Dame Caroline Haslett is the International President.

In all Europe only one Bank—the Branch Office for Lady Clients of the Rotterdamse Bank in Holland—is managed by women. A number of successful business women have come from France, where wives and mothers maintain a long-established tradition of practical shrewdness, and are not assumed to be financially incompetent. According to *Le Droit des Femmes* (quoted by *The Catholic Citizen*), a meeting of the Council of the Republic in May 1951 received a report on the part played by French women in commerce from a successful business woman, Madame Thome-Pettenotre. She stated that no fewer than 3,500,000 were in business, as against 4,400,000 men, and estimated that women owned eighty to eighty-five per cent of such retail businesses as grocery, confectionery, and dairies.

The most conspicuous among commercial Frenchwomen have been the so-called 'champagne widows', of whom the best-known, La Veuve Cliquot, built up a world-wide reputation during the reigns of Queen Victoria and Edward VII. One of her successors, Madame Olry Roederer, became Chairman of the important French firm of champagne-shippers in 1949. Madame Roederer's contemporaries in this picturesque occupation include Madame Bollinger and Madame Piper Heidsieck.

Scandinavian business women appear to prefer the less festive but more cultural activity of interior decoration. A leading personality in the Swedish furnishing trade, Mrs Greta Ljungberg, decorated a new Stockholm cinema entirely with British materials during the nineteen-thirties. More sinister has been the hereditary enterprise of a German woman, Frau Berta Krupp, the owner of

Krupp's Armament Works at Essen which before the Second World War employed over 100,000 men.

Commercial enterprise is not traditional amongst women of the Middle and Far East, but one of the few exceptions built up the most spectacular business career that a woman has ever made. Early in this century a Japanese widow, Madame Yone Suzuki, created a great mercantile empire out of a wealthy firm which dealt in rice, sugar and wheat in addition to steel and ship-building. The financial genius of Madame Suzuki, whose fortune was estimated at £30,000,000, made her the richest woman in the world and a powerful figure throughout the East. In 1927 her manoeuvres caused a political crisis in Japan, and brought down the Imperial Government.

These manoeuvres included speculations in rice which led to rioting, and made her one of the most-hated business magnates in her country. She controlled the Japanese steel industry and sugar-market, and owned sixty steamships which were said to have made between £10,000,000 and £40,000,000 during the First World War. In spite of the antipathy which she aroused by repudiating oriental feminine subservience, she was loved and admired by her girl factory workers, for whom she introduced such unheard of innovations as shorter hours, better wages, airy dormitories, and recreation rooms.

A business woman from another country where female subjection is still the rule recently took part in large-scale international speculation. In August 1952, Madame Sabika Gharagozlu of Persia arrived in Rome to negotiate the extension of Persian oil sales to Italian companies. Through her husband Madame Gharagozlu became one of the biggest shareholders in the Iranian Development Corporation, the semi-official body in charge of Persia's seven-year development plan. By negotiating oil contracts she worked persistently to build a closer commercial relationship between Italy and Persia. In 1953, as lady-in-waiting to Queen Soraya, she renewed her efforts to sell Persian oil to Western buyers and claimed orders for three million tons.

Such European and Eastern women are isolated birds of paradise in a world of barnyard hens. Their enterprise would appear less conspicuous in the United States and even in Canada, which has produced such remarkable business directors as Mrs Harold F. Ritchie, who succeeded her husband as President of a large Toronto firm of general manufacturers' agents in 1933. Another wealthy Canadian woman, Mrs H. D. Warren, died in January 1952 at the age of eighty-nine after following her husband many years earlier as Chairman of the Toronto Gutta Percha and Rubber Company.

During recent Presidential elections in the United States, women have dominated the Party campaigns not only by their numbers but through their commercial influence. In 1952 they owned sixty-three per cent of America's wealth, and were responsible for about eighty per cent of all spending, which included their husbands' wages or salaries in addition to their own.

American women are the best customers of great international beauty specialists, such as Miss Elizabeth Arden and Madame Helene Rubinstein, who are among the richest women in the world. Madame Rubinstein has been reliably described as the owner of seven homes, which include an apartment in Park Avenue, New York, a penthouse in Paris, and houses in South America and Mexico. In 1952 her customers were said to have bought ten million pounds worth of her products.

Most American women millionaires have inherited their wealth from their husbands or fathers; a number of heiresses have been the 'only daughters' of whom Mary Agnes Hamilton wrote in 1936: 'The authority of the female in America is largely the outcome of spending power in her sole hands'. But one woman, Hetty Green, amassed a large fortune by her own efforts, and several others have occupied positions which not only carry large salaries but give their holders an opportunity of increasing their wealth.

American admiration for abstract justice is not the sole or even the main reason for these advantages. The women of the United States bring exceptional energy and persistence to any work that they undertake, and the growing number of 'top-line' positions has outrun the men available.

An article in the *Christian Science Monitor* for February 1951 gave the names of several American women to whom such positions had recently fallen. They included Mrs Wilma S. Soss, President of the Federation of Women Shareholders in American Business, Incorporated; Miss Alice E. Crawford, the first woman to join the Board of a large commercial Bank in New York City; Mrs Douglas Horton (war-time commander of the W.A.V.E.S. as Mildred McAfee), appointed to the Directors' Board of the National Broadcasting Company; Mrs Madeleine Edison Sloane, daughter of Thomas Edison, and the first woman to be elected to the Board of Western Union; Mrs Millicent Carey McIntosh, Dean of Barnard College, chosen to be the first woman Director of the Home Life Insurance Company of New York; and Miss Beatrice Rosenberg, the first woman Vice-President of Macy's Department Store.

Mercantile history of a similar kind had been made five years earlier, when Miss Dorothy Shaver became President of Lord and Taylor, the big Fifth Avenue department store, and took charge of an organisation responsible for an annual turnover of thirty million dollars.

A trail had been laid for these modern women by a remarkable pioneer, Mrs Lillian Moller Gilbreth, born at Oakland, California, in 1878. Besides bringing up twelve children Mrs Gilbreth became a consulting engineer, and was afterwards Professor of Management at Purdue University, Indiana. Still later she acted as consultant to a New Jersey firm which made precision instruments for the Navy, and was appointed Professor of Personnel Relations at the Newark, New Jersey, College of Engineering.

In 1949, with General George Marshall and Mr Alfred P. Sloan, a prominent industrialist, Mrs Gilbreth received one of the three gold medals given for distinguished service to humanity by the American National Institute of Social Sciences. At that time the adventures of her children were the subject of a current best-seller, *Cheaper by the Dozen*.

Even in America, the commercial progress made by women can easily be exaggerated. A sober picture, comparable with the general outlook for business women in other parts of the world, emerged from a Bulletin (No. 236) on *Women in Higher Level Positions*, issued in March 1950 by the Women's Bureau of the U.S. Department of Labour.

This document stated that by 1940 nearly 27,000 women (over a hundred times as many as those reported by the American Census of 1870) had become proprietors, managers, and officials, but their numbers amounted only to about 3.5 per cent of the total. Women also represented about 4.5 per cent of the proprietors, managers, and officials in banking and other forms of finance, but this did not appear to be a striking advance upon the 2.5 per cent reported in 1910.

The Bulletin showed that women continued to be less successful than men in reaching the higher commercial and industrial posts. In 1948, apart from boys and girls under twenty, 'women's incomes averaged considerably less than men's in every age group, occupation group, and major industry'. Supplementary evidence came from a Survey of 'Class 1934' women students, conducted for the *New York Times* among the graduates of Barnard, Bryn Mawr, Mount Holyoake, Radcliffe, Smith, Vassar, and Wellesley Colleges. Women who had worked for fifteen years since graduation were receiving an average salary of $3,790 a year, compared with the $9,800 average salaries earned by their husbands.

Though 'significant numbers' of women held high positions in the four kinds of work described by the Bulletin—department stores, the home offices of insurance companies, banks, and manufacturing—only the department stores showed an even distribution of jobs between men and women. Women held one-fifth of the higher posts in insurance companies, and only fifteen per cent of the better-paid positions in banks and factories. In no category of business or industry was the ratio of women to men at the higher levels comparable to the ratio of women to men in total employment. Roughly two-thirds of all the workers in department stores and insurance companies were women, and about one-half in banks and manufacturing.

The writers of the Bulletin insisted that 'in many cases the tradition that certain jobs are men's jobs only reflects the fact that often there are few women qualified for positions which carry heavy responsibilities'. Their investigation had shown that in each occupation the managements were increasingly seeking the best person for the job, without excluding women simply because they were women. The Bulletin concluded with a brief exhortation:

'When qualified women are available for such positions, the traditional patterns are often abandoned. The women in positions of responsibility covered by this survey have themselves brought changes in traditional attitudes and by their own achievement have shown what other women can do.'

Here, it seems, lies the answer to business women's questions. Throughout the world, and not least in the United States, financially influential women have nearly all been the wives, widows, or daughters of wealthy men; those who built up their own careers from scratch were conspicuous exceptions. But doors long closed are now opening everywhere to the woman who will work, qualify herself, and through her earnings help to equip other women still handicapped by traditional feminine poverty.

This poverty, like so many of women's historic handicaps, has its roots in the Industrial Revolution. Under the previous domestic system, women collaborated with their husbands in the trades and crafts which produced social wealth. Capitalism transferred this wealth to the control of men; when industry left the home women stayed inside it, leisured, frustrated, parasitic, and poor.

In spite of the women's movement and its consequences, women of means still belong to a small minority. Any observant traveller soon perceives how small it is. The woman M.P. going to her constituency, or the woman lecturer travelling First to a distant engagement in order to arrive poised and unruffled, often finds herself the only woman in the compartment or restaurant car.

Taxi-drivers and hotel waiters still avoid the female client, in the belief that she will be spending someone else's money and will therefore economise in tips. This expectation is usually justified, for a wife is not yet entitled to remuneration for managing a household. Though her husband may be a millionaire, the money she spends is no more her own than if he were a bricklayer.

The young unmarried woman is now endowed with education and training, but in most households the larger share of the family cash still goes to her brother. The older employed woman continues, except in a few well-organised professions, to struggle for equal pay. Because she is charged for the necessities of life at the same rate as her male fellow-worker, she economises at the expense of food and leisure. A man's payment provides for others to carry out his domestic needs, but it is assumed that a woman can look after herself.

Some years ago, I lived opposite a residential club for business women in the Earl's Court neighbourhood of London. At week-ends young bachelors of equivalent status, if they had stayed in town at all, would have been reading, smoking, going to the cinema, entertaining their friends. But the women were as busy mending their underwear and preparing a series of small meals as they had been during the week with their typewriters. Every Sunday morning, 'lines' hung with stockings, gloves, and lock-knit vests festooned their bedroom windows.

A girl university student still struggles with similar handicaps. The mother who mends her son's socks and irons his shirts usually expects her daughter to wash her own nylons and press her frocks, while the college 'scout' who washes up the young man's tea-things as a matter of course would be scandalised by any suggestion that the young woman would benefit by similar service.

This burden of small duties and petty economies still piled exclusively on the backs of one sex exacts its toll. As Virginia Woolf showed in her brilliant essay, *A Room of One's Own*, it provides an answer to the critic's stock inquiry: 'If women are really the equals of men, why have we had no woman Shakespeare, Beethoven, or Leonardo?'

'Little jobs' are as much the enemy of feminine concentration as Tudor demands on women were the foe of feminine freedom. Read in the context of Elizabethan times, Virginia Woolf's imaginary portrait of Shakespeare's 'wonderfully gifted sister, called Judith', is as convincing as her thesis. This fictitious Judith killed herself after finding, as a consequence of her quest for theatrical training, that she was with child by Nick Greene, the actor manager, 'and lies buried at some cross-roads where the omnibuses now stop outside the Elephant and Castle'. Judith's 20th-century successor does not rest in peace by the Elephant and Castle; she flounders under a pile of dishes.

The effects of female poverty are not only personal but social. In spite of all the revolutionary changes at the older universities, the statutory limitations imposed upon women undergraduates at

Oxford and Cambridge mean that, so long as men hold the monopoly of money, women must submit to regulation from without. They have to submit because their own institutions—schools, colleges, clubs, causes, publications—lack the endowment so lavishly poured out for the institutions of men. And institutions that lack endowment do not only fail to provide the scholarships, trainings, and equal opportunities for which women in growing numbers are clamouring; they remain bleakly unadorned by the arts and graces of life which the male sex has cornered along with the means to pay for them.

Comfortable surroundings and well-cooked food, as Virginia Woolf insisted, are great aids to good conversation and mellow personalities. Bare chilly rooms furnished with an eye to economy rather than beauty, cold cauliflower cheese (since even the cold mutton of Mrs Woolf's essay is now seldom obtainable), cold boiled potatoes, cold stewed figs, and cold water, stimulate the mind no better than the body. The women in British and European universities today are paying, not only for two World Wars, but for the age-long deprivations of their sex. Even in the United States ten years before the Second World War, William Allan Neilson, the President of Smith College, challenged the readers of *The Forum Magazine* with the 'grave disadvantage' suffered by American women's colleges. These, unlike the men's colleges, had little chance to benefit from munificent gifts.

'The women graduates', he admitted, 'in proportion to their resources, are quite as generous, but it does not need to be pointed out that their resources are infinitely less . . . the most completely demonstrated difference between the women's colleges and the men's is this of resources.'

In the same year an article on a kindred topic appeared in the *Manchester Guardian*; it was called 'Abolishing That Five-pound Look'.

'Success', wrote the author, 'depends largely upon the power to feel on the top of the world, and it is just that power of which poverty and depression deprive the low-paid worker. She comes very soon to regard herself as worth no more than the pittance that she is paid; shabbiness and dowdiness give her a "five-pound look" which suggests to the onlooker that five pounds a week is not only all that she receives, but all that she will ever deserve.'

Today that five-pound look has become a ten-pound look, but it is not yet a hundred-pound look, still less a thousand. Only when women in sufficient numbers acquire a thousand-pound look will they endow their institutions and produce their Shakespeares.

Within the past thirty years, at least a beginning has been made. Today an increasing number of married women earn enough to provide from their own pockets for the relative comfort and efficient service upon which the quality of their work depends. Young women are learning at an early age how to handle money, as we may discover from that infallible guide to changing custom, the popular advertisement.

In March 1951 the London *Observer* published a Westminster Bank advertisement entitled 'The Younger Generation', of which the representative having a heart-to-heart talk with a bank manager about opening an account was pictured as a smartly-dressed girl. Growing numbers of such girls, as they reach adulthood, are accepting the obligation to make some responsible use of the money that they save and can eventually bequeath.

The Will of the late Winifred Holtby, author of *South Riding*, showed how much can be done by women even when, in commercial terms, a relatively modest sum is involved. Knowing, though still a young woman, that she had not long to live, Winifred Holtby made a Will leaving to Somerville College, Oxford, 'for scholarships', the proceeds of any literary work which might be published after her death.

South Riding, the chief of these posthumous works, appeared when she had been dead for six months. From approximately £10,000 that this novel made in fifteen years, the College, able as a 'charity' to recover income-tax, founded two scholarships and several grants. One of these scholarships was won by a remarkable Australian student, Miss M. E. Hubbard, a graduate of Adelaide University, who made Oxford history by becoming the first woman to win the Hertford Scholarship for Latin in 1950, and in 1951 the Ireland Scholarship, which is the most distinguished classical award open to Members of the University.

Many women writers, in the United States and even in Britain, have made much more money than Winifred Holtby. How far have they similarly helped their fellow-women? If they have done little up to date, the tax-gatherer, so inimical to all writers, is probably responsible.

Other professions have benefited greatly from the benevolent interest of a few women. The pioneer founders of the British Women's Engineering Society during the lean years after the First World War owed much of their success to the wealth of Lady Parsons, the wife of a well-known mechanical engineer. Mrs Willson, the rich owner of building sites, and Lady Moir, organiser of 'Week-end Relief Work' for operatives in munition factories, also helped women engineers to start their organisation.

Such initiative awaits imitation all over the world. Many more women's professions need galvanisation and endowment, while the scope for new and intelligent publications for women readers is almost unlimited. Here women might develop, in combination, enterprises which the individual woman could not afford.

Numerous forms of voluntary social service are also required which do not demand excessive wealth from those who establish them. Mrs M. E. Dickin, the founder and honorary Director of the People's Dispensary for Sick Animals of the Poor, which was providing a regular service for 207 British towns and villages by the end of 1950, relied as much upon courage and devotion as on financial aid. The small group which set out to serve 'Problem Families' in the East End of London after the Second World War made up for their limited means by unlimited self-sacrifice. This field of work awaits indefinite development. The patient supervision of delinquent households is a better answer to cruelty and violence than the ruthless dispersal of their members.

Without some money, and the more the better, experiments of this kind cannot rise to the present level of human need. Only when a fair share of the world wealth belongs to both sexes will women's initiative find full scope for its creative energy.

9

THE STRUGGLE FOR EQUAL PAY

In the last chapter it appeared that the efforts of a few well-to-do women, able and willing to use their wealth for social ends, might eventually mitigate the chronic poverty from which women suffer. But the struggle of the female sex to raise itself from indigence and depression is being carried on continuously, and often unconsciously, by the vast mass of women workers engaged in industrial, agricultural, and domestic occupations throughout the world.

Industrial women, though still widely indifferent to impersonal ends, are reaching the stage of social consciousness much faster than the women of peasant communities, especially in the East. Those who belong, for instance, to India's 750,000 villages, and live in the same mud-huts as their cows, goats, and hens, depend unknown to themselves upon a handful of educated women in cities to voice their primary need for hygiene and the rudiments of domestic training. At present the demand for equal pay is an aspiration mainly confined to industrial societies. The struggle in Britain pin-points the story of similar conflicts in comparable civilisations.

' "Equal Pay for Equal Work" is primarily a battle-cry', declared the five men and four women members of the British Royal Commission on Equal Pay who presented their Report to Parliament in October 1946. 'In a battle-cry', they added, 'it is proper to expect power rather than precision.'

The attempt to introduce precision involved a series of definitions. 'Equal Pay', they decided, meant for its advocates 'a policy of raising the women's rate to whatever is, at the relevant time, the male rate of remuneration', but 'equal work' could be defined 'by commonsense only'. Those who used the battle-cry were asking, in effect, for 'the rate for the job'.

Later in their Report, the Commissioners gave two tentative explanations for prevailing differences in the pay of men and women. Different rates in any occupation were determined, they said, 'by the conditions prevailing outside it'. But those conditions were themselves produced by the most powerful influence in human affairs—the force of tradition. They went on to develop their theme.

'The answer in terms of "force of tradition" will not be lightly dismissed by anyone with experience of the immense part played by inertia in the governance of human affairs. Economic behaviour is determined not merely by national calculation but by assumptions derived from the sociological background—by the prejudices of a previous age embodied in the customs and traditions of the present.'

In no area of women's work were the prejudices of a previous age more rampant than in the vast field of industry. For years amateur sociologists had been so busy arguing whether women ought to work, wanted to work, or could work, that they disregarded the coming of economic and social changes which had already decided that women must.

The female workers driven into the factories by economic pressure during the 19th century suffered acutely from the low valuation of their own capabilities by women from sheltered homes who subscribed to the 'pocket money' tradition. Mrs Strachey has described in *The Cause* how completely Emily Davies and Elizabeth Garrett Anderson failed when they attempted, in 1872, to persuade the London County Council to adopt equal pay for men and women school visitors.

At this time the women visitors were only too glad to accept a rate of £50 to £70 a year, as against £80 to £100 paid to the men, since it was their cheapness and docility which helped them to find employment. As Chapter 7 of this book has shown, educated women have had the hardest struggle to obtain 'the rate for the job' in professions where the compulsion to work occurred before equal pay became 'a battle-cry'.

In the middle of the last century women were not admitted to Trade Unions except in the textile trades, where their position has always been strong. The hope of voluntary self-protection did not exist for the others until 1875, when Emma Paterson founded the Women's Protective and Provident League which became the Women's Trade Union League fourteen years later. After Emma Paterson died in 1886, Mrs James Ramsay Macdonald carried on this attempt to mitigate the growing conflict between men and women in industry until her own death in 1911.

When unskilled women began to take the place of skilled men at half their rate in the light metal and kindred trades, the men opposed their employment and tried to restrict their work to a few industries and processes. Women's place, they maintained righteously, was the home, though four million women had to find work or starve. The Trade Union movement became a large-scale endeavour to prevent women from under-cutting men, without any apparent realisation that the best way to achieve this purpose was to pay the rate for the job.

Between 1900 and 1914, neither the volume of trade in Britain nor the labour market changed substantially. The position of the workers, as in other countries which had grown rich through the Industrial Revolution, did not reflect the national prosperity. In 1906 the average wage of the British working man was about 30/-, but the skilled and relatively privileged woman textile worker averaged no more than 18/8d. Even she was better off than women in other trades; some figures quoted in 1919 by the Women's Employment Committee showed that in 1906 the average weekly wage for women in the linen and silk trades was 9/9d., in the printing trade 9/8d., and in the glass trade 8/6d.

An exhibition of sweated industries, organised that year by the *Daily News*, proved that women home-workers in equivalent trades were even worse off than women in factories. Amongst other sensational 'revelations', it disclosed that the rate for carding hooks and eyes was 1d. for 384; one person, working eighteen hours a day, could earn about 5/- a week. The match-box maker, paid at 2d. a gross, was expected to find the paste, hemp, and firing needed to dry the wet boxes out of these starvation wages. Yet no second Thomas Hood arose to challenge, with a new *Song of the Shirt*, the wealthy indifference of Edwardian England.

The Birmingham investigation into women's work and wages, made in 1906 by Edward Cadbury and his colleagues, showed that wherever women replaced men 'the former always received a much lower wage'. This wage, they stated, was not proportionate to skill or intelligence, but approximated to a fixed level of 10/- to 12/6d. per week.

'The wage that the man previously received gave no criterion as to what the woman would get . . . a woman would get from one-third to half the wages of a man.'

The women questioned regarded their inferior position as 'right' because they had known nothing better; 'the pathetic drudgery of the ordinary working man's wife is accepted as the proper thing'. Even outside the factories, among the shop-assistants, teachers and clerks where the work of men and women was more clearly equal, 'it is generally taken for granted both by men and women that a man *ought* to have more than a woman'.

Both in industry and the professions, organised men still regarded women as competitors to be handicapped rather than comrades to be encouraged. The number of processes reserved for men in various trades was calculated to depress women, and cause their work to be classified as 'incidental'. Their best prospects sprang from the women's Trade Union movement, which numbered 167,000 members when Mary McArthur founded the National Federation of Women Workers in 1906.

By 1913 the total number of women trade unionists had risen to 878,000, of whom two-fifths came from the textile unions. But this intelligent minority represented only a tiny proportion of all industrial women. In 1914, according to the subsequent War Cabinet Committee on Women in Industry, women's wages amounted to rather less than fifty per cent of men's.

The number of women workers in agriculture bore little relation to the millions in industry. Britain has not been primarily an agricultural country since the Industrial Revolution; outside the rural areas of Scotland the employment of women on farms had almost ceased by 1880 except among the relatives of small owners. A talk given by Mrs Wintringham, one of the first women Members of Parliament, in the United States in 1927 threw some light upon the payment of agricultural workers during the first quarter of the century.

In sixteen English counties, she stated, women only received

agreements were now suspended by which male unionists had arbitrarily divided various industries into 'men's and 'women's' work, and though they were eventually re-imposed by the Restoration of Pre-War Practices Act, industry could not wholly eliminate the lessons of wartime experience. Trade Boards which fixed minimum wages now protected workers in the old sweated industries, and many industrial women acquired new skills in such modern trades as light electrical engineering.

Figures given in 1919 by the War Cabinet Committee showed that the 5,966,000 employed women of July 1914 had increased by July 1918 to 7,311,000. The diplomats assembling in Paris represented nations compelled by four critical years to revise their attitude towards women, upon whom three-quarters of Europe's population had depended for the production of their food, the maintenance of their industries, and the enormous supply of munitions demanded by their fighting forces.

The Minority Report of the War Cabinet Committee has become an industrial classic. Its author, Mrs Sidney Webb, summarised in uncompromising language the position of women in British industry.

'They have habitually been paid at lower rates than men for equivalent work, on the pretence that women are a class apart with no family obligations, smaller needs, less capacity, and a lower level of intelligence—none of these statements being true of all the workers thus penalised. . . . For the production of commodities and services, women no more constitute a class than do the persons of a particular race or creed.'

She added one practical recommendation, which was to become a subject of unresolved controversy during the next thirty years.

'I think . . . that the consolidation of the Factory Acts should be made the occasion of sweeping away all special provisions differentiating women from men. These special provisions arose during a period when the male Trade Unionists objected to having the conditions of their employment regulated by law. This objection has now entirely ceased.'

But the Factory Act of 1926—the first consolidating measure since 1901—gave no proof that its architects had considered

Beatrice Webb's advice. In so far as its restrictive regulations applied to women only, it raised in an acute form the question whether protective legislation was not the chief antagonist of equal pay, and therefore imposed a special burden upon the very workers whom it was intended to safeguard. This controversy had already been carried into the international sphere by the establishment of the International Labour Organisation, which by treating women as a class apart appeared to nullify its own Equal Pay resolution in Principle 7.

Many important trades were virtually closed to women in those countries which ratified the Washington Convention of 1919 forbidding night work to 'women and young persons'—a classification from which women were to spend much energy during the next thirty years in struggling to escape.

The Washington Night Work Convention was actually revised in 1935 after seven years of feminist activity in the I.L.O., the Permanent Court of International Justice, and numerous international congresses. The revision excluded from the provisions of the Convention 'persons holding a responsible position of management and who did not ordinarily perform manual work'.

This alteration of the original document formed an international precedent and dated back to an incident in 1928. One night during that year, the managing director of M. Partridge & Co. Ltd, a British firm of women engineers who supplied electricity to rural areas, was caught with her partner and four girl apprentices working in Brampton Power Station at 10 p.m., and thereby contravening factory legislation.

The Maternity Convention also adopted at Washington provided for six weeks' leave of absence before and after child-birth; and a Recommendation on Employment in Unhealthy Processes forbade women to work in industries which used lead oxide. In 1921 nineteen States ratified the White Lead Convention, which denied to employed women the use of paint containing white lead. Britain, which did not ratify, gave effect to the Convention by the Lead Paint (Protection against Poisoning) Act of 1926.

According to the War Cabinet Committee, British industries, excluding domestic service, agriculture, and transport, employed 2,178,600 women in July 1914. A Report on Equal Pay for

Equal Work, prepared in 1930 by the Standing Joint Committee of Industrial Women's Organisations, showed that this number had increased to just under three million in 1923, and by nearly another half-million six years later. The Report indicated that though the difference between men's and women's work was continually decreasing owing to the installation of weight-lifting machinery and similar devices, the difference between their rates of pay remained.

The woman worker was still the victim both of Trade Unions endeavouring to restrict or prohibit women's employment in order to protect the 'men's' rate, and of employers insisting that women's labour should be cheap owing to their poorer physique and their liability to give up work on marriage. The speciousness of these attempts to justify lower rates for women on the ground of dissimilar work or inferior physical strength became evident in a number of light occupations and small shops where the distinction between 'men's' and 'women's' work virtually disappeared. In such trades as sugar confectionery, cocoa and chocolate, soap and candles, and tobacco manufacture, the agreed time rates which determined piece-rates were respectively 51/6d., 53/-, 56/-, and 74/- for men, and 29/-, 28/-, 30/-, and 44/6d. for women.

By 1938 the wages of industrial women had reached an average of 32/6d., as against 69/- for men. During the War of 1939-45, the restrictions upon women's processes, like night-work regulations, were allowed to lapse. The obvious absurdity of clauses designed to 'protect' women who manned anti-aircraft guns or descended from parachutes behind enemy lines became apparent even to Trade Unionists, and where it could be proved, as in the Air Transport Auxiliary, that women were doing 'men's' work without help or supervision, they received the rate for the job.

In September 1942, the Trade Union Congress pledged itself 'to take all possible steps to secure recognition of the principle of equal pay for equal work, both during the War and the post-war periods . . . in order to maintain the standards both of men and women workers and to safeguard the position of men when they return from the Services'. The following year, completely reversing its pre-war policy, the powerful Amalgamated Engineering Union admitted women as members. But the average weekly earnings of women by the end of the War amounted to only 62/3d., compared with 119/3d. for men.

Six years later, with nearly seven and a half million women doing paid work and over three million of these (two factory workers out of every seven) in basic industries, the average earnings of women over eighteen with a working week of 41.5 hours had reached £4 10s. 1d., compared with £8 6s. 0d. for men over twenty-one with an average working week of 47.8 hours.

Though the figures did not yet reflect it, a new tendency to meet female competition by paying the rate for the job rather than by imposing restrictions began at last to appear within the Trade Unions, in the form of resolutions favouring equal pay and equal opportunities. In three different years women were Chairmen of the Trade Union Congress itself, and in 1948 Dame Anne Loughlin became the first woman to be appointed General Secretary of a large mixed union, the National Union of Tailors and Garment Workers.

Compared with the numbers in industry, women doing paid work in agriculture are still very few. The Women's Land Army, re-formed in 1939, was disbanded in 1950; only 100,000 women, or one in every seven workers, remained on the land. In 1946 their minimum pay, as fixed by Agricultural Wages Boards, amounted to seventy-five per cent of men's rates in England and Wales, and sixty-seven per cent in Scotland.

A major industrial revolution has occurred in domestic service, which became increasingly unpopular as a career for women during the nineteen-thirties and forties. Though the population had greatly increased since 1914, only 169,700 resident domestic women workers were shown in the 1951 Census under the section reporting on the character and composition of private households. This table revealed that only 1.1 per cent. of British households employed resident domestic servants in 1951, compared with 3.7 per cent. in 1931; the oppressed attic-dweller of Edwardian England has gone for ever. The drift away from domestic work, intensified during the War, caused the Labour Government of 1945 to set up the National Institute of Houseworkers in order to raise the prestige of domestic employment and attract more women to the job.

Though organisation is peculiarly difficult in domestic service, the shortage of workers has created a revolution in pay. Householders have been obliged to offer high enough wages to tempt women back from other forms of work, and the occupation is now so well paid that a number of men (including some ex-servicemen's groups) have established agencies for domestic help.

Where supply falls so short of demand, the question of equal pay hardly arises; even without Trade Union support, the individual worker has unlimited bargaining power. The basic minimum wage laid down by the Houseworkers' Institute varied according to experience from 34/- to 41/6d. (resident) for a forty-eight-hour week, and from 64/- to 71/6d. (non-resident) for a forty-four-hour week. The Institute demanded reasonable living accommodation for resident women and a fortnight's paid holiday each year.

Since the Second World War, organised women from many countries have maintained their protests to governments and Trade Unions against the denial to women of the rate for the job. In November 1952 a meeting of the British Open Door Council, founded in the nineteen-twenties to promote 'the economic emancipation of the woman worker', passed an Equal Pay Resolution which expressed indignation at 'the continued postponement of the application of the principle of the rate for the job for all public servants'.

The organisers of the meeting stated that out of 140 Trade Unions which supplied the Council with information in the years 1949-51, only fifteen gave women equal opportunities with men, and 115 confined them to the lower-paid and less skilled branches of their industry. Ten excluded women altogether. The meeting sent Her Majesty's Government a reminder that in 1948 Britain signed the Declaration of Human Rights, of which Article 23 contains the following clauses:

'Everyone has the right to work, to free choice of employment, to just and favourable conditions of work, and to protection against unemployment.'

'Everyone, without any discrimination, has the right to equal pay for equal work.'

In the year that the Declaration was approved, a body known as the Equal Pay Campaign Committee, representing some fifty national organisations, published a pamphlet summarising the record of successive British Governments on Equal Pay. This paper showed that, as far back as 1914, a Royal Commission on the Civil Service had recommended without result that 'the pay of women should approximate to equality with that of men'. Equally fruitless had been a recommendation of the War Cabinet Committee in 1919 that 'the Government should support the application of the principle of Equal Pay for Equal Work by applying it with the least possible delay to their own establishments'.

Between 1919 and 1929, the House of Commons piously accepted several resolutions supporting the 'principle' of Equal Pay contained in Article 427 of the Versailles Treaty without taking any action. In 1929, after more pressure from organised women, another Royal Commission on the Civil Service was appointed, but its Report published in 1931 made no recommendation on Equal Pay as the Commissioners were equally divided for and against it.

During a House of Commons debate in 1935, Equal Pay again received lip-service from leading members of all parties. The following year Ellen Wilkinson moved a Resolution on the Vote of Supply, calling upon the Government to place women employed in the common classes of the Civil Service on the same scales of pay as the men. The Resolution was passed by a majority of eight votes, but the defeated Government took advantage of a temporary confusion about procedure to obtain a second vote which reversed the decision. When Mr Baldwin, then Prime Minister, reopened the subject on the Vote of Supply he made it a question of confidence in the Government, and obtained the inevitable majority.

After the outbreak of war in 1939, the Government scheme for civilian war injuries awarded a higher rate of compensation to men than to women. Insistent agitation during the air-raids, in which bombs disobligingly failed to discriminate between the sexes, led to Equal Compensation being established in 1943. The following year Mrs Cazalet-Keir M.P. carried by one vote against the Government her amendment to Clause 82 of the Education Bill, to abolish inequality of pay between men and women teachers.

As in 1936, the National Government forced a reversal of the vote by making it a question of confidence in their conduct of the War, but subsequently appointed a Royal Commission on Equal Pay with Mr (later Lord) Justice Asquith as Chairman. When the Commission reported two years later it appeared to recommend Equal Pay for Civil Servants, teachers, and local government officers, but failed to agree on industry. A minority consisting of Dame Anne Loughlin, Dr Janet Vaughan, and Miss L. F. Nettlefold submitted a Memorandum showing that Equal Pay would benefit alike the workers, the industries, and the country as a whole.

In 1945 came the decisive victory of the Labour Party, which in its official Report (1930) on Equal Pay for Equal Work had stated that 'the principle that a man and a woman doing the same work shall receive the same pay has always been accepted by the Labour Movement'. But Labour in power spoke with a different voice from Labour merely in office, and showed the same skill as all other governments in evading the consequences of previous inconvenient declarations. In 1947, the Chancellor of the Exchequer announced the Labour Government's verdict on Equal Pay.

'The Government accepts, as regards their own employees, the justice of the claim, but they assert that in incurring additional expenditure the Government must be the judge of priorities, and they will not apply the principle at the present time on the ground that it would be wholly inflationary in its results.'

When the Conservative Party resumed office in 1951, the new Chancellor, Mr R. A. Butler, adopted a similar line of righteous obstructionism. In September 1952, while promising that the Government would introduce Equal Pay 'when circumstances permit', he told a deputation from the Civil Service National Whitley Council that he saw no prospect of making this encouraging start in the near future. The Government, however, issued no official denial of persistent reports that a scheme for giving Equal Pay by instalments to women Civil Servants would in fact be launched in 1953. An example was set them in the summer of 1952 by the London County Council, which then agreed to give Equal Pay in all clerical grades where both men and women were employed.

A prolonged correspondence on Equal Pay in *The Times* during 1951 and 1952 brought a letter from Sarah Ayansu, a Gold Coast teacher, who stated that in her own country the principle 'has long since been accepted and applied'. The women of the Gold Coast have doubtless benefited from the vigour shown by women from another part of the African continent. The South African Trade Union leader, E. S. Sachs, wrote of them in *The Choice Before South Africa:*

'With the development of manufacturing industries from 1925 onwards, ten of thousands of women, the overwhelming majority being Africaner women driven off the land by poverty, entered industry and commerce. For reasons which the writer is unable to explain the Africaner women have proved themselves in many respects far superior to their men folk. In the past twenty years most of the struggles among workers for higher standards and a better life were carried on by women.'

The Members of the Royal Commission on Equal Pay devoted one section of their Report to a comparative study of the struggle in four other countries. From both the professional and industrial standpoint, the United States and the U.S.S.R. offered, as usual, better prospects to women than countries with older traditions.

In American industry and commerce two Federal Acts, the Public Contracts (Walsh-Healey) Act of 1936 and the Fair Labour Standards Act of 1938, laid down equal rates of pay. Between 1919 and 1944, six States—Michigan, Montana, Illinois, Washington, Massachusetts and New York—passed Equal Pay Acts prohibiting sex discrimination in wages. New York enforced these Acts with characteristic vigour, employing 122 investigators to cover all establishments in eighteen months. Owing to the greatly increased employment and new types of work offered to women during the Second World War, many agreements incorporated 'the rate for the job', and the gap between the pay of men and women diminished.

A resolute theory of sex equality underlies the constitutional provisions of the Soviet Union. After the 1917 Revolution women became eligible for all posts, and have actually held a number of high positions in which they received the same pay and promotion as men. A minimum wage-rate established by Decree applied to all industrial occupations regardless of sex, but as late as 1930 the average earnings of women were only about two-thirds of the earnings of men. Between 1928 and 1935 over six million women entered the labour force, and by 1939 women represented 43.4 per cent of all wage-earners. The ratio of women's earnings to men's had probably risen by 1946 from the two-thirds of 1930, but recent figures were not available to the Commissioners.

In Australia, women Civil Servants and teachers received salaries varying from sixty-five per cent of men's rates to the relatively high ratio of ninety per cent paid in Queensland. Between the Wars industrial women received about fifty-four per cent of men's wages, and out of numerous Enactments, both Commonwealth and State, only two, in Queensland and New South Wales, made any provision for Equal Pay. During the Second World War, which saw the customary increase in women's work, the Women's Employment Board fixed the payment of women at ninety per cent of the men's rate after a trial period at sixty per cent.

Industrial wage rates in France before the Second World War resembled those of Britain in differentiating widely between men and women. During the wartime military occupation, the Germans fixed women's wages at seventy-five per cent of men's. With the restoration of the *status quo* after the War, the new minimum wage-rate provided for Equal Pay. It was also recommended by the General Confederation of Labour in conjunction with three forms of family allowances.

In Belgium, which the Commissioners did not mention, the women employed in public administration lost the right to Equal Pay after the Second World War. They contested the Government decision successfully, and after six months their rights were restored.

The reasons given for denying Equal Pay to women, like those alleged for refusing them the vote, have varied from the wholly fantastic to the apparently rational. In his *Unpopular Essays*, Bertrand Russell quoted an example of the first category from a pamphlet published by 'a schoolmasters' association':

'We gladly place her first, as a spiritual force; we acknowledge and revere her as the "angelic part of humanity"; we give her superiority in all the graces and refinements we are capable of as human beings; we wish her to retain all her winsome womanly ways. . . . This appeal' (i.e. that women should be content with lower rates of pay) 'goes forth from us to them in no selfish spirit, but out of respect and devotion to our mothers, wives, sisters and daughters. . . . Our purpose is a sacred one, a real spiritual crusade.'

The Equal Pay Commissioners dismissed the perpetrators of this document in a few laconic lines. 'It is worth noting . . . that the National Association of Schoolmasters, the one organised body of teachers in England and Wales to oppose the claim for equal pay, do not rest their case on an allegation that the work of men is superior or more onerous, but on considerations of a quite different nature.'

More usual arguments assert or imply that women should be paid at a lower rate because they are physically weaker than men, and have no dependants. The convenient tradition of feminine frailty has disguised the fact that the real handicaps of the working woman have been poverty, depression, underfeeding, and overwork; the direct connection between women's lower pay and higher sickness rate has been overlooked.

Evidence submitted to the Equal Pay Commission by Dr Sybil Horner, Dr Aubrey Lewis and Professor Lane showed that the effect on industry of 'gynaecological disturbances' in women was negligible, and caused neither loss of time nor second-rate work. When the Commissioners asserted, with reference to women's muscular inferiority, that the tendency of modern invention is to diminish the importance of sheer physical strength, they were echoing the older judgment of the Women's Employment Committee in 1919: 'Women's future industrial kingdom . . . is hardly limited by her weaker muscles, for this is a boundary which is fast disappearing'.

The familiar argument that men have dependants to support while women work only for themselves has lost much of its weight in countries, such as Britain, which have introduced a system of family allowances. It was always a 'traditional' rather than a precise contention, in which the theoretical 'wife and three children' of the industrial male came about as close to reality as the 'three acres and a cow' of the Lloyd Georgian agricultural worker.

In *The Disinherited Family*, Eleanor Rathbone estimated that less than fifty per cent of adult male workers have children to support at any given time; since most men remain at work from the age of eighteen to sixty-five or seventy, 'dependants' are a burden for only half that period. A wife cannot properly be regarded as a dependant, since by housekeeping and saving she contributes to a working man's income. If she dies or leaves she has to be replaced, as many husbands discovered during the evacuation periods of the Second World War.

A substantial percentage of women workers have dependants who are less easily classified; most middle-aged unmarried women support elderly parents, or help to educate younger brothers and sisters. Even if they do not, the rate of wages has never been fixed by family responsibilities; a man with twelve children receives the same pay for the same job as a man with one.

Only two reasons for refusing equal pay stand up to serious examination. The convention that a woman retires from her work on marriage and is thereafter maintained by her husband has always been a strong deterrent to 'the rate for the job'. It is likely to remain one so long as the worker's unplanned home involves hours of wasteful labour, and the lack of organised part-time work in both industries and professions compels women to abandon their employment for the whole period of child-bearing and rearing.

When a woman regards her job as 'incidental' to marriage, her employer cannot be expected to take the risk of training and promoting her. But her working life, like a man's, covers over fifty years, and may last even longer owing to her greater expectation of life, while twenty years is usually the maximum period in which her children will need constant attention. The loss of a capable person's services for thirty years is an unnecessary form of economic waste which calls out for remedy.*

* See Chapter 11.

The critics of differential sex-legislation have always insisted that such regulations, instead of actually protecting women, herd them into a few poorly-paid occupations and segregate them permanently at the bottom of the labour-market. During the past thirty years a large controversial literature has grown up round this subject, which rouses fierce class-passion owing to the apparent contrast between middle-class theory and working-class anxiety. Experience seems to justify the opponents of 'protection' in their belief that employers tend to regard special regulations as a substitute for equal pay, which by improving the health and amenities of working women would itself remove the need for differential legislation.

During recent years in which the justice of equal pay has become increasingly difficult to deny, governments have turned to the economic austerities of the post-war period to find a new argument. Successive Chancellors of the Exchequer have pleaded, like the Socialist Chancellor in 1947, that deeply as they desire to be just to women voters, the country cannot afford to give the rate for the job.

Yet the very administrations which make poverty their excuse for withholding equal pay have found no difficulty in budgeting additional millions for 'defence' or conscription, or even in raising the wages of well-organised male workers who would create trouble if an increase were refused. In 1947 the estimated £7,000,000 required for Equal Pay in the Civil Service was said to be out of the question, but the following year an increase of 7/6d. per week in the wages of railway workers cost Britain £40,000,000. Nor did the fear of 'inflation' deter the Government from sanctioning further wage-increases in the nationalised industries which amounted to £171 millions by the end of 1948.

The real explanation of unequal pay comes from women's weaker bargaining power due to lack of organisation. Up to the Second World War their work lay largely in occupations, such as personal service, clerical work, and repetitive industrial processes, where organisation has always been poor even among men. Before 1939, less than one in every seven employed women were members of Trade Unions. One quarter of these came from the textile trades, in which women by custom continue their work after marriage.

'The main cause of the low earnings of women', stated the Minority Report of the Equal Pay Commission, 'is their exclusion from a number of trades in which they would be efficient workers (given opportunity and training), combined with weak trade union organisation.'

In many countries women have now attained political, legal, educational and professional equality, but economic equality is long delayed. The present picture of world economy shows each community using little more than half its potential strength at a period in which no community can afford to maintain unproductive workers.

The remedy lies, as it has lain in every kindred situation during the past fifty years, in the hands of women themselves. When they have learned the lesson of organisation and found a solution for the present wastage of training and ability by traditional conceptions of marriage, the most obstinate form of sex inequality may finally disappear.

10

WOMEN AND SEX MORALS

In December 1936, the Churches of Britain celebrated the abdication of King Edward VIII by launching a new campaign for the revival of religious influences in national life.

Archbishop Lang of Canterbury made the first appeal over the radio, and summoned the nation to consider 'a return to religion and to the standards of morality laid down by our forefathers'.

His hearers were evidently intended to compare themselves unfavourably with their paternal ancestors, who built the structure of British chastity upon the granite rock of Victorian family life. But a few, unable to listen with the repentant acquiescence clearly expected of them, wondered precisely what a return to the morality of our forefathers would mean. In so acute a national crisis, the matter obviously demanded examination.

The Victorians, it appeared, thought of 'immorality' as purely sexual. Fifty years later the word was also to be applied to hatred, cruelty, falsehood, and ignorance, and quite a substantial number of citizens were to find these qualities more immoral than the yielding up of virginity by one sex. But the journey from the narrow to the wider perspective has been long and hard.

Years before and even after 1901, our predecessors seemed moral only because the evils of a double standard were hidden beneath the smooth surface of pseudo-respectability. Even where individual morality was genuine, a prudish reluctance to call things by their names left many social wrongs unfaced and unremedied. Just as periodicity was described as 'a certain time' and pregnancy as 'a certain condition', so prostitution was evasively known as 'a certain profession'. The neutral term 'certain' qualified for classification as a 'dirty word'.

Our forefathers referred facetiously to women as 'the sex'. In the eyes of most men it was her sex, and not her courage, faith, or intelligence, which represented a woman's chief characteristic, and sex was a subject for secret nudges and furtive sniggers.

'The belief that the personalities of men and women are of equal dignity in the sight of God is necessary to a right moral standard', wrote Dr Maude Royden years afterwards in *The Church and Woman*. But in the early nineteen-hundreds only a few women were intrepid enough to repudiate the social values taken for granted by both sexes, and to show them up in their true perspective. Among those few was Emmeline Pankhurst.

'Why is it', she demanded passionately in *My Own Story*, 'that men's blood-shedding militancy is applauded and women's symbolic militancy punished with a prison-cell and the forcible feeding horror? It means simply this, that men's double standard of sex morals, whereby the victims of their lust are counted as outcasts while the men themselves escape all social censure, really applies to morals in all departments of life. Men make the moral code and they expect women to accept it.'

At her Old Bailey trial in April 1913, Mrs Pankhurst denounced the laws which made it possible for her to be sentenced to fourteen years' imprisonment for damaging property while two years was the maximum penalty for criminal assaults on children. Ten and even twenty years later, the British legal system perpetuated this indifference to the sacredness of human life. In 1922, when organised women were agitating for the passage of the Criminal Law Amendment Bill, the Press reported two judicial sentences side by side. One condemned a man to twelve months' imprisonment for snatching a woman's handbag; the other imposed one month's detention upon a husband who had violently assaulted the nurse attending his wife in her confinement.

Eleven years afterwards, *The Times* recorded sentences, of two years and eighteen months' imprisonment respectively, passed by the Recorder, Sir Ernest Wild, upon a father and a procuress responsible for an offence against the man's daughter, a girl under sixteen. The Recorder added that had the prisoners been found guilty of stealing a domestic fowl the law would have allowed him to pass a sentence of five years' penal servitude, but for the criminal act described, the punishment given was the maximum permitted.

Modern psychology may doubt whether punishment, inadequate or otherwise, is the right response to sexual offences. It is unlikely to question the Recorder's condemnation of values which rated handbags and hens above women and young children. In the 19th and early 20th centuries those same values assumed the necessity of prostitution as an unacknowledged safeguard for the virtue of 'good' women, who had at all costs to be preserved from an unwelcome knowledge of biological facts.

'Silence was thought to be the great duty of all', stated Josephine Butler, whose campaign against the Contagious Diseases Acts appeared so shocking to the dons and clerics of the eighteen-seventies. It had revealed the deadly poison beneath the decorous surface, lifting the lid from the noisome obscurity of the underworld into which women were pushed by the losing battle to live on sweated wages. When Mrs Pankhurst visited the United States in 1911, and was taken to see the New York Night Court for Women where all but one delinquent faced charges of soliciting, the magistrate told her that most of the women found themselves there from economic causes.

'The whole dreadful injustice of women's lives seemed mirrored in that place', she commented, remembering the unmarried child-mothers of thirteen who had come to her office in Manchester to register their babies. Two decades later, the Seabury Report of 1932 showed the New York Night Court to be a centre of corruption, and illustrated the futility of attempts to suppress prostitution by law.

Before 1875, the 'age of consent' in Britain had been twelve. It was then raised only to thirteen, and four years afterwards an investigation by two Quakers confirmed Mrs Butler's statements that young girls were decoyed abroad and placed in brothels. In 1882 a House of Lords Inquiry again acknowledged the existence of this traffic. Among men of a vicious type it was then fashionable to hire virgin children for purposes of indulgence, and notorious procuresses, such as the infamous Mrs Jeffreys of Chelsea, made a livelihood by supplying minor girls to foreign royalties. But nothing was done, since our forefathers tolerated brothels which catered for all classes and types.

After the Contagious Diseases Acts of 1864, 1866, and 1869 had introduced into Britain the State regulation of vice started in France under Napoleon I, prostitution acquired the status of a lawful trade but the prostitute was excluded from common law protection. These Acts represented 'a state certificate for the double standard', recorded Alison Neilans in her contribution to *Our Freedom and Its Results*. The 'Morals Police' employed to enforce the Acts came perilously near to the 'Thought Police' of George Orwell's satire, *Nineteen Eighty-Four*.

Under the Contagious Diseases Acts, venereal disease in the Home Army rose from the high figure of 200 cases per 1,000 to 246. Drink and women were then assumed to be the only recreations suited to soldiers; had anyone foreseen the present-day public-house, with its dart-boards, flower-vases, and cheerful pictures, he would have been discounted as a foolish idealist. These figures show a remarkable contrast with the recent six per cent incidence of venereal disease in the Home Air Force, where the modern standards which the Archbishop deplored have operated exclusively.

A comment from *A History of Modern Culture* (1930) by the late Professor Preserved Smith of Cornell University, U.S.A., seems relevant here. Discussing Prohibition, which he regarded as anything but 'a noble experiment dictated by a lofty sense of duty', Professor Smith continued: 'The amount of indulgence in drink depends somewhat upon the relations of the sexes. The more the pleasures of love are permitted by social conditions and encouraged by public opinion, the less will the pleasures of the bottle be sought or even tolerated.'

Drunkenness became the shamefaced vice of a double-standard society, in which sex-relationships supplied the theme for sordid jests, and legitimate intercourse was rendered tedious by the docile subordination of wives. In Britain the decline of intemperance has coincided with the gradual repudiation of the double standard, and prohibitionist fanaticism has diminished with the excesses that it sought to cure.

The degradation of the double standard was not only responsible for the hideous underworld accepted by our ancestors; it impaired the nobility of legal marriage, and until 1923 wrote inequality on the Statute Book with the Marriage and Divorce

Act of 1857. Since respectability was the chief asset of the subject spouse, she and society guarded it with a ruthless zeal which often involved gross cruelty towards unmarried mothers and their children, and the pitiless ostracism of adultresses and divorcees.

As a girl I heard my father, a generous and kindly but conventional man who did not question existing standards, gleefully relate to his luncheon-guest a tale intended to illustrate the uncompromising morality of his mother. My grandmother, it appeared, had found her unwedded cook in labour and turned her out of the house at midnight. The baby was born in the cab summoned to remove her to the Workhouse.

In such Workhouses, as Mrs Pankhurst discovered after her election to the Manchester Board of Guardians in 1895, an unmarried mother could stay to earn her living by scrubbing only when she agreed to separation from her child. If she kept the baby, she was obliged to leave after two weeks without money, home, or job. The man responsible for her predicament could escape all future liability by paying £20, which purchased immunity from legal inspection for the boarding house that received his bastard child. His legitimate children remained almost wholly in his power, but an illegitimate offspring was known to the law as 'filius nullius', and its mother had to assume the entire responsibility for its support.

Before 1873, no action for maintenance could be taken against a soldier or sailor, and the maximum amount obtainable by an unmarried mother from a civilian father was 2/6d. a week. In the debate on the Bastardy Laws Amendment Act of 1873 which raised this sum to 5/-, Dr Lyon Playfair M.P. stated that out of 50,000 illegitimate children born annually in the United Kingdom, 30,000 died within the first twelve months.

After 1900, the further Amending Acts of 1914, 1918, and 1923 raised the unmarried mother's claim to 20/- weekly against a civilian father, and made the Courts responsible for collecting the money. The First World War revealed many illegal but permanent unions, and these mothers and children received the same separation allowances as orthodox families. In 1926 the Legitimacy Act made a child legitimate by the subsequent marriage of its parents, except for children born through adultery. Public opinion had become anxious to protect the offspring of illegal unions, and to retain for them whenever possible their mother's care. An unmarried mother is now received in hospital or at homes run by moral welfare societies, and the child's birth certificate no longer discloses illegitimacy.

By 1933, the illegitimate infant death-rate had fallen to 107 per 1,000, as against 62 per 1,000 for legitimate births. It was a high enough figure, but it no longer represented, as in 1873, the loss of three-fifths of all illegitimate children born in Britain.

Modern society owes an incalculable debt to the concerned minority of men and women who between 1870 and 1930 sought to raise the moral values of their time. The struggle to eliminate the double standard outside marriage began with Josephine Butler's fight against legalised prostitution, and was carried on in the 20th century by the Association for Moral and Social Hygiene. This organisation succeeded the Lady's National Association in 1915, and became the lifework of its Secretary, Alison Neilans, who died in 1942.

Josephine Butler's campaign against the Contagious Diseases Acts had caused their suspension in 1883, and their repeal three years later. Though Parliament had raised the 'age of consent' in 1875, it did nothing to stop the traffic in girls for another decade. In 1885 the Editor of the *Pall Mall Gazette*, W. T. Stead, who later perished in the *Titanic*, deliberately 'bought' for alleged immoral purposes a young girl whom he placed under the protection of the Salvation Army. The facts published in his subsequent series of articles, *The Maiden Tribute of Modern Babylon*, roused even the House of Commons, and the Criminal Law Amendment Act of 1885 embodied the first measure of protection given to minor girls by English law.

The next similar reform came in 1922, when the First World War had annihilated once for all the conspiracy of silence. By this time the appointment of women magistrates, and the installation of women police, had followed the Sex Disqualification (Removal) Act of 1919. The new Criminal Law Amendment Act protected both girls and boys against seduction up to the age of sixteen, and under it in 1933 a woman was sent to prison for seducing a boy.

In 1929 a League of Nations inquiry publicised the low age of marriage in Britain, and from twelve for girls and fourteen for boys it was raised to sixteen for both sexes.

By 1930, the number of British prostitutes annually arrested for alleged annoyance still ranged from three to four thousand, and the conscience of thoughtful citizens found expression in some lines from Humbert Wolfe's *Requiem*, published in 1927:

'All the world over in every town and city
there is a furtive shuffle of tired feet,
and the invisible hounds that know no pity
pad after them in alley-way and street.
All men are whippers-in of that foul pack,
and follow them to life's supreme disaster
as certainly as if you heard them crack
the huntsman's whip, or halloa like the Master.
Their sin is all our sin, ours is their shame,
and while a single woman earns her bread
by blasphemy committed in love's name
not only she, but all our world, is dead.'

Other countries besides Britain produced their Josephine Butlers. In France, Madame Avril de St Croix fought against the State regulation of vice, and was succeeded in this work by Marthe Richard, an agent for the Allies in both World Wars. Her campaign against *maisons tolerées* began in 1944, and ended with the closing of houses of prostitution throughout France. Italy's Signora Cajumi di Silvestri, and her woman successor, Senator Merlin, similarly succeeded in abolishing Italian brothels.

During 1921 the Second Assembly of the League of Nations discussed, for the first time, the 'White Slave Traffic', which Lord Balfour described as 'the most abominable stain upon civilisation which it is possible to conceive'. In a book on this traffic, *The Road to Buenos Ayres*, published during the nineteen-twenties, the French author, M. Albert Londres, issued a challenge to the conscience of society similar to that of Humbert Wolfe.

'Enough of morality. It is not brothels and pimps that we must contend against. . . . As long as women cannot get work: as long as girls are cold and hungry: as long as they do not know where to go for a bed: as long as women do not earn enough to allow themselves to be ill: or enough to buy themselves a warm coat in winter. . . . As long as we allow the pimps to take our place and offer the mess of pottage: the White Slave Traffic will exist. Burn the brothels and lay a curse upon their ashes. You will only have made a bonfire and a futile demonstration. The responsibility is ours; we cannot get rid of it.'

The League's Fifth Committee on Social Questions, which had accepted this challenge, extended the inquiries of its special body of experts to countries, particularly in the Far East, 'where no investigation had taken place before'. During one of the Committee's discussions, Madame Hainari of Finland emphasised the connection between the status of women and the international traffic. Its victims, she stated, were drawn chiefly from countries where women's standing was low, and it represented a notorious example of the degradation to which women could be reduced by poor pay and unequal opportunities.

In 1925, the first Convention designed to eliminate the Traffic in Women was signed by thirty-three States and ratified by twenty-one. Those abstaining included France, and most of the Latin American States apart from Brazil and Uruguay. The British Government signed this Convention in 1933, but could not ratify until it had amended an Act of 1885, dealing with procuration, which excluded prostitutes from legal protection and thus refused them the normal rights of citizens.

The initial League of Nations Report gave a sinister picture of underworld machinery, complete with the procuresses, intermediaries, and *souteneurs* responsible for the intimidation and exploitation of ignorant youth. National communities which twenty years earlier could hardly bring themselves to admit that a traffic in women existed, now began to study without squeamishness the sordid details of international vice.

Like most of the League's social work, the campaign against the traffic survived the Second World War. It was taken over by the Social Commission of the United Nations Organisation, which completed and codified the various Traffic in Women Conventions adopted at Geneva.

Long before U.N.O. was founded, the national protection of young people had reached new levels in Britain owing to additional legislation and the better sex training of boys and girls. The legal penalties and social ostracism imposed on backsliders had diminished with the belief that sex offences belonged to a special category of wickedness. As the new science of psychology developed, it taught lawyers and magistrates to give as much thought to the causes of delinquency as to its consequences, and young offenders were sent more often to the Probation Officer than to a prison cell.

The Children and Young Persons Act of 1933 protected both sexes up to seventeen from widely-defined 'exposure to moral danger'. Brothels became illegal, and severe penalties were imposed upon those who maintained them. Such problems as homosexuality and premature sex experience emerged from horrified silence into the light of day.

The controversy which raged in 1927 round Radclyffe Hall's novel, *The Well of Loneliness*—surely one of the dreariest books ever to cause a literary sensation—seems in retrospect almost as incredible as the Lord Chamberlain's original ban upon the performance of *Young Woodley*, and the prosecution of Mrs Mary Ware Dennett in the United States for a pamphlet entitled *The Sex Side of Life*. Assistant Federal Attorney James E. Wilkinson condemned this pamphlet as 'dangerous because it did not teach repression'.

In September 1929, an International Congress held in London by the World League for Sexual Reform increased public awareness of a crisis in morals throughout the civilised world. Month after month, publishers' lists advertised the arrival of new students in a field where Havelock Ellis so long worked alone. Books dealing with every aspect of morality poured out of the United States, and a huge symposium, *Sex in Civilisation*, appeared in New York and London. On both sides of the Atlantic a succession of lively booklets known as the *To-day and Tomorrow Series* gave publicity to young writers who discussed the changing outlook on sex questions with uncompromising frankness.

Even venereal disease—the hidden 'plague' of Edwardian England—followed homosexuality into the open after many young volunteer nurses from sheltered homes discovered its existence in the military hospitals of the First World War. By 1934 it had taken its place among the social ailments which demanded cure rather than punishment; 117 centres for its treatment had been established in Britain, clinics for seamen were opened in home ports, and facilities for diagnosis established in several hospitals. The cost was borne by a State which no longer regarded sexual tragedy due to poverty and ignorance as a fit subject for salacious giggles.

A simultaneous campaign against the double standard within marriage itself took several different forms. Some uncompromising critics of the past attacked the institution of monogamy as 'a hypocritical sham', and produced books and articles which extenuated polygamy and commended such experiments as 'semi-detached' and 'companionate' marriage. Orthodox unions, these critics maintained, had too often been ruined by the misleading identification of wifehood with household management. 'Preparation' for marriage had consisted of lessons in cooking and domestic economy while omitting all instruction in sex-technique.

In 1929, this questioning analysis of conventional matrimony found expression in Bertrand Russell's *Marriage and Morals*, which ascribed the subjection of wives to the determination of husbands to make sure of paternity, and deplored the ruin of marriage by 'the emphasis on sex which we owe to St Paul and the Romantic Movement'.

'Sex', he insisted, 'cannot dispense with an ethic . . . but it can dispense with an ethic based solely upon ancient prohibitions propounded by uneducated people in a society totally unlike our own.'

The struggle of women against the marriage-bar in the professions and public administration was one consequence of this changing view of marriage. To an increasing minority from both sexes, the compulsion upon a woman to choose between permanent spinsterhood and the loss of the occupation which gave her scope and independence seemed unbiological and immoral. It denied motherhood to intelligent women who cared for their work, and strongly encouraged irregular unions. The discovery that frustration lay at the root of much human stress was also modifying the social condemnation of divorce.

To Victorian and Edwardian England the fidelity of the body, especially in women, appeared to be more important than the loyalty of the mind. For generations the divorce laws had perpetuated the idea that the enforced sterility of a wife, owing to her union with a convict, deserter, invalid, or lunatic, contributed more to public welfare than any form of escape from the entanglement. Even the Matrimonial Causes Act of 1923, though it conferred equal rights of divorce, had emphasised adultery in either sex as the chief reason for matrimonial breakdown.

Twenty years afterwards, even equality seemed to provide an incomplete answer to the problems raised by marital conflicts. Was it really beyond the power of an adult society officially to recognise that a marriage had failed, without further penalising one of the partners by the attribution of 'guilt'? And was it genuinely in the interests of Christian morality that one partner should have to accuse and disparage the other before either could be free?

In March 1951 a private Member, Mrs Eirene White, brought before the House of Commons another Matrimonial Causes Bill which sought to establish a new principle in divorce legislation by admitting the actual breakdown of a marriage as sufficient reason for divorce. To the existing grounds recognised by the law—misconduct, cruelty, incurable insanity, desertion for at least three years, and a husband's guilt in specified sexual offences—she proposed to add separation for seven years on the petition of either partner. As the London *Evening Standard* commented in a leading article, 'This new Bill will not break one single home which is not already broken. Rather should it help to bring new and happier marriages from the ruins of the old.'

The House of Commons so far endorsed this view as to carry the Second Reading of the Bill by a large majority. Mrs White subsequently withdrew it in response to the Government's promise of a new Royal Commission to study the whole field of British marriage. This Commission began to hear evidence from witnesses towards the end of 1952, and expected to publish its Report in the Autumn of 1953.

Side by side with the Divorce Law Reform organisations supporting Mrs White's Bill, a number of Marriage Guidance societies which tackled 'matrimonial causes' from a more constructive angle had grown up through the years. Instruction in sex technique and the knowledge gained from birth-control clinics* brought a new principle of prevention rather than cure to ease marital tensions. Many of these, according to a statement by Dr Alfred Torrie, war-time Director of Army Psychiatry, at the National Marriage Guidance Council at Harrogate in 1951, were due not to sex difficulties but to 'emotional immaturity'.

The repudiation of the double standard has not led, as some pessimists prophesied, to a decline in the status of monogamous marriage, but to sincere endeavours to make it work. The highly-publicised successive polygamies of Hollywood might appear to justify a more cynical view, but behind the broken unions written up in American tabloids a solid core of fidelity remains.

Public respect for happy lifelong marriage has increased precisely because there are now so many recognised exits which our forefathers failed to provide or regarded as disreputable. The wife who stayed with her husband because no alternative existed but starvation or the streets bore witness not to the loftiness of morality, but to the cruelty of society. The self-respecting, self-supporting woman who continues by choice to live with the partner of a lifetime alone provides reliable evidence that monogamy can and does succeed.

In such a union, as Havelock Ellis wrote, 'all the finer activities of the organism, physical and psychic, may be developed and satisfied. The test of a true marriage is that it does produce a doubling of experience and an intensification of life. This satisfactory result cannot be achieved if one partner is deeply frustrated or habitually regarded as the inferior of the other. Mutual respect, which cannot live in an atmosphere of condescension, is the first ingredient of a lasting love.'

Since 1930 the moral changes towards which the previous half-century was moving have become more definite. These changes reflected the growing influence of women in public life and the disappearance of the woman whose whole existence was conditioned by personal relationships and narrow domestic duties. They embodied the democratic outlook which especially in

* See Chapter 11.

Britain has triumphed over Fascism, Communism, and heresy-hunting; they also owed a debt to both the candour of modern biological education and the emphasis placed by contemporary psychology upon understanding rather than condemnation.

Externally this new morality may be less decorous than the old; at the core it appears to be far sounder. In Britain and similar countries young people of every type live in a safer and more rational world than that of our Victorian forbears, with their rigid distinctions between men and women, rich and poor, morality and immorality. The new approach to a single standard has sprung, amongst its other origins, from one unexpected source. Birth-control has set women almost as free as men have always been from the physical penalties of unorthodox conduct, and there are now alternatives to prostitution which do not involve the exploitation of a degraded class. Today it is ethical standards, rather than the fear of consequences, which challenge both sexes alike. Amongst the young men and women of the nineteen-fifties, there are many who regard the right response to that challenge as a social obligation.

The emergence of these modern values became clear during the Abdication Crisis of 1936. Much of the sympathy for the King which sprang from the violent and confused emotions of that time originated in the disgust felt by ordinary decent people for the ecclesiastical hierarchy. The Archbishop and his supporters appeared to be condemning marriage while condoning a return to the double standard of the pre-war Edwardian Court. Popular reactions to the self-righteous authority of Primate and Premier were summed up by Macaulay's comment on Moore's *Life of Byron*: 'We know of no spectacle so ridiculous as the British public in one of its periodical fits of morality'.

In case after case reported from the Law Courts, the revolution created by fifty years of change in the official attitude towards sexual misbehaviour appears so often that we have ceased to notice it. One recent notorious action for breach of promise not only provided evidence, by the reduction of damages on appeal, of a declining sympathy towards women who seek to capitalise a broken love-affair; it was even more remarkable for the behaviour of the jury towards the woman involved. Half a century ago no jury would have been tender to her reputation, but in 1951 it was the man who met with condemnation for his sorry part in the sexual compact. British juries have ceased to look upon women, however unorthodox, as 'ancillary to the interests of men'.

The revival in 1952 of Noël Coward's play, *The Vortex*, first performed in 1924, startingly emphasised the altered perspective in which sexual offences are now regarded. Those histrionic agonies over adultery and drug-taking seemed utterly disproportionate to the misdemeanours represented, and illustrated, by the very impression of hysterical exaggeration that they gave, the growing conviction of ordinary people that morals as a whole, and not merely sex morals, are the basic concern of men and women today.

A society which has witnessed the criminal actions of two great wars—mass-extermination by bombing, mass-murder in concentration camps, the world-wide debasement of moral currency and the deliberate disparagement of spiritual values—no longer feels able to condemn adultresses and drug-addicts as the most shameful practitioners of immoral behaviour. The worst sinners are seen as those whose wrong-doing is a threat to the survival of civilisation itself.

With the recognition of an urgent need to lift the level of all morality, the over-emphasis on sexual delinquency which especially penalised women is disappearing into the past. In spite of clerical denunciations and the war-time return to medieval barbarism over large areas of the earth, human society has gone forward since it stepped into daylight from the foetid atmosphere of Victorian hypocrisy.

The history of the past fifty years has shown that human nature does change in its attitude towards cruelty and injustice, though it may not always receive much assistance from episcopal charity. It has still far to travel along the road of understanding and compassion, but few men and women today would join the late Archbishop Lang in demanding a return to the morality of our forefathers.

11

THE MARRIED WOMAN'S STRUGGLE

As Chapter 5 of this book has related, the status of women was first internationally discussed at the League of Nations Assembly in 1935, and again in 1937. The mass of information then supplied by governments and women's organisations revealed not only the subordinate position of women in general, but the special disabilities suffered by wives and mothers.

The Assembly learned that in some countries a woman could still be bought and sold, physically chastised by her husband with the law's blessing, forbidden the use of her own property, denied rights over her children, refused the power to divorce her husband though he could repudiate her at will, and excluded from all political means of seeking reform.

In his famous legal classic, *Ancient Law*, Sir Henry Maine wrote that human society normally progressed 'from status to contract'. For men, marriage had long been a contract, but for women everywhere it still involved the acceptance of a status. Round this status, myths, taboos, and conventions continued to circulate with obstinate persistence. The idea even of relationship was submerged in that of ownership. Married women still lived in the shadow of the Ten Commandments, which placed a man's wife in the same category as his house, his servant, his ox, and his ass, and did not even put her first among these.

By 1935 the unmarried women of Britain had stormed most of the citadels hitherto held by men, but the wife, in a majority of marriages, seemed content to accept the position of her husband's chattel. Even so, her standing was far better than that of her Victorian predecessor. For over fifty years she had been able to control her property, and for twelve had possessed equal rights of divorce. In 1925, after nearly a century of agitation, she had obtained the right to equal guardianship with her husband over their children.

Above all, thanks to the spreading knowledge of contraceptives, she had acquired the power to plan her family, choose her work, and organise her future. The magnitude of the revolution which this knowledge created in the lives of married women cannot be exaggerated; it substituted the civilised faculty of conscious choice for victimisation by haphazard fate.

Today the prolific millions of the East await the same salvation. In 1951 Mr Nehru, referring to India's population increase of forty-two millions within ten years, said that birth-control 'from being the fad of some individuals has become one of the important issues before the country'. Already, for India and other Eastern countries, family planning represents a policy, to be accepted or refused. In Britain it just happened—and began to happen with dramatic effect at the very time when the current trend towards large families might have been expected to continue indefinitely.

During the 19th century, the small island which had been agricultural became industrial; within three generations a population of 10½ millions grew to 40 millions, and seemed destined for limitless increase. But in 1876, with a long era of prosperity apparently ahead, the birth-rate began suddenly to fall. Except for slight interruptions at the end of the two World Wars, it continued to fall headlong.

In 1876, the British birth-rate was 36 per 1,000 of the population. By 1901 it had dropped to 28.6, by 1931 to 15.8, and by 1940 to 14.6. The later years of the Second World War and the first post-war years showed a rise up to 20.5 in 1947. By 1948 the number of births had again declined to 17.9. As Lord Beveridge put it, one out of every three married women under forty-five had a child in 1876, but only one out of every eight in 1930. By 1950, the birth of a child in nearly all sections of the community had become a relatively rare and carefully planned event.

What caused this change? In 1876, a document famous in the history of birth-control was published, *The Fruits of Philosophy*, by Annie Besant and Charles Bradlaugh. A celebrated trial and a £200 fine on the two authors followed, but Mrs Besant and Bradlaugh did not invent family limitation. It had been known to the Romans, preached by Malthus in 1798, and advocated by the reformer, Francis Place. Even *The Fruits of Philosophy* was an old pamphlet re-published.

Why was this propaganda so suddenly effective? Sociologists themselves cannot say; they only know, without knowing why, that from 1876 onwards the British people began to practise birth-control. They are also aware that this change in the size of families became a chief cause of woman's liberation, giving her the power to choose how many children she had and to decide when to have them.

The rapid decline of population in a highly industrialised country raises problems which are outside the scope of this book. But the use of contraceptives does not prevent the birth of large families to those who desire them; it eliminates only the unwanted family and the over-burdened mother, whose children are a menace rather than an asset. Amongst woman's four freedoms, which include freedom to be educated, freedom to be a full citizen, and freedom to work, the freedom to regulate the size of her family claims an outstanding place.

In an anonymous article on Dr Marie Stopes, the birth-control specialist, published on December 9th, 1933, the *New Statesman* commented appropriately: 'It is she, above all others, who has brought to women the right to be mistresses, and not slaves, of their own fertility, and to children the right of coming as invited guests, and not as gate-crashers, to the banquet of life'.

In spite of many continuing handicaps, British married women are probably freer than those of any territory except Scandinavia, and possibly the United States and Russia. Nearly everywhere else, the law demands only that a man shall provide his wife with food, clothing and shelter; the standard of such provision is left to his judgment.

From a financial angle, a wife's contribution to national life is regarded as worthless. So little value is placed upon her work that in several countries parents are still expected to give their daughter a marriage dowry, which becomes the property of her husband. She is also denied the separate taxation of her income and the right to her own legal domicile.

Scandinavian law has long given to women a better status than that of any other system. In Sweden, divorce by consent has existed for many years without disastrous consequences. Some comparative statistics for the year 1922 show that the number of divorces per 100,000 Swedish marriages was then 24. In the United States, where no State administration had ever permitted divorce by consent, the divorce figure per 100,000 marriages was 136.

For thirty years, Swedish women have enjoyed economic equality in marriage. Under the Swedish Marriage Act of 1921, husbands and wives are legally bound to pool their incomes and divide them equally. The same type of obligation applies to property, debts, and wills. On a husband's death, half the estate goes to his widow, and the other half to his children—a rule which applies similarly on the death of a wife. The State grants a maternity bonus of 75 Kroner to all families—about 92 per cent of the population—with a taxable income of less than 3,000 Kroner.

In Norway a wife is likewise entitled by law to a share of her husband's income and property. The Scandinavian Code provides for the regular payment of a proper sum for housekeeping, and a wife is legally entitled to anything that she can save from this allowance. In a *News Chronicle* article published in November 1950, Doreen Gorsky, Vice-Chairman of the British Married Women's Association, quoted Article I of the enlightened Norwegian Marriage Act:

'Husband and wife, through contribution in the form of money, through activity in the home or in any other way, to contribute each according to his/her ability to such maintenance of the family as must be considered to be in accordance with the financial means and social position of the spouses.

'Such maintenance is supposed to comprise what is needed for the joint household and upbringing of the children as well as what is necessary to meet the particular demands of each of the spouses.'

But, 'in the rest of Europe', as Susan Deacon reported in the *Sunday Express* of February 18th, 1951, 'the matrimonial manacles are pretty tight'. In France a woman who has her own income must be careful to get a legal agreement with her husband before marriage; otherwise he can sell her securities, furniture or car without consulting her. A Swiss wife may take a job only with her husband's consent, while a Portuguese husband can dispose of any 'movable' property in the home whether his wife agrees or not.

For many years the only country where the State allocated a maternity bonus was Australia, which gave £5 for each confinement that produced a living child provided that the joint income of husband and wife did not exceed £299 for the previous twelve months. Before the Second World War, New South Wales was the only State to give child endowment, paying 5/- a week for each child after the first under the age of fourteen.

In the United States, where women own so large a percentage of the national income, theories regarding the work and status of married women are reasonably advanced, but in practice the combination of marriage and career has been difficult owing to the scarcity and heavy cost of domestic help. American middle-class homes are well-equipped with labour-saving devices which sometimes involve a larger expenditure of time than their designers intended, and American husbands, well-trained by social necessity, are probably more co-operative than husbands and fathers in any other civilised community. The homes of many Negroes and 'poor whites' remain very primitive, especially in the South.

Reliable facts about married life in Soviet Russia are as difficult to obtain as other types of social information, but after the Revolution of 1917 Russian women emerged from complete bondage to their husbands, and reached a position of relative equality and respect. According to *Women in Soviet Russia*, published by Fannina Halle, a German writer, in 1933, the codification of Russian family laws took place in 1925. This achievement meant that divorce was simplified and both spouses were permitted to choose their occupation. Woman's economic independence came to be regarded as normal; illegitimacy was abolished as a legal conception; and a man was held responsible for all his offspring, whether born in wedlock or not.

In 1910 two-thirds of all Russian children, like Britain's illegitimate children in 1873, died within twelve months of birth. These figures must have been drastically reduced by the maternity and child welfare work begun after the Revolution, and by the provision of cash payments for nursing mothers and the mothers of large families. In so far as accounts of the social revolution in the Soviet Union can be trusted, motherhood does appear to rank as a service to the State rather than as a disadvantage and handicap to the mother. Experience there, as in Scandinavia, suggests that where a woman's economic independence obtains official recognition, her standing as a mother is appreciated and respected.

It is the lack of precisely this appreciation and respect which has dominated the story of motherhood in Britain. Even in the 20th century, the tradition of subordination in marriage survived with an obstinacy only rivalled by that of women's industrial subjection.

Marital subservience revealed itself in several forms, of which the most costly in life and health has been the persistent undervaluation by the State of the functions of wives and mothers as such. Even in the 1951 Census, as in previous surveys, the 12,818,300 housewives of Britain are described in the Table of 'Status Aggregates' as 'unoccupied'.

Until the National Health Service was established in 1948, Maternity and Child Welfare services for these overworked mothers were supplied by local authorities, which varied in their attitude towards their obligations, under the Maternity and Child Welfare Act of 1918. Mr Arthur Greenwood contemplated a National Maternity Service as Minister of Health from 1929-1931, but 'expense' invariably supplied governments with an excuse for postponement though ample funds were always available for armaments.

After the First World War, Field-Marshal Sir William Robertson estimated that the three bombardments before the battles of Messines, Arras, and Passchendaele had cost the British Government £52,000,000. In 1930 Mr Greenwood put the cost of a National Maternity Service at £2,750,000 per annum. It was this comparatively trivial sum which the Socialist Government of 1929-31 'could not afford'. Presumably it regarded as adequate the £2,000,000 spent annually on maternity and child welfare by local authorities, though half this amount was raised by the rates and did not constitute a burden on the National Budget. The total sum was approximately the same as the yearly expenditure on public baths and washhouses.

Mr Greenwood himself described the maternal mortality figures of that time as 'a nightmare', though they showed some improvement on the 4,000 maternal deaths of 1900 and the 3,028 deaths of 1919. In spite of pioneer work in maternity and child welfare and a general improvement of the social background, the loss of 2,787 mothers in 1929 meant, as Arthur Greenwood realised, that 'the death-rate . . . is higher than in any other calling'. Motherhood was an occupation more dangerous than a miner's.

During the same period Sir George Newman, Chief Medical Officer of the Ministry of Health, gave a series of lectures on 'Citizenship and the Survival of Civilisation' in which he referred to the additional heavy burden of maternal suffering, sterility, and permanent invalidism which vital statistics did not reflect, In 1932 a Departmental Commission on Maternal Mortality admitted that forty-seven per cent of the annual deaths were preventable and probably resulted from unskilled attempts at abortion.

At that date gynaecology was still the despised Cinderella of the medical sciences. Compared with other branches of medicine, no remarkable advance had been made since the death in 1817 of the Princess Charlotte, whose sacrifice to obstetrical conservatism was graphically described by Sir Eardley Holland in the William Meredith Fletcher Shaw Memorial Lecture delivered at the Royal College of Obstetricians and Gynaecologists on September 28th, 1951.

The fashionable doctors of the nineteen-twenties still regarded 'these baby cases' with ill-disguised contempt, while reports issued by the Ministry of Health between 1924 and 1930 revealed insufficient training and low standards among practitioners attending the poor.

In spite of four Acts between 1918 and 1928 designed to improve the position of nurses and midwives, their pay and status remained extremely low. Mothers had to wait till 1936 for the Midwives Act which set up a comprehensive service of salaried midwives by local authorities.

An outdated attitude towards motherhood has existed up to the present day even amongst those feminist groups which fought for a mother's right to be regarded as a normal human being. The early controversialists who opposed protective legislation failed to perceive that maternity, far from being an uncomfortable handicap liable to exaggeration, was an important national service, comparable from the State's point of view with conscription, which deserved special privileges.

The majority of mothers themselves accepted this traditional undervaluation, and regarded the production of their children as an 'interruption' rather than an important social task to be joyfully fulfilled. Their feminist sponsors endeavoured to minimise the interruption, instead of realistically accepting it as an essential human fact and boldly demanding part-time employment and refresher courses of training to enable the valuable mother to perform her function without being penalised.

Owing to this universally false perspective, British motherhood remained unendowed by the State until Family Allowances became law in 1945. Instead the State assumed responsibility for the well-being of the male wage-earner, and left his wife totally dependent upon his benevolence whether extensive or non-existent.

From the beginning of her battle for Family Allowances, Eleanor Rathbone recognised how completely British wives and mothers had lost the economic security which was theirs when they shared in producing the wealth of an agricultural community under the domestic system. Both she and Beatrice Webb believed that the Exchequer should help to provide for children, and agreed on the importance of motherhood as an occupation. But their campaign proceeded slowly owing to the prevalent indifference towards 'women's questions'.

Home-makers were even excluded from the National Health Insurance scheme until the Socialist Governments of 1945-51, though Sir George Newman had commented in 1930 on the excessive sickness rate revealed by the National Insurance Acts among married women working for pay and claiming medical and maternity benefits. 'Motherhood and womanhood were at a discount when the National Insurance Acts were passed', Sylvia Pankhurst asserted that same year in her book *Save the Mothers*.

She referred to the original disregard of 'gainfully employed' married women in the National Health Insurance Act of 1911, passed by an all-male House of Commons which ignored disabilities due to pregnancy and childbirth in its estimates for sickness. The omission threatened with early insolvency all Approved Societies composed of married women, and compelled the Government to revise the Act in 1912.

This invalidism arising from overwork, though lightly overlooked, was hardly surprising, since successive governments had felt no obligation to provide public assistance for the mother with a large family, or to help the wife who worked outside her home. The number of crèches, nursery schools, communal kitchens and municipal laundries available for workers and their families was minute in relation to the need, while the domestic duties perforce abandoned by a child-bearing woman had often to be carried out by the midwife for lack of other domestic help.

The callousness of the State towards overburdened mothers had extended also to their children until Infant Welfare Centres were set up under the Maternity and Child Welfare Act of 1918. The establishment of these Centres, an immediate consequence of women's enfranchisement, led to a swifter decline in the infant mortality rate, which had been 154 per 1,000 registered live births in 1900. By 1919, when the Ministry of Health was founded, this figure stood at 89 per 1,000, and was almost to be halved in the next twenty years (51 per 1,000 in 1939).

The mothers and children of the workers were not the only or even the worst sufferers from medical lethargy. In 1934 a *News Chronicle* map illustrating the incidence of puerperal fever in London districts significantly showed the 'black' areas as Hampstead, Lewisham, Islington, Battersea and Wandsworth, while the 'white' included Rotherhithe, Bermondsey, Southwark, Clerkenwell, and St Giles. The continued mismanagement of middle-class babies had already led to the founding in 1927 of the Chelsea Babies' Club, an Infant Welfare Centre for Subscribers which still functions in Danvers Street, S.W.3. This useful experiment was leading to the foundation of other centres and would probably have become a national movement, had not the evacuation of bomb-threatened areas in the Second World War redistributed children all over Britain.

The British wives and mothers of the nineteen-twenties and

thirties suffered almost as much from legal as from medical discrimination. They had, and still have, no right to any share in a husband's wages or salary, though a housekeeper looking after an unmarried man can claim payment for services far less devoted and conscientious.

The master-servant relationship of most 19th-century marriages changed very slowly into a companionship between equals, since educational talks on marital obligations were given even more rarely to boys than to girls. Though a more co-operative partner did eventually replace the selfish male who thought all forms of housework beneath his dignity, the husband really able and willing to share responsibility for home and children belonged to the future. In Britain he remained free from the obligations demanded of husbands by Scandinavian law.

During 1943 Lady Violet Bonham Carter and Dr Edith Summerskill M.P. published letters in *The Times* expressing dissimilar views on the housewife's right to payment. Dr Summerskill urged in conclusion: 'If £1 a week comes to be regarded as the monetary worth of a housewife, and children are brought up to think of father as being worth, say, £5 a week, and mother only £1, the cause of women will be harmed irreparably'.

In 1951 the Vice-President of the Married Women's Association, Lady Helen Nutting, uncovered some peculiar case-histories in the course of a campaign to give every wife a legal right to part of her husband's income. According to a Press article by Joseph Garrity, she and her colleague, Mrs Jean Mann, M.P. for Coatbridge in Scotland, interviewed the widow of a company director who had given his wife only £5 a week for all household and personal expenses, including the upbringing of two sons. When he died after twenty years of marriage, she learned that he had enjoyed a net income of £2,000 a year.

Foremost among the married woman's handicaps has been the primitive home still imposed upon her owing to the convention which regards her as a domestic slave, and her own explicable failure to organise and protest. More mute inglorious Miltons—or Jane Austens—have been drowned in the kitchen sink than were ever buried among the rude forefathers of the hamlet. The failure of male architects and engineers to replace obsolete designs and antiquated plumbing has been mainly responsible for the 5 a.m. to 10 p.m. day of the working-class wife and mother.

'In a hundred ways', wrote Eleanor Rathbone in *The Disinherited Family*, 'our social customs, our domestic architecture, our ideas of decoration and dress, show signs of the undervaluation of domestic work . . . an average of an hour a day for every British housewife is a modest estimate of the waste of human brain and energy caused by ill-planned homes, lacking in even the cheaper and more obvious kind of labour-saving devices. . . . Assuming there to be roughly about eight million separate dwellings in the U.K., this implies a waste of fifty-six million hours per week, which if the modest value of sixpence an hour were put on the housewife's services would be equivalent to a loss of £73 million per annum.'

The Disinherited Family was published in 1924. Today, in the mean streets behind city thoroughfares and the dreary wastes of suburbia, homes such as Eleanor Rathbone described have been perpetuated by war, bombing, and a chronic housing shortage. Sample surveys made as recently as 1951 showed that six per cent of British homes were without an internal water supply, five per cent had no cooking stove, twenty-three per cent shared one, seven per cent lacked a kitchen sink, fifteen per cent had no water closet, thirty-eight per cent no fixed bath, and fifty per cent no vacuum cleaner.

The energy and initiative of 20th-century science has gone into contrivances for large-scale destruction, while a substantial percentage of houses throughout the world remain ill-adapted to the purposes of a home. Here, perhaps, lies one explanation for the widespread juvenile delinquency of which modern sociologists so anxiously seek the cause. Children compelled to play in bomb-damaged streets can hardly be blamed for failing to develop a respect for property.

Protests by both women and men have not been lacking. 'Pray Silence for the Middle-Class Wife' was the title of a *cri du cœur* in 1948 from Honor Croome, novelist, lecturer, and the mother of five children, who complained that family responsibility and sheer exhaustion barred present-day middle-class housewives from every activity but cooking, shopping, and child-rearing.

'Why Should Women Slave to Let Men Lead Easy Lives?' inquired John Gordon in a *Sunday Express* article which explained in August 1952 how scientific research, industrial invention, and business enterprise had lifted the burden of housekeeping from the backs of American wives. He did not however remind his readers that even gadgets can become tyrants if, like American washing machines, they replace laundries and other external aids which enable a woman to get rid of 'chores' altogether.

Until sufficient British counterparts of the garbage-disposal installations, 'nappy services', and all-nylon underwear habitual in the United States bring relief to the married women of the Commonwealth, the valuable time swallowed up by household tasks will be used as an excuse to tie wives to the home and to oppose their use of their gifts outside it.

For years the general over-emphasis on domesticity in marriage was responsible for the marriage-bar maintained by the Civil Service, the teaching profession, local authorities, and commercial employers. Subjection continued for wives long after it had been abandoned for spinsters. Whatever a woman's tastes or talents might have been before marriage, her male relatives and social acquaintances comfortably assumed that after it she would settle down to be somebody's wife, or somebody's mother, and never wish to be herself any more.

Only one or two percipient women, such as Sylvia Anthony in *Women's Place in Industry and Home*, explained how wasteful was the convention by which one wage-earner was supposed to require the full-time unpaid services of another person. The home-centred woman, often frustrated, possessive, and over-anxious, won the moral approval of neighbours and friends who saw no immorality in treating the training and skill of an intelligent person as 'expendable'.

This conception of a wife as her husband's 'appendage' has affected the relative positions of men and women in the highest as well as the lowest occupations. An Ambassador's wife, for example, is expected to act as her husband's honorary hostess. However exacting her social duties, her status remains that of an unpaid worker since the whole salary is given to him.

Now that women can enter the Diplomatic Service, the time seems to have come for recognised prestige and a proper allocation of pay to be made for the functions performed by the wife of an Ambassador or Minister. The same principle might with advantage be extended to the wives of bishops, vicars, doctors, and all other married women upon whom professional duties are imposed by their husband's occupation.

Owing to the pressure of custom and the lack of modern facilities in most British homes, the minority of wives who go out to work have carried up to date a heavy double burden. They have been the most harassed members of the interrupted sex, perpetually confronted by the choice between overwork and frustration. In the past even their husbands felt little obligation to help them, for the idea that wifehood and motherhood involve sacrifice and renunciation dies unwillingly amongst those who benefit.

Working wives have also been impeded by the irrational jealousy of other married women who have made the care of their households an excuse to relinquish outside occupations, and resent a practical demonstration that home-management and wage-earning can be successfully combined. A further handicap has been the inability of elderly relatives to realise that an employed woman's time has the same economic importance as that of an employed man.

During the first third of the century, the only support usually available to working wives was that of organised women, who repeatedly called attention to the 'dysgenic' effect of marriage-bars upon a society where the number of children produced by healthy, intelligent, and disciplined mothers was already far too few.

The belief that intellectual women were all plain and dowdy had largely disappeared after the First World War; as Rebecca West commented in an American magazine, the same vital qualities which carry a woman to the top of a profession are also those which make her desirable and successful in marriage. But most men continued to believe that, faced with the choice, a woman would always prefer marriage to a career. Only the exceptions acknowledged the compulsion of the view once expressed by Florence Nightingale: 'Some few sacrifice marriage, because they sacrifice all other life if they accept that'.

The frustration so readily dismissed as 'nerves' when suffered by married women was not, of course, confined to the gifted. To the observant eye it was as clearly apparent in the farmer's lonely wife marooned in an isolated village as in the peevish ex-stenographer suffering from 'suburbanitis' after her marriage to a bank clerk. Organised women endeavoured to meet the needs of the one by Women's Institutes, and of the other by Townswomen's Guilds.

A different approach to the problems which persisted when marriage and motherhood remained 'at a discount' began soon after 1918.

During the War, the separation allowances paid to the wives of working men had given a new security to mothers, whose family income at last bore some relation to their needs. Their improved health owing to better nourishment led Eleanor Rathbone to start her campaign for Family Allowances. She perceived that such a scheme would end the anxiety and malnutrition of mothers, and often also of their older children, whenever a new baby arrived to impose further strain upon an impoverished household.

Throughout the period between the wars, this fight to introduce a 'new deal' for mothers and children continued. Under an Act of 1921, benefits were first paid to dependent wives and families. In 1925 the widows and orphans of insured workers began to receive pensions, and after the Midwives Act of 1936 each expectant mother, whatever her means, could obtain the services of a trained midwife, and when necessary of a doctor whose fee was paid by the local authority. By the end of 1937, 3,462 child welfare centres, municipal and voluntary, had been established in England and Wales. Health Visitors encouraged mothers to take their families to these centres, and during 1937, 477,903 children, of whom 357,121 were under a year old, attended for the first time.

These practical reforms produced a more co-operative attitude in husbands and fathers, and a realisation by the community itself that other services were needed. The nineteen-thirties saw the extension of meals for school-children, instituted for undernourished children in 1906, and a development of the medical services for both infants and older boys and girls which had started in 1907. Industrial canteens for men and women workers became customary in large factories, and a limited number of service flats were built for the middle classes. The nursery school movement initiated by Rachel and Margaret McMillan made some slight headway, though up to 1939 the idea of the co-operative nursery school so long accepted in America still appeared extravagant to the British official mind.

Before the outbreak of the Second World War the results of this new concern, limited though it was, had become apparent in vital statistics. In addition to the fall in the infant death-rate, maternal deaths had dropped to 2,000 a year by 1939.

The Second World War itself brought further changes. Under a system of universal rationing the claims of mothers and children to special treatment became evident, and were met by a Government again sensitive to the value of women's work during a potentially disastrous shortage of labour. Under the Ministry of Food, the Welfare Foods Service provided mothers and babies with extra milk, free cod-liver oil, and orange juice at moderate cost, while food subsidies guaranteed for most families a minimum of the foods essential to health. Free school milk and cheap school dinners lifted much of the burden of catering and cooking from the mother's shoulders.

The evacuation of young mothers from towns to country districts involved much impromptu provision for maternal needs. The Ministry of Health staffed and equipped Emergency Maternity Homes in reception areas, and in 1941, when 3,000 expectant mothers left London every month, appointed twenty women Welfare Officers to their regional headquarters. By March 1944 ninety-eight of these Maternity Homes still existed, with nearly 1,000 women as nursing staff. Over 160,000 babies were born in them, and throughout England and Wales midwives attended about ninety per cent of all births.

An occasional lack of organisation in some areas showed the

old belief that anything was good enough for a mother to be far from extinct. During November 1943, a letter to *The Times* from Surrey recorded some facts which the writer described as 'interesting' in view of the general desire to increase the birth-rate.

'An evacuee in this district was expecting her seventh child on the 11th instant. The hospital eight miles away could not take her until the actual beginning of labour, although a bed had actually been booked for her there on the 10th, with the result that the baby was born before the local doctor, midwife, or ambulance could arrive. The birth was in no way premature. The birth took place by the light of a single candle, with the help only of a friendly neighbour, and with two children of eight and nine crying in the next room. They had been left in the house because their mother had no one else to help her in any way by day.

'I have no doubt that many women are in like case all over the country, and that only a big increase in the number of maternity homes giving pre-natal accommodation will guarantee to the mothers and babies the skilled attention and comfort that they deserve. When is this grateful country going to get moving?'

Good intentions, though not always fulfilled, were now a normal response to the needs of evacuees. More remarkable, and to the cynically-minded very instructive, was the sudden official change of attitude towards married women's work.

Mothers who had been told for years that their place was the home were now urged to leave it just when children needed constant supervision owing to the danger from bombs. Though the mother of a child under fourteen living at home escaped industrial conscription, inducements such as good pay, part-time work, and day-nurseries for her younger children tempted her to volunteer for the labour market. Women began to realise that a tender concern for the sacredness of motherhood existed so long as they were potential competitors, but was liable to cease in emergencies which created full employment for both sexes.

The number of childless wives at work now amounted to eighty-one per cent, and many mothers voluntarily undertook whole-time or part-time employment. By 1945 a total of 2½ million married women were working, more than five times the number of those 'gainfully employed' before the War. Wives and mothers largely staffed the 2,000 Civic Restaurants which had developed out of communal feeding during the air-raids. These restaurants, like industrial canteens, nursery schools, and the School Meals Service, went far to solve the problems of the married woman worker, and could always have done so had the State and society been concerned to help rather than impede her.

In the final spring of the War, Eleanor Rathbone's long and patient campaign at last showed results; the Government brought forward a Family Allowances Bill to provide a weekly payment of 5/- for each child after the first. The original measure had arranged for this payment to be made to the father. In Mary Stocks's biography of Miss Rathbone, some lively paragraphs describe the personal campaign, supported by women's societies, by means of which she caused the Government to accept an amendment making the payment to the mother.

'They were impressed by her vehemence', a senior Civil Servant remarked of this capitulation by the Ministry of National Insurance. When the Bill made its final appearance in the House of Commons on June 11th, 1945, Eleanor Rathbone was acclaimed with enthusiasm by all the Members. Like other pioneer women, she had proved to be immortal until her work was done.

The period which followed the Second World War saw a prolonged rebuilding of family life, shattered for six years by the absence of men in the Forces and the evacuation of mothers and children from their homes. This process involved many tragedies both of divorce and of juvenile crime.

Seven years after the War, moral casualties among adolescents were still a source of deep concern to magistrates, clergy, welfare workers and parents. In December 1952, after the trial of a sixteen-year-old boy for shooting a policeman, the *News Chronicle* published a series of articles examining the causes of juvenile delinquency, and found no simple explanation.

Though housing and child-rearing raised difficult problems in a hazardous period, post-war marriages occurred earlier than marriages between the Wars. In 1947 the most popular age for boys was twenty-three, and for girls twenty-one. The percentage of women who married during the child-bearing years rose steadily

N

as the sexes approached numerical equality. Advances in medical science, which drastically reduced the infant mortality rate to 29.8 per 1,000 births in 1950,* meant that a growing number of vulnerable boy-babies survived to adulthood.

The 1951 Census showed an actual surplus of boys up to the age of 14 (1,639,300 males between 10 and 14, and 1,589,600 females) and a virtual equality up to the age of 30 (1,796,500 males and 1,828,600 females between 25 and 29). At the later ages women became 'surplus' owing to the earlier death-rate of men. Between 65 and 69 only 866,700 men were recorded, against 1,153,300 women. The maximum number of married women occurred between 35 and 39, and of married men between 40 and 44.

Young and older married couples alike lived and worked against backgrounds too varied for generalisation. The scarcity and increasing cost of domestic help meant that most middle-class wives had to work harder than ever before, and penalised especially the gifted woman whose talents demanded a measure of freedom from trivial anxieties.

Slow and much-hampered post-war building programmes furnished luxury flats for the well-to-do, and a somewhat larger allocation of modern council houses for wage-earners. Most professional women fell between these extremes, being unable to afford luxury flats, yet ranking as too affluent to occupy council dwellings. A number of married couples, who had homes of a kind before the War, found themselves when it was over living uncomfortably with relatives and unable to escape. Though most households were better off financially than they had ever been, prices rose steeply and budgeting became a source of real anxiety for the housewife.

The new respect for wifehood and motherhood, shown in legislation initiated by women voters, was reflected after the War in the willingness of local authorities to share the burdens of parents. By the municipal provision of 'home helps' and 'baby-sitters', mothers were freed from the emergencies which once left them dependent in illness or childbirth upon the good will of

*Similar improvements occurred elsewhere. In 1951 the Italian death-rate of children under twelve months old was reported to have fallen by 26.4 per cent from the pre-war figure.

neighbours. Largely owing to the use of sulphonamides in cases of puerperal sepsis, the striking decline in the infant death-rate was accompanied by an even more dramatic fall in maternal mortality. By 1947,the 2,000 maternal deaths of 1939 had dropped to 1,059. In 1950 the rate descended still further to 0.37 per cent and began to reflect the benefits due to the institution of a National Health Service.

In social attitudes the greatest change affected mainly middle-class women. Though three out of five women at working ages were still housewives and statistically not 'gainfully employed', the growing tendency of married women to take up or remain at work had come to be generally accepted. The emergency which made their employment patriotic, and the subsequent removal of professional marriage bars, had set middle-class wives free to pursue careers without the nervous tension created by popular disapproval and jealous prejudice. It could hardly be argued that a choice which was desirable amid the dangers and difficulties of war-time became suddenly impossible or anti-social when peace returned.

The contrast between the three best-known Queens in British history illustrates this change in popular opinion. The first Elizabeth achieved success by remaining a spinster, if not indubitably a virgin. Victoria won contemporary acclamation by producing a large family, and later retiring into prolonged widowhood consistent with 19th-century notions of domestic morality. Elizabeth II, a Queen at twenty-five owing to two major accidents of history, combines wifehood and motherhood with a public life of very hard work.

The married woman's struggle is not yet near its end; she still awaits the reorganisation of industry and the professions to meet her needs.

A suggestion that half-time work should be regularly available for married women first came from Miss Van den Plas of Belgium when the International Labour Organisation was set up after the First World War. In 1922 a pioneer group of American citizens opened bureaux for part-time women workers in New York and Philadelphia, and placed 13,000 during the next seven years.

As valuable members of the community performing an essential service, rather than second-class auxiliary workers upon whom governments find it expedient to call in times of crisis, mothers have the right to demand that conventional employment regulations should be modified for their sake. Part-time work would enable a mother to retain whatever skill she possesses and with it the confidence that independence brings. By this means she would save herself from the poverty and monotony which often limits her outlook, and causes her, in too many families, to be despised by her adult children.

Though home-helps and baby sitters may solve some of her domestic problems, she still needs to organise in order to claim a legal proportion of her husband's earnings, and to gain other advantages given to wives by the Scandinavian Code. An example of effective organisation comes from Chile, where the National Association of Housewives, under Señora Rosa de Gonzales, wife of the President, made it their business to fight inflation and keep down the price of food.

More co-operation is still required during child-bearing and child-rearing periods both from the State and from fathers. Even in the final years of the Second World War, which represented the peak period of State assistance to British mothers, the total accommodation for children under five in day-nurseries and nursery schools amounted to less than a quarter of a million places, though the pre-school child population was two-and-a-half million.* The lectures and classes on Fathercraft given at the Chelsea Babies Club between the Wars might well be developed on a national scale, for fathers and children have everything to gain and nothing to lose by a better understanding of one another. A still greater paternal share in domestic responsibility might even speed-up the long-delayed modernising of the British home and the rationalisation of the services upon which it depends.

In February 1951, the Anglo-American Council on Productivity published a report drawn up by British representatives of the rigid box and carton industry who had recently visited the United

* Many schools and nurseries have since been closed owing to the withdrawal of children on account of the high charges made by local authorities. An official inquiry seems to be called for into the administration of the funds allocated for this purpose.

States. This industry was largely staffed by women in both countries, but more of the American workers were married owing to the longer hours available for shopping. The report might also have described recent American developments in the provision of Automats and self-service stores.

As Maureen Owen prophesied in the *News Chronicle's* 'World Beyond Tomorrow' series of articles, the future may see large one-floor underground stores, linked with Tube Stations and over-ground structures serving as landing places for aerial delivery vans. Food universally kept under glass, cooked meals in thermostatic containers, slot machines stocked with eatables in tablet form, and illustrated catalogues televised into the home, added graphic details to this halcyon outline of a housewife's dream. But the key to the married woman's future does not rest with gadgets, useful though they may be. Nothing less than a revolutionary conception of motherhood and its functions will redeem the callous indifference of the past.

Women have not yet achieved equal opportunities with men, but the woman who stays single can overcome by energy and determination most of the obstacles that remain. It is the married woman who still flounders in the morass of inequality. Yet the continuation of the race depends upon mothers; their position determines its achievements, and the fate of their daughters is related to their own.

For this reason the future of all women demands a dynamic solution of the married woman's problems. How shall she bear children, and yet remain a self-sufficient human being? How can a community ensure that tomorrow's children will be produced and reared by the finest mothers, as it cannot if the best-qualified women feel compelled to sacrifice marriage?

At present the idea of a 'Sabbatical year' for a mother, combining temporary freedom from her family with a continuing salary related to her worth, would appear to most communities a costly and fantastic arrangement. But why is it more important for a professor to write a book, or for a young conscript to undergo twelve months' military training, than for a woman teacher or doctor or artist to take an endowed year off duty in order to bear a child without anxiety?

Every woman who solves this problem for herself hastens the day when mothers will shed their traditional inferiority complex, and demand as a right that concern for the most fundamental of 'women's questions' which even half a century of struggle has not yet secured.

12

WOMEN AND WAR

BETWEEN 1901 and 1952, the two greatest wars yet experienced by mankind deeply affected the history of women. The latter part of this chapter will examine the claim so often made that it was the war work of women in Britain and other Commonwealth countries which gave them the vote. First it is necessary to describe the practical effect of the two wars upon women's work and status.

When war broke out in 1914 and ended for ever the safe, prosperous and unequal society associated with Queen Victoria, it seemed to emphasise the national value of men and the dependent uselessness of women. But that opening phase was brief. The hospital and nursing services were the first to reveal the new opportunities for work that would come to women through war.

France and Serbia quickly accepted the help of Dr Elsie Inglis and her staff of fully trained medical women whom the British War Office had scornfully repudiated, and the fourteen units known as the Scottish Women's Hospitals went out to assist the Belgian, French, Russian and Serbian Armies. Dr Inglis herself, involved in the retreat of Serbian troops during the chaos which followed the Russian Revolution, died in 1917 after bringing the remnant of the Serbian army safely to England.

By 1915 the War Office had already changed its mind about women doctors. Dr Louisa Garrett Anderson, the daughter of pioneer Elizabeth, and Dr Flora Murray, who had started medical work in Paris in September 1914, were put in charge of a hospital of 520 beds in Endell Street, London. This hospital, staffed by women surgeons, physicians, dentists, nurses, and orderlies, worked with maximum efficiency till the end of the War, and at peak periods took in 1,000 patients. But the War Office refused all appeals to give women doctors official status, and they carried on as civilians without commissions.

The first twelve months of the War saw a rapid expansion of Nursing Services and Voluntary Aid Detachments, which had been started at the Army Council's request in 1909. The Territorial Force Nursing Service increased from 3,000 to over 8,000 members and Queen Alexandra's Military and Naval Nursing Services from 1,000 to 10,000, while 23,000 V.A.D. nursing members and 15,000 orderlies entered Service Hospitals. These semi-trained women ranked as officers, and about 10,000 served abroad.

Of the most famous among the First War nurses, Edith Cavell, Mrs Strachey reported a comment made by Mr Asquith in 1915: 'There are thousands of such women, but a year ago we did not know it'. He meant, of course, that he did not know it. Even before 1914, quite a few individuals in key positions had realised what women could do.

Between 1914 and 1918 Britain did not introduce conscription for women either military or industrial, but in 1915 the spectacular process of women's absorption into industry began. 'They were willing to do "everything",' recorded Mrs Strachey, 'but they did not know how to do anything.' Their chief disadvantage lay in this lack of training for work which required a long apprenticeship. Work-shops were opened to provide the training, but it was less easy to overcome the reluctance of employers to use women and the hostility of male Trade Unionists.

The 'Treasury Agreement' of March 1915 between the Government and the Trade Unions finally arranged that 'the rate for the job' should not be lowered owing to the temporary performance of the work by women, juveniles, and unskilled workers. It was also agreed that restrictions on other types of labour should be suspended only for the duration of the war. The Munitions of War Act (1915), the Munitions of War (Amendment) Act (1916), and after the Armistice the Restoration of Pre-War Practices Act, further implemented this agreement.

Nearly half a million women 'did their bit' in munition factories. Others accumulated a vast miscellany of industrial and semi-industrial jobs, which included ship-building, house-painting, grave-digging, chimney-sweeping, and bus-conducting.

Women were first engaged as auxiliaries with the troops when the Women's Legion began in July 1915. In 1917 the Women's Army Auxiliary Corps was established, followed by the Women's Reserve Naval Service and the Women's Reserve Air Force. Also in 1917 came the Women's Land Army, which farmers at first received unfavourably. Its total full-time force never exceeded 20,000, though 300,000 women in England and Wales gave part-time service. Meanwhile the huge temporary Ministries in Whitehall absorbed about 162,000 women, and they were also widely employed in banks and business houses.

Between 1914 and 1918 the number of British women working for pay rose to one and a third million, of whom it was estimated that 700,000 directly replaced men. Of these women 400,000 came from domestic service, and 80,000 were diverted from clothing and textiles. Thousands who had never previously worked entered industry or offices from patriotic motives. Many more ran canteens, entertained the troops, organised welfare schemes for war prisoners or munition workers, collected salvage, administered war charities, and supervised the distribution of pensions and separation allowances.

Great surprise greeted the success of women in these varied enterprises. Most astonishing of all seemed the skill and energy of the factory workers, who for the first time in their lives were enjoying relative equality with men, and owing to better wages had at last enough to eat. The Home Office Report on the Substitution of Women for Men in Non-Munition Factories admitted that women had shown an unforeseen capacity to take up processes hitherto reserved for men, 'and have displayed unexpected readiness for work which at first sight seemed wholly unsuitable for them'.

In 1919, the Report of the War Cabinet Committee on Women in Industry acknowledged that women's supposed inability to perform certain categories of work was not the real reason why this work had been monopolised by men. Some employers and managers who gave evidence before the Committee confessed that, especially in processes needing dexterity, women had proved more valuable than the men whom they replaced, though these jobs had been classed as 'men's work' before the War.

This transformation of women's lives and the disconcerting revelation of their strength and ability had several concrete results. A crescendo of praise began in 1916, and two years later came the first instalment of the vote. In social and welfare work the war accelerated changes which without it would have occurred more slowly. The provision of canteens, rest-rooms, first-aid services and recreations followed the government control of many munition factories and the continuous publicity given to women's work in war industries.

A minor revolution in psychology accompanied these practical benefits. Amongst the women workers themselves a new confidence sprang to life; they had acquired skills, carried responsibility, earned and spent their own money, and now realised the power that this independence gave them over their own and their children's lives. At the same time some medical reports, such as that of Dr Janet Campbell for the War Cabinet Committee, emphasised the improved health of women owing to 'adequate nutrition', while the reduced infant mortality rate in 1916 and 1917 testified, in the Committee's words, that 'poverty and an insanitary environment may have an even more injurious effect than the mother's absence'.

Another unforeseen consequence was the new approach to a single moral standard when many women discarded 'virtue' and adopted the morals of men. For the younger generation life had grown short, and death was always imminent; the postponement of love to a legal occasion might mean its frustration for ever. In *Our Freedom and Its Results*, Alison Neilans described how previous teaching about the sacredness of the body lost its meaning for the young men and women who saw it destroyed by Christian nations in the name of Christ. Victorian inhibitions gave way before the desperate determination to eat, drink and be merry with those who to-morrow might die. When life itself had become so precarious, a mere loss of chastity seemed trivial indeed.

This new conception of morality transformed especially the middle-class girls for whom the contrast with their previous sheltered lives had been more violent than any experience which the Second World War could provide. To go as a V.A.D. nurse or W.A.A.C. 'private' to France or the Mediterranean might not appear much of an adventure to the young women of the nineteen-forties who lived for months under bombardment, or joined underground movements as secret agents. But even these hazards offered no such novelty as the First War brought to the girls whom it transferred from comfortable homes and private schools, where they had hardly been allowed to go out alone, to front-line hospitals and overseas camps.

The dangers that they faced should not be minimised merely because the weapons that killed or injured them had not reached the same stage of 'perfection' as the guided missile and the atomic bomb. Many women, young and older, went down in hospital ships; others died on duty in air raids against which they had no defence system of underground tunnels and concrete shelters. The nurses who lost their lives in the bombing of Étaples were buried beneath crosses marked 'Killed in action'; it was perhaps the first time in history that such an inscription had appeared on a woman's grave.

Yet the thousands of women who went into the Services or war factories left small impression upon their new surroundings. A year after the War ended three-quarters of a million had vanished into voluntary retirement, and traditional influences resumed their sway. Other women who quit their homes for war work did little to alter the subjection of wives, or to challenge the convention which chained even the most able married woman to the kitchen stove.

In 1916 Mr Walter Long, a former political opponent of woman suffrage, actually said in addressing the Women's Land Army: 'There are still, unfortunately, villages to be found where the women have become imbued with the idea that their place is the home. That idea must be met and combated.' But when the War was over the official desire to combat it abruptly ceased—until the next period of fighting. Then again it became *comme il faut* to leave exposed to wartime perils those young children who had been regarded as so infrangible a tie when the alternative to their care was a well-paid civilian job.

Not least surprising was the failure of the war books which began to appear in the nineteen-twenties to give any adequate picture of the part that women had played. One category regarded war as an exclusively male business; a second displayed woman in the Andromache-like role of 'smiling through her tears'; and a third represented her as the meanest type of war-profiteer, battening upon the sufferings and savings of the fighting soldier.

Edmund Blunden's *Undertones of War*, R. C. Sherriff's *Journey's End*, and Siegfried Sassoon's *Memoirs of an Infantry Officer* presented, for all their beauty and poignancy, entirely a men's war. Robert Graves, in *Goodbye To All That*, found women typified by the young wife who stayed at home and bore his children; Erich Maria Remarque, in *All Quiet on the Western Front*, saw them as passive victims who starved on civilian rations in a small German town. Richard Aldington's Elizabeth and Fanny, in *Death of a Hero*, were callous parasites who described their shell-shocked husband and lover as '*un peu gaga*'. The story of the women who worked in hospitals and factories seemed to be relegated to casual references or hidden beneath soulless statistics.

'Why are we, who served with the armies, so inarticulate that we cannot transform these dry memorials into literature?' I inquired in an article published in 1930. 'Who will write the epic of the women who went to the War?'

The fact that I was forced to make the attempt myself says little for the enhancement of women's prestige by the events of those violent and tragic years.

When the Second World War began,* the idea of women as engineers, aircraft-pilots, munition-makers, medical officers, journalists under fire and members of the Armed Forces had long ceased to be revolutionary.

The earlier demand for women's services recurred, but it affected more countries and followed a larger pattern. Much of the work required was more dangerous and dramatic. Women manned anti-aircraft guns, took charge of barrage balloon sites, ran the Women's Section of the Air Transport Auxiliary Service

* For most of the facts and figures in this section, I am indebted to Miss Vera Douie's comprehensive survey, *Daughters of Britain*. (Oxford, George Ronald, 1950. 7/6.)

which included such celebrated pilots as Amy Johnson and Pauline Gower, and in many parts of the world were dropped by parachute to join resistance movements behind enemy lines.

Women civilians faced comparable emergencies as air-raid and shelter wardens, and women doctors, like men, had often to crawl under perilous ruins carrying hypodermic syringes to relieve the injured. Instead of being attenders and comforters of male casualties, many women became casualties themselves.

Between 1939 and 1946, large contingents of women served under commissioned officers as part of the Armed Forces of Great Britain, the British Dominions, and the United States. American Service women, unlike British, received the same pay as men. In the Soviet Union some women functioned as officers and a few as combatants, but women's units were not formed and the majority worked behind the lines.

Most of the belligerent countries, like neutral Switzerland, recruited Women's Services with women officers. Numerous women also ranked as officers in the organised resistance movements of enemy-occupied countries. When the War ended, both Britain and the United States made their Women's Services permanent, with voluntary enlistment.

At the outbreak of war, the total number of British women between fifteen and sixty-five available for employment amounted to about seventeen million. Like women in the First War they represented the country's main reserve of labour, but they were no longer a wholly new source. Between 1914 and 1918 the majority of women had not been transferred from one job to another, but from idleness or domesticity to war work. In 1939 most single women were working already, and had merely to be removed from 'non-essential' jobs to positions regarded as more important by the peculiar standards of war-time. Married women now represented the chief new reservoir of labour.

At first, as in 1914, women did not appear to be needed, and unemployment figures rose as luxury trades were curtailed. But these figures soon fell when the Registration of Women began in April and May, 1941; from that time onwards women registered at Employment Exchanges in age-groups up to fifty. In December 1941, the National Service (No. 2) Act made unmarried women and childless widows liable, for the first time in British history, for compulsory service with the Armed Forces.

Only those born between 1918 and 1923 were actually conscripted, though women were liable up to the age of thirty and had the same right of conscientious objection as men. A small number refused their call-up and went to prison. Women with children under fourteen and pregnant women received automatic exemption; so did housewives looking after evacuated children or billeted war-workers. The mothers of families were responsible for an emphatic rise in the birth-rate, and medical and social progress for the fall in maternal and infant mortality figures below all previous records.

Modern war demands a huge non-combatant force to maintain the men at the front. This work devolved chiefly upon the three Women's Services, which had reached a combined total of 467,000 by the summer of 1944. The largest was the Auxiliary Territorial Service, with a peak figure of 212,000 recruits, including 6,000 officers. Their first Chief Controller was Dame Helen Gwynne-Vaughan (until 1941). When the Women's Reserve Naval Service and the Women's Auxiliary Air Force were founded in 1939, Mrs (later Dame) Vera Laughton Matthews became Director of the one, and Miss Jane Trefusis-Forbes Senior Controller of the other. In the A.T.S. and W.A.A.F., women received two-thirds of the pay of men, rank for rank and trade for trade. The W.R.N.S. included only two grades of work, specialised and unspecialised.

These Services released men for fighting to an extent unknown in any other country. Army women became substitutes for men in eighty trades, and ninety-five per cent of W.A.A.F. airwomen directly replaced airmen. A.T.S. girls took over nearly all the Home Searchlight Batteries, and managed every type of vehicle from baby cars to three-ton lorries. During the Battle of Britain, they drove bomb-disposal officers with their loads of unexploded bombs.

Many naval air stations were staffed almost exclusively by women, of whom some stood by in asbestos suits ready to save the crew if a crashing plane caught fire. By 1944 the Service Meteorological Officers were nearly all women, and in all three Services women packed parachutes with full responsibility for the lives of those who wore them. W.A.A.F. women helped to develop radiolocation, as radar was then called; twelve were chosen for this work in 1939, and 4,000 had taken part in it by the end of the War. They also learned to interpret aerial photography; a W.A.A.F. Interpretation Officer first noticed unusual details in pictures taken over Peenemunde in May 1943 which led to the identification of the flying bomb.

For the first time in history, British service women became eligible for certain military decorations; these included the Victoria Cross and the Military Medal. The George Cross and George Medal were also available to women for heroism behind the lines. Two women received George Crosses during the War, and two more when it was over. Mrs Samson and Mrs Szabo, to the second of whom the Cross was awarded posthumously, had both been captured and tortured by the Gestapo after dropping from parachutes into France as members of the Women's Transport Service.

When the bombardment of Britain began, the work of whole-time Civil Defence absorbed thousands of women. The peak period came in 1942, when 80,000 women served as full-time wardens, ambulance-drivers, storekeepers and firewomen, or staffed First Aid Posts and Rest Centres. Part-time Civil Defence claimed 350,000 women, of whom 47,000 were auxiliary fire-fighters. At the height of the raids, the Fire Guard Service included five million civilians of both sexes.

Outside the direct war services, munition-making acquired an importance similar to that of the First World War. The maximum number of women in munition factories was recorded in 1943, with a total of 1,928,000 occupied in iron and steel manufacture, ship-building, engineering, and the making of aircraft, tanks, instruments, chemicals, and explosives. About six women to every ten men worked in an industry which had been largely masculine before the War, and together with the men put in some excessive overtime after the loss of British ammunition at Dunkirk.

In May 1940 various agreements provided, as in the First World War, for a temporary relaxation of pre-war Trade Union conventions, so that skilled processes could be divided between a larger number of unskilled workers, and women might undertake 'men's work'. On May 22nd an agreement was signed, and endorsed by all the Unions affiliated to the Trade Union Congress, which secured to trained women engaged on 'men's work' the skilled men's rate of pay. By the end of 1943, 1,961,000 women had become members of Trade Unions, but as male Trade Unionists then numbered over six million, the proportion of organised women was still far from equal.

With so large a choice of spectacular occupations before British women, the care of the sick and wounded inevitably attracted less limelight than that of the First World War. Medical women working with the Forces now held commissions in the appropriate Women's Services and received the same rank and pay as male Medical Officers. They shared their Officers' Messes, were welcomed as professional equals, and sometimes acquired distinguished reputations. Dr Janet Vaughan, the haemotological specialist who later became Principal of Somerville College, Oxford, organised Blood Transfusion Services; Dr Genevieve Rewcastle was the first woman to join the Director-General's Staff at the Admiralty with the rank of Surgeon Lieutenant-Commander; and Dr Laetitia Fairfield, as Lieutenant-Colonel, occupied a similar position at the War Office.

Members of the regular Nursing Services travelled all over the world, with Sisters ranking as officers. Their proportion of casualties became higher than that of any previous war, though casualties among men never reached the huge figures of 1914-18. Over 1,000 nurses shared in the evacuation of Dunkirk, and learned a new realism; in 1944, when the Army Nursing Services returned to France, they discarded their grey and scarlet uniforms for khaki battledress, gum-boots, and tin hats.

The Voluntary Aid Detachments never recovered their First War status; their members ranked as privates, performed only inferior duties, and were finally enrolled in the Women's Forces. Much of the work done by V.A.D. members between 1914 and 1918 fell to the Civil Nursing Reserve, which was recruited from retired nurses and partially-trained auxiliaries. These women were responsible for the better care given to civilians in the Second

WOMEN IN TWO WARS

Supervisors of the Forage Branch of the Army Service Corps (First War) and (*left*) a Ferry Pilot of the Air Transport Auxiliary

MADAME YONE SUZUKI

MADAME KOLLONTAI

World War, and especially to mothers, factory workers, and children.

No fewer than 4,786,000 women were statistically described as engaged in 'other work', and in addition over one million served under the Dowager Marchioness of Reading in Women's Voluntary Services. A further 225,000 worked in Forces canteens all over the world, including the jungle areas of Burma. Advisory bureaux for Soldiers', Sailors' and Airmen's Families sprang up in every belligerent country, including 1,400 staffed by 20,000 voluntary workers in Britain alone. Members of E.N.S.A. gave performances for troops throughout the British Isles and abroad; British Red Cross workers organised welfare for prisoners, libraries for the sick, wounded, and prisoners, and inquiry departments for the relatives of the missing. Every type of transport and communication fell largely into the hands of women, who kept trains, buses, telephones and postal services going throughout the air raids.

From the standpoint of the struggle described in Chapter 11, the most significant figure was still that of the largest group. 'The rest' of the female population, composed mainly of housewives and domestic workers, amounted to 10,901,000 in 1939. By 1945 this number had fallen to 8,869,000; in those six years, more than two million housewives had gone out to work. Women who could not leave home carried the responsibility for nine million children under fourteen.

Apart from the new categories of work open to women and the larger numbers employed, two other relevant changes distinguished the Second War from the First. Between 1914 and 1918, no women Members of Parliament had existed to share in national planning and watch the interests of women. Though women M.P.s never exceeded fifteen before 1939 and only twelve sat in the House at the outbreak of War, they made themselves responsible during the next six years for such major problems as the mobilisation of women, welfare in the Women's Services, and Equal Compensation for War Injuries.

Two women Ministers, Ellen Wilkinson and Florence Horsbrugh, bore heavy responsibilities throughout the War. Ellen Wilkinson, at first Parliamentary Secretary to the Ministry of

Pensions, moved to the same position in the Ministry of Home Security and took charge of Civil Defence. She drove her own car so fearlessly through heavy air raids to visit shelters that the strain was suggested as a possible cause of her premature death in 1947.

Florence Horsbrugh served as Parliamentary Secretary to the Ministry of Health under four different Ministers, and supervised the casualty and shelter services, evacuation, and rest-centres. After the bombing of Coventry in November 1940, she was one of the first officials to arrive on the scene. The choice of twenty-four women—the largest number ever elected—from eighty-seven candidates in 1945 suggested that the wartime work of political women had impressed the electorate.

The many distinguished European women who took refuge in Britain from Nazi-occupied countries brought a further contrast with the 1914 War. To help them, the British Federation of Business and Professional Women set up International Women's Service groups with Caroline Haslett as Chairman. One group studied the problems of reconstruction; another examined the world status of professional women, and discussed how best to prevent the reimposition of artificial sex restrictions on women's work after the War.

How far did the work so widely performed by women in two World Wars contribute to their enfranchisement and the relative independence which they now enjoy?

Undoubtedly the wars of this century gave women an opportunity to display their powers, and proved that the claims made before 1914 were well founded. The First War completed women's struggle to escape from the tyranny of Victorian homes; by making paid employment both patriotic and normal, it ended the convention that work was 'unladylike' and virtually abolished the old category of 'lady' altogether. The practical revolution that it created in the lives of once-sheltered women gave them a new awareness which enabled them to produce organic social changes by their votes.

The Second War further established the right of women to equality and their capacity for full comradeship with men. In

Britain it incorporated the changes which followed the First War in the policy of the State, making the once despised 'women's questions' an important part of the programme by which the Labour party won popular support in 1945.

In both Wars the sexes mingled as co-workers, and the artificial distinction between 'men's' and 'women's' work almost disappeared. Women shared with men the values and activities of the wider world, and mingled with all types of humanity. This levelling of classes became even more drastic in the Second War owing to its widespread social upheavals. If any 'ladies' were left, they quickly became 'women' in the democratic cameraderie of air-raid shelters and the enforced privations of refugee camps.

Wars on the 20th-century scale were convulsions which shook all life to its foundations; they exploded antiquated prejudices and traditions at the same time as they debased such once-respected virtues as courtesy, honesty, and imaginative compassion. They stirred up minds inhibited by social lethargy and destroyed many outworn myths, such as the legend of feminine weakness and the belief in women's 'unsuitability' for skilled and well-paid occupations. Like all times of testing, the wars were also periods of opportunity.

Yet when this fact is acknowledged, the current conviction that British women owe their advance to war still appears to be not so much a paradox as an illusion. War may shatter the structure of society and with it many obsolete patterns. It may accelerate, and in Britain did accelerate, processes set in motion by other historic forces long before its outbreak. But it did not create those progressive forces, and usually appeared to be hostile to them owing to the anti-social and anti-biological policies to which it led.

Wartime improvements in the position of women have seldom been due to any new realisation of woman's dignity and needs; they originate in the selfishness of States seeking additional workers for temporary and unconstructive ends. The insecurity of the wartime prizes conferred on women became clear from the reversion to old habits and conventions which followed the First War, though they were less easily re-established after the Second. In so far as war changes practices which cannot be restored it brings progress, but the progress is incidental, and springs neither from principle nor from a revolution in values.

The history of Scandinavia reinforces this conclusion. Here women advanced more rapidly than anywhere else in Europe, yet Norway, Sweden and Denmark had avoided war for more than a century before the Nazi invasions of 1940. New Zealand and Australia were also among the first countries to enfranchise women, though war has touched them only from far away.

Convulsions that do appear to further women's progress are great national enterprises or constructive revolutions which demand the utmost from all citizens. The share of women in the early pioneering of American families underlies the respect felt for women in the United States. India's leading women owe their present international status to the Civil Disobedience campaign, into which Mahatma Gandhi took the educated women of his country and gave them political experience.

The military values which dominate most 20th-century States can hardly fail to be prejudicial to women's interests, since money spent on armaments cannot also be used for health, education and the care of childhood. Wars have contributed in large measure to the poverty of the female sex by absorbing resources which could otherwise have been used to reconstruct homes, furnish modern tools, endow schools and colleges, and provide social services.

The reader of Chapter 11 will have observed that, for the cost of three First War bombardments which made pulp in a few hours of thousands of mothers' sons, Britain could have financed a National Maternity Service for nearly twenty years. It has been estimated that the First World War cost the four chief Allied Powers alone more than ten billion pounds. A calculation of the constructive uses which could be made of this sum suggests that modern civilisation has transformed itself into a mad-house.

Chapter 9 describes a similar contrast after the Second World War between the national expenditure lavished on rearmament, and the trivial saving effected by refusing Equal Pay to women Civil Servants. An even more startling example of waste comes from the East. For some years after they gained their independence, Pakistan and India respectively spent seventy per cent and sixty per cent of their Central Revenues upon defence measures against each other, while urgent national schemes for health, education and industrial welfare cried out for endowment.

Within the memory of all adults, Nazi Germany and Fascist Italy showed how militarised nations could undervalue women while sentimentalising motherhood. Their concern for mothers was not inspired by respect for the maternal status, but by the expediency of increasing the population and finding new sources of labour for the war machine.

In Britain the small, abnormal Fascist movement led by Sir Oswald Mosley caused occasional repercussions out of all proportion to its relative insignificance. The suggestion by Sir Herbert Austin in the nineteen-thirties that women should be removed from industry as a 'solution' for the unemployment problem showed the influence of the Fascist creed, while certain types of young womanhood thought it 'modern' to proclaim, like their Victorian great-grandmothers, the second-class humanity of women.

Behind the political antics of British Fascism, a literary cult associated with the names of D. H. Lawrence and John Middleton Murry revived the idea of 'auxiliary' women. In their peculiar society no real meeting place for the sexes existed; it worshipped the instincts, emphasised sexual differences and functions, and encouraged much talk (by men) about woman's 'normal' place. Into the wide areas where perpetual sex-consciousness is pointless and inappropriate—the regions of art and science, scholarship, politics, and sport—women, they suggested, must not enter and share essentially human experiences with men. They must remain for ever in spheres where their womanhood, hanging over them like a perpetually opened umbrella, excluded them from the sunshine and the clear sky.

The values and ethics of essentially non-military communities, such as the Society of Friends, show a remarkable contrast. Male Quakers, having voluntarily surrendered the primitive advantages of physical force, recognise the spiritual equality of women members, and demand no armaments other than the moral weapons available to both sexes.

Whether women were Fascists, Quakers, or members of more representative communities in Europe and Asia, they had only to use their eyes and ears during and after the Second World War to perceive the devastating effect of global conflicts upon family life. This, they had always been assured, was their special preserve, which it was their duty to build and protect.

In 1942, on the twenty-fifth anniversary of his consecration as a Bishop, the Pope made a remarkable broadcast. Behind the war front, he said, rose another front—the front of family anguish.

'We should like', he continued, 'to address a fatherly warning to the rulers of nations. The family is sacred. It is the cradle of children, and also of the nation, of its force and its glory. Do not let the family be alienated or diverted from the high purpose assigned to it by God. . . . We think of the separation between husbands and wives, and of the destruction of family life; of famine and economic misery. There are heart-breaking and unending examples of every one of these. This is one of the most terrific and terrible things which has ever happened to mankind.'

The Pope's words did not exaggerate the suffering of families torn apart by conscription, imprisonment, injury, and death, and by the wholesale evacuation of children in bombed countries to rural areas or overseas while their mothers were urged to put the claims of the war machine before the sacredness of domestic ties. No one troubled about two incomes, or five, going into one home if they were made by war work; only when they came from such creative occupations as teaching and medicine had objections been raised.

Modern war struck more fiercely than ever before at those things which meant life to the majority of women—children, homes, education, healing. In Europe and many parts of Asia, starvation increased the horror of massacre by bombing. All over the world, as in the First War, women were condemned to spinsterhood and sterility by the loss of the young men who would have been their husbands.

After the War, Sir Arthur S. Macnalty's contribution to the British symposium, *Rebuilding Family Life in the Post-War World*, described further consequences for all the belligerent countries. He stressed the removal of bread-winners by death, the forfeiture by sons of a father's guidance, the wretchedness of children reared by relatives or public institutions after the loss of parents and homes. In recording that 80,000 such children had been affected in Britain and 107,000 houses destroyed in London alone, he prophesied all too accurately the emergence of young social misfits unable to settle down to a normal civilian routine.

Commenting that 'the evils of war, like old sins, cast long shadows', Sir Arthur also described their effect upon the race itself. Through conscription and the *levée en masse*, the best physical specimens had been taken from every country. The decimation of French manhood in the Napoleonic Wars, the Franco-Prussian War, and the First World War with its toll of nearly 1,500,000 Frenchmen killed, had left France an easy prey to Nazi invasion. He might have added that those 1,500,000 men, like the anonymous hordes of helpless refugees obliterated in Dresden, had all been borne and brought up by women.

Sir Arthur's essay was written before thousands of children in Hiroshima and Nagasaki had been burned to death by atomic bombs. To prospective mothers those bombs were far more deadly than the lead paint industry, forbidden to the women of many countries by International Convention in the nineteen-twenties. Preaching on the commemoration of the Holy Innocents in the last week of December 1952, the Vicar of St Martin-in-the-Fields reminded his London congregation of the slaughter of innocents then going on in Kenya and Korea. From 1939 onwards, the almost uninterrupted tale of death and destruction has offered little inducement to motherhood.

In her speech at the Old Bailey Conspiracy Trial, Mrs Pankhurst used some memorable words.

'We cast about', she said, 'to find a way, as women will, that would not involve loss of human life and the maiming of human beings, because women care more about human life than men, and I think it is quite natural that we should, for we know what life costs.'

Years afterwards, in *The Church and Woman*, Dr Maude Royden by chance added a postscript to this comment.

'A religion or society which bases itself on militarism and exalts the use of physical force must in its very nature be opposed to the freedom and authority of women, and this for two reasons. . . . Not only are women inferior to men in muscle, they are by a deep-seated instinct debarred from soldiership . . . there *is* an instinct which convinces us that those who bear life should not be life's destroyers.'

The women of the nineteen-fifties are no longer 'debarred from soldiership', but the military demands of States do not eliminate deep-seated instincts. As Mrs Pankhurst and Maude Royden perceived, war violates a profound biological urge in women. The woman who shouts for war, whatever her temporary gain, has been perverted by propaganda from her natural impulse to create and to save.

13

THE STRUGGLE FOR PEACE

In Chapter III of *The Feminine Point of View*, the authors comment on a curious omission in Professor Arnold Toynbee's treatise, *The Study of History*.

'He is seeking far and wide for explanations of the repeated breakdown of civilisations through war and conflict; but among the similarities he finds in the characteristics of these civilisations he does not mention the position of women. One concludes that he has never even considered whether there might be any connection between the subordination of women in all these doomed civilisations and the glorification of war.'

The failure of an important historian to relate two significant historic factors is doubtless regrettable. Yet even some feminist leaders have perceived no special significance in woman's aversion to physical violence, nor found a key to the future in her resistance to the fascination which sheer power so often exerts over men. In the Washington of the nineteen-twenties the American feminist, Alice Paul, did not hide her distaste for younger women who allowed their energies to be diverted into work for the League of Nations.

She did not care, she declared, if the League failed and the world had to face another war; equal rights for women were her sole concern. Her powerful one-track mind had evidently not reflected that the women's revolution, like the similar movements for class and race equality, began only when a sufficiently large minority perceived reason to be superior to force as an influence in human affairs.

Two decades earlier, Olive Schreiner had recognised that respect for reason was unlikely to prevail in military societies; for her the campaign against war, the most vicious expression of force, was fundamentally inseparable from feminism, socialism, slave emancipation, and the liberation of subject races. In *Trooper Peter Halket* she had connected the women's struggle with the race conflict; in *Woman and Labour*, published in 1911, she identified it with the crusade for peace. Her fourth chapter, 'Woman and War', contained a famous and much-quoted passage.

'We have always borne part of the weight of war, and the major part. . . . Men have made boomerangs, bows, swords, or guns with which to destroy one another; we have made the men who destroyed and were destroyed! . . . There is no battlefield on earth, nor ever has been, howsoever covered with slain, which it has not cost the women of the race more in actual bloodshed and anguish to supply, than it has cost the men who lie there. *We pay the first cost on all human life.*'

To the women of two war generations, those words have come home with bitter reality.

'Never in the world's history', wrote Howard Spring, reviewing a volume published between the wars entitled *Letters to Mother*, 'were there so many mothers as there are today who saw the whole matter of a man's life from the cradle to the grave and found at the last little to show for it save a few letters to "Dear, dear Mother" from "Your loving son".'

Yet the prophecy with which Olive Schreiner followed her assessment of war's cost to women is still unfulfilled.

'That day', she continued, 'when the woman takes her place beside the man in the governance and arrangement of external affairs of her race will also be that day that heralds the death of war as a means of arranging human differences.'

During the four decades since *Woman and Labour* was published, the biological truth implicit in Olive Schreiner's statement has been reinforced by historical and scientific developments. All over the world, women are more intimately affected by war today than they could have been in 1911. As civilisation has advanced—if that is the correct expression—the difference between the parts played by men and women in periods of conflict has rapidly diminished.

The economic demands of modern war now loom so large that endurance at home, and the maintenance of key industries which fall largely into women's hands, have become as important to ultimate success as victory at the front. Simultaneously the radius of the weapons used has extended, until the Second World War saw non-combatants universally involved, and the former contrast between a man's and a woman's war virtually extinguished.

What evidence exists that partially emancipated womanhood perceives in this altered picture any obligation to support the struggle for peace?

In 1939, when war appeared inevitable, a large and agitated correspondence reached peace societies from women all over Britain. Some letter-writers wanted to help, others to be helped, but all agreed in their desire to find a means of preventing the War. Many of their suggestions were admirable; they merely forgot that burning sincerity is seldom effective without large-scale organisation.

Perhaps it was the difficulty of organising, combined with the unremitting pressure of war propaganda, which so soon thrust these protests underground. Most women reverted to the pre-war attitude of dumb acquiescence which Bertrand Russell had described in *Which Way to Peace?* (1936). There he quoted a cinema commentator describing a bomber shown in a news-reel: 'If we must be bombed, and it seems we must, we might as well be bombed by an up-to-date machine'. The audience, he reported, displayed neither pleasure nor pain. A resigned apathy appeared to be their only emotion.

The war years suggested that women's capacity for resignation had become a menace to the civilisation which their united efforts might have saved. A negative reaction so different from the first spontaneous resistance was hard to explain, but three causes probably contributed. The first was common to both sexes; the other two were peculiar to women.

One outstanding consequence of modern war has been its numbing effect upon human sensibilities. In the collection, *Falsehood in Wartime*, which exposed the atrocity stories circulated between 1914 and 1918, Lord Ponsonby remarked that truth was the first casualty in war. He might have added that the power to feel is certainly the second.

In the First World War, many young V.A.D. nurses who had previously seen no mutilations quickly developed a defence-mechanism of callousness from perpetual contact with horror. A similar imperviousness to the sufferings of air-raid casualties in the Second was mitigated for the individual only by the possibility of joining them. Women, like men, must possess unusual powers of compassion if their sensitiveness is not to be blunted by an awful but too-familiar succession of tragedies.

A second explanation arose from certain shortcomings still typical of women's education. Even in 1939, all but the youngest generation of wives and daughters had grown up with little knowledge of political problems. After the First World War the teaching of current events to girls had been limited to 'progressive' institutions, while the Edwardian school-rooms once attended by the middle-aged had inculcated the curious theory that women whose interests were confined to their homes, husbands and children possessed a unique moral worthiness.

The near approach of an epoch in which such indifference to contemporary history would appear both selfish and irresponsible was not even visualised. Political ignorance usually accompanied a ruthless training in the virtues of meekness, self-effacement, and submission to misfortunes described as 'inevitable', since up to 1914 women were regarded as powerless to defend themselves against the larger assaults of destiny.

A third ingredient of women's acquiescence lay, as it still lies, in the liability of all women to be mentally anaesthetised by domestic details which provide continuous antidotes to thought. In total war, rations, coupons and food queues absorb women's time, occupy their minds, and dominate their conversation. Between 1939 and 1945, the suburban wife waking up on a Saturday morning was unlikely to ask herself if she could do anything to end the war and save millions of her fellow housewives from further suffering. She probably speculated whether, by getting up early and standing in a queue, she could secure some synthetic cream puffs for her Sunday tea-party instead of falling back on the usual currantless buns.

This domestic form of anaesthesia was not confined to the Second World War, nor to the years just before and after it. In 1952 the preoccupied small-town housewife still did not care whether the United Nations forces in Korea had crossed the 38th

Parallel so long as there was plenty of dry soap in the cupboard. The fulminations of Mr Vyshinsky, and the Mau Mau murders in Kenya, left her unmoved in comparison with the discovery of a new recipe for tomato salad. Invitations to attend political meetings met with a discouraging response.

'I'm not interested in politics. Looking after the house and children takes up all my time.'

Not even two World Wars and the threat of a third had convinced some women that the duty of keeping their homes clean and their children tidy was small compared with the moral obligation to be intelligent about the future. Blinded by the details of living, they failed to perceive that the very right to live was menaced by powerful governments armed with lethal weapons capable of destroying not only civilisation but life on this planet.

Fortunately the conversion of majorities has never been a prerequisite of human progress. An awakened minority responded to the challenge of the 20th century, especially in countries unmenaced by invasion, bombing, and famine, where daily life remained relatively free from the tedious small-change of war-time existence. It included women from the United States, Canada, and Sweden, and the unintimidated feminists of Latin America who were so logically to connect, in their work for the United Nations, the status of women with the organisation of peace.

The concern of this growing minority could be expressed in a fashion for which precedents existed. During the First World War the menace of militarism to life itself seemed less ominous than it was to appear after thirty more years of scientific progress, but the climate of countries rudely shaken out of complacency favoured the development of political consciousness. Especially active were small groups of women who realised that such consciousness depended upon the exercise of elementary political rights.

In February 1915 a Dutch woman, Dr Aletta Jacobs, summoned an international gathering of women to Holland, then a neutral country, in order to discuss how women could hasten the return of peace. When this Congress met in April, women from twelve countries, belligerent and neutral, came to The Hague. Over forty from the United States risked a journey across the mine-strewn Atlantic; they included Carrie Chapman Catt and Jane Addams, whose powerful influence had caused the American Government to modify its attitude towards foreign immigrants.

The American contingent included Mrs (later Lady) Pethick-Lawrence of Great Britain, who had been speaking in the United States on woman suffrage. Only two other English delegates were able to attend, for the British Government closed the North Sea to 180 women waiting to cross. The French Government issued a similar prohibition, but a thousand members from all over the world nevertheless managed to join the Conference. President Wilson subsequently used its peace proposals, drawn up at The Hague, in drafting his Fourteen Points.

From this Conference was born the Women's International League for Peace and Freedom, with Jane Addams as its first International President. Both she and another American, Emily Greene Balch, who held the same office in 1952, have been among the few women to receive the Nobel Peace Prize.

With fifty thousand members drawn from many countries, the W.I.L.P.F. is still a force in politics. Its American and Scandinavian Sections especially are large and influential; it has a long-established international headquarters at Geneva, and is included amongst the voluntary bodies which have been given Consultative Status on the Economic and Social Commission of the United Nations, and also on U.N.E.S.C.O. and the Food and Agricultural Organisation. After a second international conference held at Zürich in 1919 and attended by the representatives of twenty-one nations, the League organised similar gatherings at three-year intervals apart from a break during the Second World War. Today its main purpose is to develop a world conscience in support of the Declaration of Human Rights.

A kindred group had been at work before the Women's International League was born. Carrie Chapman Catt, who attended the Conference at The Hague, had herself become President in 1904 of the International Women's Suffrage Alliance. This organisation was also concerned to secure enfranchisement and equal opportunities for the women of all nations, and to take part in constructive work for peace. Now re-named the International Alliance of Women, much of its present propaganda is based on the Declaration of Human Rights.

A British woman, Mrs Margery Corbett Ashby, who stood several times for Parliament as a Liberal, followed Mrs Catt as President in 1923. In 1946 the new President was Dr Hanna Rydh, the Swedish archeologist who organised relief for Norwegian and Finnish children during the War. A Danish woman, Miss Ester Graff, followed her in 1952.

Other international bodies of women which work directly or incidentally for peace include such organisations as the International Council of Women, the International Federation of Business and Professional Women, the International Federation of University Women, the Associated Countrywomen of the World, the International Co-operative Women's Guild, the World Union of Women for International Concord, the World Association of Girl Guides, and the Young Women's Christian Association.

Similar work is done by the international sections of national and religious bodies, such as the All-India Women's Conference, the Catholic Women's League, and the American United Council of Church Women. In 1948 the United Council launched its own peace crusade, on lines similar to Canon H. R. L. Sheppard's post-card campaign which initiated the British Peace Pledge Union in 1936. It circulated 'commitment cards' in the hope of obtaining a million women's signatures, and urged the United Nations to support the abandonment of atomic bomb production.

During the past fifty years, the combined influence of these international women's groups has been valuable and extensive. It is none the less true that a limit is set to the work which women's organisations can do, while women's peace campaigns as such have usually been failures. At any moment the aggressive impulses of the statesmen who still dominate political bodies may take control of human events and frustrate women's constructive endeavours.

The time is past when women have to prove their ability to work politically by organising themselves into separate groups. A more modern phase of the women's struggle is the attempt to achieve equal and friendly co-operation between the sexes, in which the self-consciousness of national woman suffrage movements has virtually disappeared. Some organisations, such as the International Alliance, regard even the Status of Women Committee as a tactical mistake which perpetuates the idea of women as a class apart. The chief value of women's associations today probably lies in their support for the larger role of women on mixed international bodies, where the struggle for peace and freedom is best continued.

The experience of women in the League of Nations, the International Labour Organisation, and the United Nations suggests that this task of co-operation is likely to prove harder than the more encouraging but sometimes abortive achievements of feminists working alone. In spite of the reputations made at Geneva by such individual women as Dame Rachel Crowdy, Frau Anna Bugge-Wicksell, Froken Henni Forschhammer, Miss Agnes MacPhail, Dame Edith Lyttleton, and Miss Karin Jeppe, the League of Nations was dominated by male values from the beginning to the end of its history.

In September 1924, the first British Labour Government sent Mrs H. M. Swanwick to the Fifth Assembly of the League as substitute-delegate for Great Britain. For seven years Mrs Swanwick was Chairman of the British Section of the Women's International League for Peace and Freedom, and in 1924, on the death of E. D. Morel, she became Editor of *Foreign Affairs*, a monthly magazine published by the Union of Democratic Control.

In spite of her intimate acquaintance with the international scene, the organisers of the Assembly expected Mrs Swanwick to confine her attention to such time-honoured feminine topics as children, invalids, and refugees. She was therefore appointed to the Fifth (Humanitarian) Committee, which she described in her autobiography, *I Have Been Young*, as 'a sort of rag-bag of miseries and forlorn hopes'.

Before the Assembly ended, she received a deputation from the women delegates of several governments asking her to speak on the Geneva Protocol. With the consent of the British delegation, she made the closing speech to the Assembly on Disarmament. A

LA VEUVE CLIQUOT
Famous in the annals of Champagne

MARY WOLLSTONECRAFT
1759–1797
from a painting by Opie

OLIVE SCHREINER
South African Writer

SELMA LAGERLÖF
Swedish Nobel Prizewinner

JANE ADDAMS
American Nobel Prizewinner

VIRGINIA WOOLF
British Writer

Frenchman who heard her described it as one of the only three great speeches ever delivered before the League.

Mrs Swanwick, who died shortly after the outbreak of the Second World War, was made a Companion of Honour for her work at Geneva. The majority of women delegates were less expert and less determined. Ten years after the foundation of the League, when Dame Rachel Crowdy left her key position as head of the Social Section, women's influence at Geneva began to diminish.

By that time a tendency had developed to replace by men the women who had transformed small posts into great administrative offices, on the ground that these positions had become too important for women to fill. Many of the League's critics remarked that to dismiss women because they had been too successful seemed a strange interpretation of Article 7 of the Covenant, but they were powerless to arrest either the growing monopoly of offices by men or the decline of the League itself.

Some administrative changes subsequently affected the position of women in the United Nations Organisation, which replaced the League after the Second World War. Under the League it had been possible to invite to Geneva any woman whose attendance seemed desirable, but owing to the government domination imposed upon the United Nations by the U.S.S.R., the initiative now lies with the individual governments, which appoint women to Commissions. In spite of this retrogressive step the U.N.O., as Chapter 5 has shown, pays far more attention than the League of Nations to the position of women and to Human Rights.

Though the number of women on official delegations has seldom exceeded twenty, Britain appointed Alderman Evelyn Emmet as a full delegate to the Assembly in 1952, and Pakistan subsequently gave a similar status to Begum Liaquat Ali Khan. A few conspicuous women—such as India's Health Minister, Rajkumari Amrit Kaur, who was President of the World Health Organisation in 1950-51—have occupied positions never held by women before.

On many voluntary international bodies with peace programmes, women have more scope for co-operation with men. Groups which support such programmes include the United

Nations Student Association, the Council for Education in World Citizenship, the War Resisters' International, the International Friendship League, the International Fellowship of Reconciliation, and the International Voluntary Service for Peace, founded by Pierre Cerésole in the nineteen-twenties.

Since these groups are unofficial, the women who join them, though more numerous, must necessarily be less effective than the minority which serves on U.N.O., U.N.E.S.C.O., and the I.L.O. But they are not wholly ineffective, for women's service for peace is best carried on today by the leavening process of creative values through teaching, writing and speaking; by examples of private conciliation within families; and by the persistent infiltration of women into public life. At present only the few who have qualified themselves to enter are there, and the minority is still very small which realises its special function of creating awareness and bringing the principle of reconciliation out of the home into the wider world.

Political consciousness is none the less growing among women, and so is the appreciation of their special qualities by men. When women have a fifty-fifty share in the councils of States the struggle for peace will be nearer fulfilment, for peace means escape from the mental paralysis characteristic of modern governments with their large male majorities.

It will be born from the conviction that, notwithstanding the terrifying world created by modern science and technology, men and women have still the power to control their own destiny, and to unite in fulfilling the great purposes inherent in the nature of man.

14

WOMEN WRITERS AND THE WOMEN'S MOVEMENT

At the end of the last chapter, it appeared that the inculcation of creative values through teaching, speaking and writing probably represents the best form of service that women can offer today to the cause of peace. Some proof of this seems to lie in the contribution made by these methods of spreading ideas to the women's movement itself.

'Preaching and teaching', wrote the late Bishop of Lichfield in his diocesan letter for December 1940, quoted by *The Times* in January 1953, 'is not mere "utterance", it is powerful to change the hearts of men and, indirectly but very really, to affect the course of history.'

These comments are even truer of the written than the spoken word. Amid all the female practitioners of the arts, women writers have most directly influenced the women's revolution. Certain great skills—acting, dancing, executive music—have brought little change to the position of women because they are traditionally accepted feminine attainments. The triumphs of a Sarah Bernhardt, an Anna Pavlova, or a Jenny Lind do not create the surprise which is the first ingredient of a new train of thought.

Such women are unrevolutionary in spite of a few individual exceptions. Sybil Thorndike, for instance, has proved by her own life that a woman can remain for years at the top of the theatrical profession without sacrificing personal fulfilment as wife and mother. Among great actresses she has especially succeeded in making the idea of courage and leadership in women acceptable to both sexes by showing it on the stage. The changing 20th-century ideal of womanhood owes a particular debt to her interpretations of Hecuba in *The Trojan Women* and Joan of Arc in Bernard Shaw's *St Joan.*

In spite of such British personalities as the late Dame Ethel Smyth, the late Dame Ethel Walker, and the living painter Dame Laura Knight, women have not yet made, as women, any special impact on music and painting. Dame Ethel Smyth went to Holloway Prison after some athletic stone-throwing in Downing Street, and wrote 'The March of the Women' to Cicely Hamilton's words, but neither the judical sentence nor the rousing tune can be regarded as part of her creative work. Her distinctive contribution to the women's movement was probably her fight, both in musical circles and with her trenchant pen, for recognition as a serious composer.

Fortunately for this endeavour, Dame Ethel lived to be eighty-five years of age. After graduating through the years from a 'lady composer' to a 'woman composer', she would have welcomed with delight the symbolic victory accorded to her in the opening sentence of *The Times* obituary: 'We regret to announce the death of Dame Ethel Smyth, the composer'. Her bust executed by Gilbert Bayes and unveiled by Sir Malcolm Sargent now stands in the vestibule of Sadler's Wells Theatre to remind all music-lovers of that ebullient campaign.

Apart from this example of claims staked with blithe determination, neither music nor painting seems to be an appropriate medium for conveying the essence of a democratic revolution. The prejudice against women as composers, and their exclusion as executive musicians from important orchestras, stamped music for many years as the most conservative and recalcitrant of the arts which they tried to practise. Much was done to modify this traditionalism by Marion Scott. As England's leading authority on Haydn she formed the Society of Women Musicians in 1911, and in 1930 won recognition for women's work in music from the B.B.C.

By contrast, women writers have played an important role. Their early recognition as colleagues by male authors owed much to the personal quality of literary success, which does not exclude a man from similar achievement and thus arouses the minimum of sex jealousy.

The triumph of the women's movement was assured when a few gifted women began to make their names as writers. They showed that in at least one intellectual field they could hold their own, in the competitive market open to both sexes, by writing not as men write but with the arts and graces peculiar to women. The minority which preferred the pseudonyms of men to the despised category of 'lady author' were seldom able to conceal indefinitely their essentially feminine qualities of subtlety and keen perception.

Their significant achievements started long before women became aware of themselves as human beings and challenged the world's conscience with their demand for freedom. Unlike her contemporary Mary Wollstonecraft, Jane Austen had no thought of changing the position of women by her work; nor had the Brontës. But as soon as the women's revolution became a recognised force, other women writers, deepening and widening the channels made by their pioneer predecessors, deliberately placed themselves in the van of the movement.

During the half-century which divided the reigns of Victoria and Elizabeth II, it is possible to trace three main directions in which women writers furthered the general progress of women.

First, they helped woman to achieve her destiny merely by doing superbly what they set out to do, whether or not they were interested in her mission as woman. Without the shining precedents established during the 19th century by Jane Austen, the Brontës, Elizabeth Barrett Browning and George Eliot in Britain, Georges Sand in France, and Harriet Beecher Stowe and Julia Ward Howe in the United States, 20th-century women would have been less likely to produce their own examples of literary distinction.

The cause of women has prospered through the mere existence of such authors as Virginia Woolf, Britain's leading novelist in the nineteen-thirties; Edith Sitwell, who takes a foremost place among contemporary English poets; Colette, the first woman to join the Académie Goncourt, whose legend dominates Europe from Paris; and two great German writers, Ricarda Huch and Clara Viebig, who survived the collapse and destruction of their world, and died in 1947 and 1952 aged respectively eighty-three and ninety-two.

In Jugoslavia the Croatian writer Ivana Brlitch Mazhuranitch, author of poems and fables, was the first woman to enter, in 1937, the Jugoslavian Academy of Science and Art. From Russia the name of Antonina Koptiayeva suggests that a woman may be the first author to challenge the long reign of didacticism in Soviet literature. Reviewing her comparatively subtle novel, *Ivan Ivanovitch*, for the *Manchester Guardian* in 1951, Alexander Werth described it as 'a Soviet *Madame Bovary*'.

American women have reason for gratitude to their own conspicuous writers, such as Edith Wharton, the second woman to be elected, in 1930, to the American Academy; Ellen Glasgow, the Pulitzer prize-winner of 1941; Edna St Vincent Millay, whose poems wove spells for two generations; Willa Cather, who added an intense preoccupation with craftsmanship to a reverence for tradition; and Gertrude Atherton, whose sheer longevity linked the authors of several decades. Her creative life exceeded the length of the period considered in this book; on her ninetieth birthday in 1947 she received a gold medal from San Francisco for her services to Californian literature.

In the centre of the 20th-century picture stand the five women who won the Nobel Prize for Literature. Selma Lagerlöf, the Swedish writer whose work has been translated into thirty-nine languages, was the first woman to be awarded it, in 1909. Grazia Deledda of Sardinia, and Sigrid Undset of Norway, were prize-winners in 1927 and 1928; the American author, Pearl Buck, and the Chilean writer, Gabriela Mistral, followed in 1938 and 1945.

Sigrid Undset thus helped the cause of women in spite of herself, for like Britain's Mrs Humphry Ward she was no friend to the movement for sex equality. Long before the victory of the Nazis, who burned her books because they reminded Norwegians of their majestic past, she adopted a Teutonic view of women's domestic obligations.

No Commonwealth woman has yet received the Nobel Prize for Literature, but the Commonwealth countries with their small groups of cultured readers have been worthily represented by their writing women. Australian-born Henry Handel Richardson, who wrote *The Fortunes of Richard Mahony* and survived till 1946, acquired early the conviction that 'to a writer, experience was for one thing that really mattered'. Her peer and contemporary, the poet Sarojini Naidu, died three years later. She had then been the three decades a part of the Indian women's movement, but this meant, as it had meant for Ethel Smyth, the sacrifice rather than the practice of her art.

In Canada and South Africa, Mazo de la Roche and Sarah Gertrude Millin made international reputations as authors. It was also South Africa which produced the greatest Commonwealth woman writer, who survived the First War and lived till 1920. But Olive Schreiner stands at the head of a second category of writers: that of the women who dared to deal directly with the problems of contemporary life, and produced the great classics of feminism. If Mary Wollstonecraft, with her *Vindication of the Rights of Woman*, represented their morning star, the works of Olive Schreiner can claim, in the context of their period, to shine for the cause of women with the light of a constellation.

Twenty-five years before Mrs Pankhurst and her followers began their campaign, Olive Schreiner was speaking as uncompromisingly as any of them on 'man's inhumanity to woman', and emphasising the right of all women to freedom and equality. Her *Story of an African Farm* was linked with the performance of Ibsen's *A Doll's House* as a milestone on the road to women's emancipation.

Woman and Labour, which appeared nearly thirty years later, sounded a clarion call to the generation of girl children who, unknown to themselves, were about to be flung from sheltered school-rooms into the maelstrom of the First World War. Olive Schreiner did not merely repudiate outworn tradition; her fiery vision of a new relationship between men and women presupposed a totally different code of morals from that which dominated both South Africa and Britain at the time of her birth, and had not wholly disappeared from either by the date of her death.

Not all the useful creators of feminist literature could claim the eminence of Mary Wollstonecraft and Olive Schreiner. They included the historians of the women's movement, such as Ray Strachey and Sylvia Pankhurst; the feminist leaders who wote autobiographies though their gifts were mainly political; and the woman biographers of eminent women. Amongst the best-known of these were Millicent Garrett Fawcett's *Life of Josephine Butler;*

Ethel Smyth's moving vignette, in *Female Pipings in Eden*, of Emmeline Pankhurst, who 'set as the sun sets, undiminished in power and glory'; Mary Stocks's spacious and scholarly study of Eleanor Rathbone; and Cecil Woodham Smith's best-selling portrait of Florence Nightingale.

Literature was not always better served by the lively but tendentious novels which used the women's struggle as a theme. The more memorable included Elizabeth Robins's suffragette story, *The Convert* (1907), and Jo van Ammers-Küller's *The Rebel Generation* (1925). This novel, one of the most widely read in Holland for fifty years, traced the story of Dutch women from repression to freedom through four generations of the Cornvelt family of weavers.

Virginia Woolf's deliberately feminist essay, *A Room of One's Own*, took propaganda back to high literary levels. So, in Sweden, did *The Alarm Clock* by Elin Wägner, the biographer of Selma Lagerlöf and the second woman to be elected to the Swedish Academy, who was working on a study of Frederika Bremer when she died in 1950.

Literature too in its different fashion was Winifred Holtby's *Women and a Changing Civilisation*, a combination of history and essay published in 1934. This short book showed the same zest for a life soon to be prematurely extinguished as her posthumous novel *South Riding*, which won the James Tait Black Memorial Prize in 1937. Other makers of literature whose work occasionally dealt with the women's movement included Cicely Hamilton, Stella Benson, Pearl Buck, and Rebecca West.

The final category of women writers who served the feminist cause is the largest, and therefore the least susceptible to detailed treatment. It contains the authors—chiefly novelists and dramatists, but sometimes the writers of such creative autobiographies as Storm Jameson's *No Time Like the Present*—who have portrayed without special bias the sheer process of change as it has affected the lives of modern women.

Because that process has been especially swift and dramatic during the 20th century, the least controversial work of fiction which covers two or three generations cannot help but reflect the alteration in women's status. Every novel or play which describes a problem of contemporary woman also belongs to this third literary division.

Occasionally a trifle, of small importance in itself, illustrates a whole era of social change. In 1946, for example, a play entitled *Love Goes to Press*, by Martha Gellhorn and Virginia Cowles, was put on by the Embassy Theatre at Swiss Cottage in London. The authors were American war correspondents who had met while reporting the Civil War in Spain, and now collaborated in a drama dealing with war correspondents, of whom two were women, on the Italian front.

Without the women's movement and the peculiar impetus given to it by two wars, this play could not have been written or produced. Florence Nightingale and these two young American women would probably have had much in common, but a virtual century of mental and social tradition separated *Love Goes to Press* from the romanticised portrait of Florence as the angel of Scutari in Reginald Berkeley's popular drama staged in 1929, *The Lady With a Lamp*.

'Is there a feminine point of view distinguishable in literature?' inquired the compilers of *The Feminine Point of View*. 'Are women writers even today, when they write so much, influenced by a masculine pattern and masculine prejudices?. . . . Our literature and our social ideas would gain enormously if we had more women writers with the confidence and originality to force their readers to open their eyes on a new picture of life—its values, joys, sorrows and sensations as they are experienced in the lives of women.'

It seems clear that a conscious feminine point of view did begin to emerge from 19th-century writing, notably in the work of Olive Schreiner. During the 20th century this view has struggled increasingly for expression, but has not yet found it on a large enough scale or with sufficient public appreciation of its saving value.

In the writing of books (as distinct from their work as journalists) women have not only achieved equality with men but have sometimes surpassed them, both from the standpoint of their earnings and in status, recognition, and power. Without detracting from the great political and social effect of those Victorian-born Titans, H. G. Wells and Bernard Shaw, it is probable that of all 20th-century British writers Virginia Woolf had the greatest influence on literature as such.

The results of her work illustrate the difference between equality and identity, for to her has largely been due the novel of insight, where the theme springs from the unfolding of character, which has superseded the romantic novel based on external events. That this fundamental change of treatment should come through a woman lies in the logic of 20th-century writing.

The reasons for women's present conspicuousness as authors are more difficult to define than they appear. In the two wars, and especially the first, many young men died who were potentially great writers, and like Julian Grenfell, W. N. Hodgson, Charles Hamilton Sorley, and Roland Leighton, were able to display only their promise in a few valedictory verses from the battlefield. Their women contemporaries took the place that they would have filled, and were helped in doing so by an incidental consequence of war. The development of science and technology, particularly after the second upheaval, offered prizes of increasing value to young men of talent, and caused them to yield, as America had long yielded, the world of art and culture to women.

Here again the effects of war can easily be exaggerated. Women could not even have attempted to compensate for the 20th century's lost men of genius had not the preceding revolution in women's education widened their perspective and enlarged their scope as authors. Few 19th-century women possessed the background knowledge of economic and social history required for the novels of Yorkshire's illustrious trio, Phyllis Bentley, Storm Jameson, and Winifred Holtby, or the understanding of dynamic national events which made Margaret Mitchell's *Gone With the Wind* the biggest best-seller to be published up to date.

Apart from such exceptional books as Elizabeth Gaskell's *Mary Barton* and the works of George Eliot, whose intellectual outlook belonged to the 20th rather than the 19th century, most women novelists from Jane Austen to Mrs Humphry Ward used drawing-rooms and vicarages as the settings for their stories because these were the only world that they knew. They could not have found their way about a textile factory or a shipbuilder's yard, or have unravelled the complicated agenda of a Yorkshire county council.

A new phenomenon of the 20th century has been the acknowledged influence of writing women upon their successors. With some feminine authors brought up in an older tradition it was fashionable to admire only the work of men and take pride in themselves as exceptions to the general rule of female futility, but this appears to be an Edwardian rather than an Elizabethan attitude.

In 1951, when *John O'London's Weekly* quoted Ruby M. Ayres as saying in an interview: 'I can't stand women authors. I seem to know what's coming next, so I stop. All the books I read are by men', Madeleine Henrey (Mrs Robert Henrey) was ready with a reply from a younger generation.

'I have exclusively been influenced by writers of my own sex. And what a heritage we have! . . . As I grow older, and read more, and think more clearly, I am increasingly proud of being a woman.'

In a personal letter, the French-born author of *The Little Madeleine* further defined the modern woman writer's appreciation of literary women.

'It is very important to realise that we no longer live in an age of Kipling, Wells and Shaw *versus* Marie Corelli. Today the great and thoughtful man writer has a counterpart in some woman writer who is *equally* thoughtful and great. There are even signs that there are more women of eminence in letters than men. Does not the pendulum swing violently to correct a previous fault?

'This, then,' she continued, 'is surely the most sensational development since 1900. The reasons are many and complex. The giving of higher education to young women, and the hurling of them into near-men jobs from 1914-1918, brilliant moments mixed with bitter sorrow, produced the experience they needed for writing great works. Women have been gaining their advantage by the inherent seriousness of their writing. As the great Edwardians like Shaw and H. G. Wells withdrew into the clouds, I mean by that mostly rested on gigantic reputations, women quietly took their places but being women, never became quite so fabulous in the public imagination. . . . If the serious woman writer is today so noticeable in literature, it is chiefly because there are more and more serious women readers.'

She concluded on a note of surprise that male writers should so readily have accepted women's new pre-eminence.

'What is curious is the way that men have allowed themselves to be ousted from the top places in literature, for when you hear a man deplore that literature is not what it used to be, what he really means is that it's not what it used to be for the men—but for you and me it's a golden age.'

The 'golden age' will not however be completely realised, nor the 'sensational development' fulfil itself, until the 20th century can find an answer to the outstanding question which still faces women.

How can a woman achieve greatness in an art or profession without sacrificing human relationships in the process? This problem is even more fundamental than the struggle for equal pay, which is already coming in response to routine pressure, because it is perpetuated by the psychological attitude of the many men and women who still believe that a woman's right to work is not quite equal to a man's, and her dedicated hours are less sacred than his.

In theory, the justice of equal opportunity is accepted; in practice the opportunities themselves are curtailed by traditional assumptions. These do not survive in men alone; the most gifted women still suffer from perennial conflict with an inculcated ideal of feminine duty which demands not achievement but self-sacrifice.

The work of women authors highlights this conflict, for sustained imaginative writing demands relentless concentration which the interruptions habitual in women's lives are liable to shatter. Without such concentration and a belief in the right to command it, could Shakespeare have produced his plays, Rembrandt his pictures, Beethoven his symphonies?

Most women writers marry, but the majority appear to refrain deliberately from having children. No woman in the first rank of British authors has been a mother except Elizabeth Barrett Browning, who like several other writing women venturing into motherhood had only one child. Mrs Gaskell, Alice Meynell, and other 'good seconds' produced large families, but they are not in the class of Jane Austen, the Brontës, George Eliot, Virginia Woolf, and Edith Sitwell.

In human society as it has so far existed they could not have been; the burden of conventional expectation is too great for the genius of a woman who becomes a mother to reach its full stature. Young children demand incessant attention; older children tend to become critics who undermine a mother's confidence with its shallow root. Among her own people a prophetess receives even less honour than a prophet; in most families the younger generation regard their claims on their mother as morally superior to those of any art or ideal.

Must we then accept the proposition that a woman writer can produce great literature only by subduing her natural desire for children? To do so would be defeatism indeed, for the sterility of the gifted is a tragedy for the race, and not least for the woman who must endure frustration and forego experience as the price of achievement. Such sacrifice is itself a challenge which demands the pursuit of new solutions.

These exist potentially in both practical and psychological directions. Much more could be done through the training of fathers in ordinary human efficiency, and by a minor reorganisation of domestic service which would save the creative woman from being perpetually at the mercy of 'the Fifth Column below stairs'. Some special State or municipal assistance, perhaps in the form of individual 'home helps', might well be officially available to the wife and mother who has proved her value as an author—and has even become a dollar-earner.

Above all else is needed the creation, through education and training, of a co-operative home atmosphere which would help the woman writer to overcome convention, and develop in herself that impervious self-confidence which insists upon the right to repudiate it. Such education is perhaps a long-term policy, but the mere half-century of enormous change which has separated our mothers' lives from those of our daughters suggests that the time required may not be abnormal.

So long as women writers and artists must sacrifice motherhood in order to fulfil the inexorable demands of a creative gift, the feminist revolution remains incomplete. With the answer to this problem the future of women now rests; the status of the many is involved in the fate of the few.

15

THE HUMAN REVOLUTION

At the close of a recent women's conference, the youngest of the few male visitors inquired with a bland assumption of naïveté: 'But has the emancipation of women *really* made any difference?'

About the same date Mr A. J. Cummings, the *News Chronicle* commentator, published an article which provided, in its maturer wisdom, a judgment on this superficial inquiry. It began as follows:

'Most of us, I suppose, were a little startled, as well as deeply impressed, by the courage and presence of mind of those two women in Kenya who defended themselves so successfully against a murderous gang of Mau Mau men.

'We ought not to have been startled. Our astonishment is a measure of our inability even now to realise fully the place civilised woman has won for herself in the modern world.

'The advance of women, in which Britain leads the way, is the most remarkable social fact of this century; yet the majority of men, and millions of women themselves, are still only dimly aware of it or do not appreciate its immense significance.'

That majority of men included the young conference guest. Not only had he learned nothing from the changing scene in Britain; he had failed to cast his eyes over the world as a whole. No nation, however backward, has escaped being affected by 'the most remarkable social fact of this century'.

As the earth shrinks, political emphasis shifts constantly from the West to the East, from the Atlantic to the Pacific. Like other major movements, the women's revolution has become a global influence in which the women of one area offer examples of human achievement to those in another. The conflicts created by change have reached different stages in different countries, but everywhere women are developing a sense of mission which is no longer men's, but their own.

This book has shown that over the past half-century the women's movement has 'made a difference' in three major directions. The first has been, in all progressive societies, the transformation of 'women's questions' into the substance of the Welfare State. This Welfare State, wherever it has developed, represents something new in the world's history, for it marks the beginning of a profound change from power-politics to welfare-politics.

It is only a beginning, for in every country the old aggressive values still dominate at the top; India alone has seriously attempted, during the thirty years of Gandhi's moral authority, to substitute on a national scale the principle of non-violence for that of force. But the Welfare State is dedicated to social service, and in it women have become ends in themselves and not merely means to the ends of men. To both sexes alike it offers new opportunities by removing such handicaps as poverty, ill-health, and the artificial barriers laid down by snobbery, which once chained whole sections of society to a subject race, category, or class.

The Welfare State has been both cause and consequence of the second great change, by which women have moved within thirty years from rivalry with men to a new recognition of their unique value as women.

Rightly, for no progress was possible without this first step, the pioneers began by repudiating the conception of women as second-class citizens unworthy of the same rights as men. Though some of the older feminists never developed beyond this point, their successors have gone on to insist that women have something to contribute which is not only rare in public life, but desperately necessary if civilisation is to survive. With growing clarity they have perceived the importance, not of educating women to equal or excel men, but of educating men to respect and adopt those women's values which emphasise the principles of love and toleration.

During 1952 this point was stressed in two publications, a pamphlet on *The Education of Girls* issued by the Education Department at King's College, Newcastle-upon-Tyne, and *The Feminine Point of View*, to which several references have already been made.

The compilers of the second document agreed after much discussion that 'the following qualities are probably more common among women than among men: compassion for suffering; intuitive sympathy; aversion to using violence or committing acts of physical cruelty; selflessness in personal service; reverence for the individual life'.

In support of their argument they quoted some British crime statistics for 1950 which showed that, among individuals convicted for 'violence against the person', 3,523 were men and only 316 women, while Broadmoor Institution for criminal lunatics contained 220 women and 809 men. They also noted that women, though the poorer sex, subscribed in far greater numbers than men to societies for the prevention of cruelty to children and animals.

It is significant that in Denmark, one of the countries in which women's emancipation began earliest and has gone farthest, educational experiments have been made for some years in 'The Education of Women as Women'. An article under this title by Debora Halfdan-Nielsen in *The Friends Quarterly* for July 1949 described the Gentofte (Denmark) Educational Project for young women which emphasises rather than minimises the psychological distinctions between the sexes.

'During the past two or three generations in our schools and colleges', wrote the author, 'women have demonstrated their ability to think and work alongside men. Why continue a battle that is already won? Why not take that ability for granted and begin to recognise that somewhere in the education there should be a recognition of the difference between them and men? Why not make some provision for the education of modern women as women?'

Only experience can show whether such projects will serve the future better than the systems which allow women to make their characteristic use of knowledge shared by both sexes. But their existence illustrates the third major consequence of the women's revolution: the changes in personal relationships within the home and outside.

Some of these changes, such as the transformation of the dictatorial paterfamilias into the modern co-operative father, are obvious and well-recognised. Others are so subtle that, as A. J. Cummings observed, we fail even to realise that change has occurred, much less that it was due to the women's movement.

The familiar lines of Arthur Hugh Clough describe the fashion in which, outside such clearly defined fields as politics and legislation, the women's revolution has changed human society throughout the world:

'For while the tired waves, vainly breaking,
Seem here no painful inch to gain,
Far back, through creeks and inlets making,
Comes silent, flooding in, the main.'

To perceive the significance of this human revolution it is necessary to examine some of those 'creeks and inlets', thereby making their shape far more definite than it ever appears to the individual who takes the tide itself for granted.

It is probably true to say that the largest scope for change still lies in men's attitude to women, and in women's attitude to themselves. But from both these angles, as this chapter will show, a major revolution which is still in progress has occurred both in and out of the home. Co-operation between the sexes in each sphere is still insufficient; it is also far greater than it has ever been.

Motherhood, especially in backward communities, remains the most despised and neglected of human territories, yet in every country the social attitude towards it has improved. In Britain midwifery, once a female profession, was lost to women when it became a subject of study at universities where they were not admitted. With the advent of the woman doctor, it became once more a dignified calling after a century and a half of virtual disregard.

A hundred years ago, as the gravestones in country churchyards testify, mothers still patiently bore at a husband's demand innumerable children whom they could not rear. When birth-control began this mass-mortality diminished, but the mother continued, in the elegant phrase of the first Lord Birkenhead, to be looked upon as a mere 'conduit pipe' whose misfortunes were negligible or comic.

Early in this century, the windows of stationers' shops even in provincial towns exhibited salacious postcards depicting the trials of motherhood and infancy, a mystery and a menace to the children who observed them. It cannot be more than thirty years since I saw the following gem of masculine egotism among the birth announcements in a leading London daily:

'On April 4th, at M— Vicarage, to the Rev. X.Y.Z., a son.'

Even today the insultingly anonymous words 'the wife of' are sometimes used to describe a newly-made mother who is not permitted a Christian name. But in most announcements she is now fully described, and the children also acquire personalities—'a sister, Susie, for Peter and Jim'.

Eleanor Rathbone's passionate reference in *Our Freedom and Its Results* to 'the criminal folly of society's whole attitude towards mothers and children' is no longer true even to the extent that it was still true in 1936. Only in isolated cases would a mother now be moved to write, as Elizabeth Fry, the least neurotic and ego-centric of women, wrote in her Journal before the birth of her youngest child in 1822: 'Let my mind not dwell on what is before me'. Maternal suffering has ceased to be a topic for obscene drawings and Parliamentary jests; nor is infant mortality a subject for philosophical resignation on the part of governments. Instead we have, in many States, National Maternity Services and Family Allowances.

Much more help is needed for all mothers, as Chapter 11 has shown; the provision of nursery schools, home helps and communal services is still grossly inadequate in every country. Nowhere, with the possible exception of Russia, has motherhood acquired the status of a national service worthy of privilege, rather than a misfortune for the mother and a tiresome handicap to commercial production. But this new esteem is coming because enough persons are now interested in seeing it come.

Not least among these is the once all-too-detached husband and father. The modern husband, in the rare instances where his wife dies in childbirth, loses not the submissive housekeeper, sick-nurse and ministress to his comfort who could so easily be replaced, but the equal and unique companion who shares his interests and tastes. The realisation that a wife can become an intimate friend has been, for men, one of the most exciting discoveries of this century. Because he has made it, his attitude towards her in most marriages has fundamentally altered even in the past twenty years.

In 1931 an article entitled *When Nurse Says Goodbye* appeared in one of those simple domestic magazines which are read in their thousands by 'the woman in the little house'. One paragraph of advice was headed 'A Man Must Be Considered', and began thus:

'You will find that your busiest time is between the first and second meals, for unless you have domestic help there will be certain household duties to perform and your own and your husband's breakfast to prepare. With Baby still in his cot, your husband can have his meal in peace. In your joy of possession do not forget that you have a duty to your husband. Unhappiness is apt to creep into a home where the man is shown quite plainly that he is of secondary consideration.'

Paraphrased in the more ruthless terms with which psychological analyses of human selfishness have made us familiar, that paragraph would run something like this:

'A man must be considered before everybody else, even when his wife, still weak after childbirth, is first left on her own to cope with an unfamiliar situation. He must be considered even before the fragile infant life, which is still at the stage when neglect, or mistakes due to agitation, may make all the difference between good health and bad. Unless he is regarded, not as a sympathetic and co-operative asset but as a liability scarcely less demanding than the baby itself, he will turn nasty and revengeful. A husband, in effect, is a peevish, unreliable non-adult, who will behave like a bear if he is asked temporarily to endure the slightest discomfort in order to relieve a situation for which he is at least half responsible.'

This non-adult British male is now as completely out of fashion as his American counterpart became a generation ago, when the change, familiar today in Britain, from an abundance of depressed domestic workers to an extreme scarcity of highly-paid help began in the United States. If he cannot assist in bathing his baby, many of his contemporaries will regard him with derision rather than respect.

A man who thinks that pushing a perambulator or carrying a shopping bag is beneath his dignity indulges an outdated attitude towards both work and women. The revolution described by the expression 'lady into woman' has its counterpart in the phrase 'gentleman into man', since a 'gentleman's' behaviour towards his wife once tended to be the exact reverse of the conduct implied by the word. In the Danish account of the Gentofte Project, it was suggested that the formal break in school work at fourteen for two years of household training 'would be just as good for boys, though it would be revolutionary in education'.

Popular advertisements and newspaper articles already suggest the coming of this revolution in attractive catch-phrases. 'KITCHEN STYLES FOR MEN' was the heading of an *Evening Standard* paragraph in November 1952.

'How can husbands be persuaded to the kitchen sink to tackle the chores?' it inquired. 'The Gas Council suggest an answer at their international cookery demonstration at the Royal Festival Hall today. They are sponsoring two outfits for the well-dressed man in the kitchen; one is a hip-length coat in dark blue denim with revers and pocket in a lighter colour; the other is an apron, striped butcher-blue, with a canary yellow waistcoat top.'

A month earlier an advertisement for Marmite, the vegetarian relish, in another London daily concluded with the reassuring masculine words: 'Three cheers for Marmite and a kiss for me before we face the washing up!' About the same date a popular article reporting a week-end 'problem quiz' arranged by the Women's Voluntary Services, carried a title, HUSBANDS THEY PREFER DO THE WASHING UP, which struck the same note of household co-operation. 'All groups agreed', it concluded optimistically, 'that husbands today are far more considerate and companionable than they used to be.'

The woman whose domestic tasks are shared by her husband has time and energy for a new understanding of her children. Into the modern small family has gradually entered a form of mutual decency—the reluctance to penalise and exploit—such as men have always shown to men, and women have learned to show to women. Where the home is securely founded upon a right relationship between husband and wife, a mother loses the desire, rooted in frustration, to possess her son. In most households the pattern of the boys' growth is now totally dissimilar from the 'regular education in selfishness' lamented by Frances Power Cobbe in the eighteen-eighties.

A small boy's nursery training was once an odd combination of demands for implicit obedience with suggestions of a future lordship of creation. Parents working assiduously to turn their daughters into good wives and mothers lost sight of the equal obligation to bring up their sons to be good husbands and fathers. Within the past twenty years many young men now at college or already earning their living have been taught that no form of work is contemptible in itself, and least of all contemptible for one sex rather than the other. As babies they learned to wash cups, polish silver, and keep an eye on their younger brother or sister. They will not despise such duties when they become the husbands of young women equally interested with themselves in the world outside the home.

Different generations inevitably have different outlooks; there is much about which they cannot agree and perhaps should not try to compromise. But the once passionate impulse of the younger generation to escape from the dead-weight of maternal dullness lost its point when the mother became an intelligent comrade, who offered guidance without imposing irrational authority, and cherished, without demanding, the freely offered confidence of a son or daughter.

The modern mother, with her daughter's friendship as one of life's best assets, has ceased even to understand the bygone period in which a girl-baby a year was the severest punishment that the Victorian novelist Charlotte M. Young could devise for her most selfish and flighty characters. Having staked her own claim to human rights as an individual, she will not violate those rights in her daughter or seek to probe into reserves such as she herself established.

When her daughter takes a post abroad or sets up housekeeping with a contemporary in her own apartment, she does not accuse her of 'indifference' or 'ingratitude'. At an equivalent age she herself knew, and still knows, the thirst for experience, and has learnt that each girl graduating into womanhood must make her own adventurous experiments and acquire wisdom through her own mistakes.

Gone, probably for ever, are the strained relations which so often developed when mother and daughter each had too much time on her hands. Today few hard-working mothers would exchange the task of adapting the home to a daughter absorbed in her first job, for the apprehensive husband-hunting by which the parent of 1901 so often hurried a girl into an unsuitable marriage lest spinsterhood should prove even worse.

These new values in the changing home add up to the disappearance of the woman, whether mother or daughter, whose life was wholly dominated by personal relationships. For modern woman, as for her ancestors, the greatest joys in life probably still depend upon the existence and affection of other individuals, but she no longer counts, any more than man has counted, upon these alone. She reckons on happiness only as the result of her own efforts in whatever field of work she chooses to enter, and knows, in an epoch unduly shadowed by death and disaster, that this is the one asset which will never let her down.

When John Galsworthy created the character of Clare Dedmond in *The Fugitive*, first played in 1913, a delicately nurtured but uneducated wife fleeing from an abhorred husband had no choice between finding another man who could keep her till his means or inclination failed, and going on the streets. Today the same type of girl has probably been to a university or received a specialist's training, and can be as independent of the male sex as her wishes dictate.

At any age under fifty—and in some rare cases over it—she will probably pay her way whether she associates with men or not. In April 1951 a Gallup Poll raised the question: 'When a young man takes a girl out, should he expect her to pay for any part of the evening's entertainment?' Amongst the replies received, forty-four per cent believed that the girl should pay her share, and forty-three per cent—largely consisting of the well-to-do and elderly—believed that she should not. The remaining thirteen per cent was made up of the usual 'Don't know'.

'The divisions', stated the report on the poll, 'run along unexpected lines. It is not a question of differences between the sexes; it is division between age-groups and social classes. The lower we go down the age-scale the more emphasis there is that the boy should not be expected to meet all the expenses.'

Like their mothers, the Clare Dedmonds were still leisured women, social phenomena which largely disappeared after the First World War and all but entirely after the Second. These hapless parasites deliberately complicated their home lives in order to provide themselves with occupation, serving elaborate formal meals, giving elegant bridge parties, and covering sofas, cushions and piano-backs with wool embroidery. Here and there, in country cottages or the drawing-rooms of ancestral mansions, the tide of time has left high and dry the pathetic collections of crochet mats, antimacassars, and elaborate lace 'bedsides' which represented the endless empty days of long-dead women.

Their successors simplify their homes in the hope of winning a perpetual battle with the overcrowded hours. Recently I asked an acquaintance—a young society woman married ten years ago —what she was doing now, and received a typical mid-century reply.

'Doing? I don't know what I'm not doing! I've got three children and no cook!'

Housework, for such busy wives and mothers, has become an obligation to be disposed of in the minimum of time. The decorative napkins and frilled table-centres have vanished with the brass fenders and silver trays of the past; plastics or wood replace metal, planted bowls the innumerable vases of flowers. Edwardian dinners served by a retinue of underpaid domestics are not even memories to the guests who attend informal sherry parties and help host and hostess to clear the plates and glasses.

The departure of the leisured woman and the futile occupation has brought, on the part of both women and men, a new attitude towards work which makes even that pioneer generation which fought for women's right to do it appear out of date.

Some years ago I was a guest at a house-party largely composed of politically-minded women. One evening a discussion arose on the value, purpose, and duration of committees.

'I like my committees to go on all day', remarked a woman who had been in the suffrage movement. 'You really feel then that you've got something done.'

A young guest who had already won considerable success in her profession appeared quite scandalised by this statement.

'All day!' she exclaimed. 'But when do you do your *work*?'

The elderly feminist regarded her with a half-amused yet rueful expression.

'But, you see', she explained after a pause, 'I think committees *are* work!'

Nothing could have better summed up the essential difference between the old and the new feminism. The suffrage movement was mainly political and legal; it demanded the expenditure of interminable hours on committees, conferences, lobbying, public speaking—incessant but largely unpaid activities for which even Members of Parliament were once not remunerated. But between the wars the women's movement became economic, and involved for younger women the idea of self-support as a moral principle.

'My first duty', announced in effect the girl of the nineteen-twenties and thirties, 'is to do sufficient work of some kind to give me a living wage or salary. After that I'll see what time I have over for committees and speeches.'

With the professional committee-woman has also departed the well-intentioned but unreliable 'voluntary worker' who once drove almost to dementia the offices of political organisations. Today, whether the work is paid or unpaid, professional standards among women are taken for granted—not only by women but by men. Male patronage has become as obsolete as the 'ladies' who were once believed to enjoy it. If the distinguished man invited to take part in a Girls' School Speech Day should confine his address—as one once did—to some jaunty advice about the cultivation of feminine charm, he becomes an object of mirth rather than irritation.

Seldom indeed is such advice now needed. In so far as 'bluestockings' and 'embittered spinsters' existed outside male imagination, they have vanished with the driving academic poverty which produced the one, and the jocund contempt for the unmarried which created the other.

The cruellest of Victorian institutions was perhaps the 'old maid', who whatever her usefulness or intellectual qualifications was thought fit for nothing better than the social scrap-heap because she had failed to acquire a husband and children. In literature she might be a potential Emily Brontë, in public service a Jane Addams or Octavia Hill, but to her relatives she remained that ludicrous figure, the maiden aunt—unsought, unloved, and unfulfilled.

Today, whether she is an aunt or not, husbands and fathers know as clearly as wives and mothers that they cannot do without her. The Newcastle pamphlet on girls' education observed that 'the Welfare State has been staffed largely by the surplus woman' —which in fact means that she is 'surplus' no longer. She ceased to deserve that description in the years immediately following the First World War, when the British Census of 1921 showed that the half-million excess of women over men recorded in 1911 had leapt to 1,700,000. Faced by that challenge, the young women whose intended husbands lay buried beneath the mud of France or the sand of Gallipoli found the independent place in society which the women's movement had prepared for them.

It is mainly the spinster whose shoulders carry the growing burden of administrative work both national and local. She runs government departments and manages innumerable businesses; she keeps factories going and still largely, though no longer entirely, trains and educates a nation's children. Without her, the married woman would produce those children to little purpose. Far from being a pathetic family incubus she has become an economic and social asset, self-supporting, happy and free.

One of the greatest changes brought by the 20th century has been this increased happiness of women.

In the past they were often miserable because their fortunes, like those of the wives of Kingsley's 'Three Fishers', were vested entirely in the lives of others. Whatever troubles we may encounter today—anxiety, ill-health, loneliness, injuries done us by others, or the deaths of friends and relatives—there is not one which work and the security that it brings does not mitigate. Women suffered more than men from these evils in the past because, if sorrow came, they had no alternative but virtuous resignation.

Ill-health was once regarded as woman's predestined fate, and was even assumed to be a religious legacy with which it was impious to interfere. Among the 19th-century middle classes the fragile, clinging type of womanhood became so fashionable that delicacy was considered to be one of a girl's chief matrimonial attractions. With a stalwart male protector in view, her whole upbringing encouraged her to exaggerate her minor ailments.

Only within the present century have men and women alike understood that a sound, vital and energetic woman is better adapted to wifehood and motherhood than the frail flower of the early *Punch* cartoons. During the past thirty years, patient and sympathetic research into women's diseases has been undertaken by women doctors and scientists, often working in co-operation with men. They soon discovered that much 'inevitable' suffering could be banished by healthy living and regular work.

The idea that women were all semi-invalids, incapacitated in varying degrees by menstruation, pregnancy, and the menopause, began to change in the nineteen-twenties. As long ago as 1923 Dr Winifred Cullis, Professor of Physiology in the University of London, heralded this change in a *Time and Tide* review of Dr Christine Murrell's *Womanhood and Health*.

'There is too great a tendency to associate womanhood with invalidism. . . . The mind has only to linger for a moment on the upheaval that would be caused in modern society if all women, whatever their avocations, domestic servants, factory workers, clerks, shop assistants, teachers, actresses, doctors, etc., took off one or two days every month from their usual work, to realise how unfounded such fears are.'

In a footnote she added: 'Recent statistical investigations with regard to these disabilities show that the number experiencing them is nearer five per cent than fifty per cent, with a tendency towards still further reduction. The chief factor in the reduction is probably the greater amount of exercise taken by women.'

Subsequent research (such as *Two Contributions to the Experimental Study of the Menstrual Cycle*, by S. C. M. Sowton, E. M. Bedale, M.A., and C. S. Myers, M.D., F.R.S., published by the Industrial Fatigue Research Board in 1928) showed the fitfulness and excitability hitherto regarded as unavoidable in women to be produced largely by the influence of suggestion—the same suggestion which had left the woman of 1910 struggling helplessly beneath the burden of her own inferiority. As still later investigations have established, it was all part of the 'whispering campaign' which made girls long to be boys, and caused sympathy to be lavished on married couples who only produced daughters.

So far has the invalid woman become a phantom of the past, that women are now universally recognised as the sex which is not only longer-lived but tougher. A touching item in the *Manchester Evening News* for February 7th, 1951, reported that 'smelling salts, the standby of elderly women of the Victorian days, and young victims of "the vapours", have now become a man's comfort. You see them in courts of law. On nearly every magistrates' bench in London there is a bottle of smelling salts, and barristers often take a whiff.'

This suggestive paragraph does not really imply a drastic deterioration in masculine health, but rather an increasing realisation by men and women alike of the value of fresh air and sunshine. Men acclimatised by their mothers or wives to sunny, airy living-rooms find less tolerable than they once did the close atmosphere of Courts designed by Victorian architects.

Sun, air and exercise have combined with the great cosmetics industry to create for all classes of women a standard of beauty which owes relatively little to wealth. Not the least of the many changes which transformed the 'lady' of 1901 into the 'woman' of 1952 has been the disappearance of the external contrast between the hereditary peeress and her personal maid.

Between the wars, women whether rich or poor began to treat their faces as pictures and touch them up daily—with excellent results not only for a nation's beauty, but for its standards of fitness. The desire to provide their families and neighbours with a pleasing work of art, however poor the original equipment, led women to take better care of their skins, hair, eyes, teeth, and finger-nails. In this laudable ambition they have been assisted by both the cinema and the 'Beauty Columns' of women's magazines.

Some women—such as the compilers of *The Feminine Point of View*—deplore this transfiguration as either a modern variant of the old slavish desire to capture a man, or a commercial male-dominated exploitation of feminine weakness. As an habitual user of cosmetics, I do not accept this view. I have always acquired them to reinforce my own self-respect and not to please anybody—though the desire to present an attractive picture to others is surely meritorious in itself. I am sure that this attitude is true of most women. In any case, the advantages of beauty culture appear to outweigh any possible disadvantages.

Almost vanished today from every social class are the blotchy complexions, school-marm spectacles, bitten nails, tombstone dentures, and wispy 'buns' which in the past made British women a by-word for 'homeliness'. Dentists and even doctors, with their prescriptions for slimming and the swift restoration of normal contours after childbirth, have been compelled to turn artist as well as scientist. Their growing care for the physical apparatus on which loveliness depends has made the prolongation of vigour not only apparent but actual. The beauty parlour, their perfumed auxiliary, has opened especially in America a vast and lucrative field of work for women.

In 1905 a young German named Charles Nessler invented the permanent wave, adopted the trade name of Nestlé, and made three million dollars. Within a few years attractive coiffures became accessible to the workers, and the quest for beauty created a great industrial enterprise.

Life magazine recently reported that the gross sales of beauty parlour products in the United States amounted to $1.25 billion a year, hardly less than the takings of the U.S. film industry in 1948. The parlours themselves became virtual clubs for women, transforming their daily lives. The presentation to Nessler, reported by *Life*, of the American Women's Voluntary Services' award for furthering the 'economic, cultural, and social prestige' of women, showed that American womanhood had perceived the revolutionary significance of Nessler's invention.

That revolutionary significance went deeper than the attractive surface, for cosmetics and the beauty-parlour had provided women with a reliable weapon against their traditional Appolyon, the inferiority complex. For years the woman in public life, whether Member of Parliament, political speaker, or professional lecturer, had to overcome a diffidence which seldom afflicted the historically dominant, socially flattered male. Beauty culture and sartorial elegance have now given to women an advantage which the less carefully-groomed masculine performer does not possess. The woman speaker, particularly in clothes-conscious America, who devotes as much attention to her appearence as to her lecture notes is neither vain nor foolish. She has merely mastered the technique by which women throughout the world are conquering their old inhibitions.

The clothes themselves, like the cosmetics, are now her allies. In Edwardian days female clothing possessed a sexual significance which the modern process of discarding garment after garment has eliminated. The historic remark of the pre-1914 bus conductor—'Ankles ain't no treat to me'—has become meaningless for the present generation, but in 1910 it represented a typical comment on the main purpose of fashion. So long as young women in their hundreds are photographed in bathing suits, there is little fear that feminine attire will resume its prurient aspect. It is equally unlikely to return to the class-differentiated shabbiness of the woman wage-earner which once guaranteed a sense of inferiority, and gave grounds for it by restricting movement.

Skirts today move up and down with fashion, but never return during working hours to the foot-impeding length which women accept in the evening, just as men accept starched shirts and the iron-clad formality of dress uniforms. Hatlessness, a post-war practice, frees the brows of women from constriction when they have to think or speak, and allows fresh air and sunlight to add vitality to well-groomed hair.

Other conveyors of emancipation are less obvious, and would probably find no place in social histories written by men. They include not only the short swinging skirt and the button-through dress, but such minor time-savers as zip fasteners, press-studs, pull-on gloves, and court shoes. Women old enough to remember the First World War can compare the short-sleeved, all-in-one overall worn by nurses today with the elaborate seven-piece uniform of 1914.

Fresh air, exercise, cosmetics, and simple fashions have produced one result out of all proportion to the expectations of their advocates. They have not only added years to women's lives, but have extended their youthfulness for decades beyond that rubicon of thirty which once spelt nemesis to the unmarried woman.

Of these changed age-perspectives Charlotte Luetkens comments that the extension of woman's range into time is as important for her as the widening vistas which give a new meaning to space. It has ended, with many other limitations, the over-emphasis on youth which narrowed the significant period of a Victorian girl's life to a few frantic years of husband-hunting.

Two other influences, more weighty in themselves than those already described, must be acknowledged in this attempt to see a human revolution in the illusory perspective of habit and custom. Each comes from a new and major science, the one being biology and the other psychology.

Biological studies—as Bertrand Russell explained in his essay entitled 'An Outline of Intellectual Rubbish'—have shown that no peculiar mental inferiority accompanies the physical attributes of the female sex. Since daughters frequently inherit from their fathers, and sons from their mothers, the hereditary qualities of a family tend to reverse sexes in two generations.

Most people know the lively limerick invented to explain the operation of Mendel's law of heredity.

'There once was a fellow called Starkie
Who had an affair with a darkie.
The fruit of his sins
Was quadruplets, not twins,
One black, one white, and two khaki.'

According to the proportions here illustrated, half the human race belongs to the 'khaki' class; that is, it inherits characteristics derived from both parents. The remaining fifty per cent are divided between those who inherit mainly from one parent, but there is, and could be, nothing in the limerick to indicate whether the 'white' offspring of the adventurous Starkie was a boy or a girl. And there is certainly no biological law which insists that a particular set of sexual organs basically transforms all the attributes inherited by a boy from his mother or a girl from her father. All that these organs do is to influence the view of each sex regarding the use to be made of his or her qualities.

Though psychological specialists, like biological experts, are themselves rare, their findings have become part of the common knowledge of mankind through the interpretations of writers, journalists, and teachers.

In *Women and a Changing Civilisation*, Winifred Holtby took the view that the work of Sigmund Freud had emphasised the sex-consciousness largely responsible for women's slow progress towards citizenship. It may well be a fact that Freud influenced the D. H. Lawrence school of instinct-worshippers, but our realisation of the unconscious mind and its operations is a valuable form of insight which we owe to Freud, and to other pioneer psychologists.

Alfred Adler, for instance, was concerned mainly with the effects of another and equally fundamental instinct, the desire for power. It is to him that we owe our comprehension of the spiritual damage wrought by frustration, and he who wrote in *Understanding Human Nature*: 'Character traits which would seem to prove this fallacious contention of the inferiority of women prove themselves on closer observation nothing more than the manifestation of an inhibited psychic development.'

A younger psychologist, Professor Floyd Allport, echoes this view in his *Social Psychology* when explaining contrasts of personality between the sexes. 'These differences', he writes, 'are more probably due to early influences and the pressure of a man-made double standard of morals than to innate factors.'

Jung and his school taught especially the influence of symbolism, and the importance of an integrated personality for men and women alike. Later specialists who have dealt with integration, such as Dr Thouless of Cambridge, have shown how the subjugation of a sex, race or class is a form of warfare which arises, just as 'shooting wars' arise, from the impulse to dominate, and can be countered only by that co-operation and respect for personality of which equal rights and opportunities are part.

Thanks to the work of these psychologists, most people now recognise that it is a major, and destructive, form of moral insolence for one group to tell another group what it ought to want. The individual, whether man or woman, who goes through life as a square peg in a round hole not only suffers personally, but causes suffering to all others with whom he or she may be associated. Self-fulfilment, the fulfilment of the *whole* human being, body, mind, and soul, is a deep spiritual need.

No amount of authoritative repetition would ever have persuaded Florence Nightingale that her place was the Victorian drawing-room. Florence, no doubt, was a Titan, and Titans of either sex are few, but many lesser women are equally unsuited to the restrictions of a home, and equally constructive, within their own limitations, in the world of affairs. They include the travellers, adventurers, aviators and scientists; the creators of literature and art; the administrators and organisers; the loyal partners in business or profession. Admittedly this minority which does not fit into a man-made domestic pattern is still small. But society would be the poorer without it, not least because its ranks provide the inspired originators of patterns totally new.

As one of the many makers of the revolution which I have described, I am frankly prejudiced in favour of the newer patterns, and have perhaps expressed that prejudice not least in this chapter. There are losses to be set against the gains, of course; they are of a type which tends to be deplored especially by old-fashioned elderly men. With the coming of female independence has gone much of the grace and charm which the dependent woman was obliged to develop in the process of persuading some male to support her.

Manners are more abrupt; language is coarser and less reserved. Men are expected by their wives and daughters to help in the performance of tedious duties which they have long found it convenient to resist as 'unnatural'. Women pay less attention than they did to this male impulse to 'get out from under' in domestic crises, and have thereby abandoned a certain elegant diffidence.

Masculine gallantry and chivalry have diminished in return; no doubt it is often difficult to feel gallant towards the self-sufficient creature who supplies half the housekeeping money and hands you the dish-cloth. But gallantry, for her, too often proved to be a false coin which was no lasting substitute for the real. Today she has learned to recognise the true gold in an equal partnership, and it has become hers, to keep and to cherish.

SHORT READING LIST

HISTORY AND SOCIAL STUDIES

Wollstonecraft, Mary.	A Vindication of the Rights of Woman. 1792.	Everyman's Library. 1929.
Mill, John Stuart. With an Introduction by Professor George Catlin.	The Subjection of Women. 1869.	Everyman's Library. 1929.
Cobbe, Frances Power.	The Duties of Women. 1881.	Swan Sonnenschein & Co. 1905.
Ellis, Havelock.	Man and Woman. 1894.	Walter Scott Publishing Co. 1904.
Cadbury, Edward, and others.	Women's Work and Wages. 1906.	Fisher Unwin. 1909.
Schreiner, Olive.	Woman and Labour.	Fisher Unwin. 1911.
Rathbone, Eleanor.	The Disinherited Family.	Edwin Arnold. 1924.
Royden, Maude.	The Church and Woman.	James Clarke. 1924.
Strachey, Ray.	The Cause.	George Bell & Sons. 1928.
Russell, Bertrand.	Marriage and Morals.	George Allen & Unwin. 1929.
Woolf, Virginia.	A Room of One's Own.	Hogarth Press. 1929.
Smith, Preserved.	A History of Modern Culture.	Henry Holt & Co. New York. 1930.
Pankhurst, Sylvia.	Save The Mothers.	Knopf. 1930.
Pankhurst, Sylvia.	The Suffragette Movement.	Longmans, Green. 1931.
Anthony, Sylvia.	Women's Place in Industry and Home.	Routledge. 1932.
Ellis, Havelock.	The Psychology of Sex.	Heinemann. 1933.
Stephen, Barbara.	Girton College.	Cambridge University Press. 1933.
Halle, Fannina.	Women in Soviet Russia.	Routledge. 1933.
Reiss, Erna.	Rights and Duties of Englishwomen.	Sherratt & Hughes, Manchester. 1934.
Holtby, Winifred.	Women and a Changing Civilisation.	The Bodley Head. 1934.
Strachey, Ray (Ed.)	Our Freedom and Its Results. By Five Women.	Hogarth Press. 1936.
Rogers, Annie M. A. H.	Degrees by Degrees.	Oxford University Press. 1938.
Williams, Gertrude.	Women and Work.	Nicholson and Watson. 1945.

Marchant, Sir James (Ed.)	Rebuilding Family Life After the War.	Odhams Press. 1945.
Luetkens, Charlotte.	Women and a New Society.	Nicholson & Watson. 1946.
United Nations.	Political Rights of Women: 56 Years of Progress.	Department of Public Information. 1949.
United Nations.	These Rights and Freedoms.	Department of Public Information. 1950.
Douie, Vera.	Daughters of Britain.	George Ronald, Oxford. 1950.
Russell, Bertrand.	Unpopular Essays.	George Allen & Unwin. 1951.
Campbell, Olwen W. (drafted by)	The Feminine Point of View.	Williams & Norgate. 1952.
Education Department.	The Education of Girls.	King's College, Newcastle upon Tyne. 1952.
Picton-Turbervill, Edith.	Should Women be Priests and Ministers?	Society for the Equal Ministry of Men and Women in the Church. 1953.

AUTOBIOGRAPHY AND BIOGRAPHY

Pankhurst, Emmeline.	My Own Story.	Eveleigh Nash. 1914.
Dorr, Rheta Childe.	Susan B. Anthony.	F. A. Stokes Co., New York. 1928.
Fawcett, Millicent Garrett and Turner, E. M.	Josephine Butler.	Association for Moral & Social Hygiene. 1927.
Webb, Beatrice.	My Apprenticeship.	Longmans, Green. 1929.
Strachey, Ray.	Millicent Garrett Fawcett.	John Murray. 1931.
Smyth, Ethel.	Female Pipings in Eden.	Peter Davies. 1935.
Pankhurst, Sylvia.	Life of Emmeline Pankhurst.	Werner Laurie. 1935.
Swanwick, H. M.	I Have Been Young.	Gollancz. 1935.
Pethick-Lawrence, Emmeline.	My Part in a Changing World.	Gollancz. 1938.
Stocks, Mary.	Eleanor Rathbone.	Gollancz. 1949.
Smith, Cecil Woodham.	Florence Nightingale.	Constable. 1950.

REPORTS

War Cabinet Committee on Women in Industry.	H.M. Stationery Office. 1919.
The Differentiation of the Curriculum for Boys and Girls in Secondary Schools.	Board of Education (now Ministry). 1926.
Equal Pay for Equal Work.	Standing Joint Committee of Industrial Women's Organisations. 1930.
Report on the Census of 1931.	H.M. Stationery Office.
Report of the (British) Royal Commission on Equal Pay, 1944-46.	H.M. Stationery Office.
Women in Higher Level Positions.	Women's Bureau of the U.S. Department of Labour. 1950.
One Per Cent Sample Report on the Census of 1951.	H.M. Stationery Office. 1952.
Access of Women to Education.	International Bureau of Education, Geneva. 1952.

INDEX